RED ■ BLACK ■ WHITE

RED BLACK WHITE

THE ALABAMA COMMUNIST PARTY 1930★1950

MARY STANTON

THE UNIVERSITY OF GEORGIA PRESS   ATHENS

This publication is made possible in part through a grant from the Bradley Hale Fund for Southern Studies.

© 2019 by the University of Georgia Press
Athens, Georgia 30602
www.ugapress.org
All rights reserved
Designed by Melissa Bugbee Buchanan
Set in 10.1/14 Kepler Std
Printed and bound by Sheridan Books, Inc.
The paper in this book meets the guidelines for permanence and durability of the Committee on Production Guidelines for Book Longevity of the Council on Library Resources.

Most University of Georgia Press titles are available from popular e-book vendors.

Printed in the United States of America
23 22 21 20 19 P 5 4 3 2 1

Library of Congress Cataloging-in-Publication Data
Names: Stanton, Mary, 1946– author.
Title: Red, black, white : the Alabama Communist Party, 1930–1950 / Mary Stanton.
Description: Athens : The University of Georgia Press, [2019] | Includes bibliographical references and index.
Identifiers: LCCN 2019020543| ISBN 9780820356167 (hbk : alk. paper) | ISBN 9780820356174 (pbk : alk. paper) | ISBN 9780820356150 (ebk)
Subjects: LCSH: Communist Party of the United States of America. District 17 (Birmingham, Ala.)—History. | Communism—Alabama—History—20th century. | Communism—Southern States—History—20th century. | Communists—Alabama—History—20th century. | Communists—Southern States—History—20th century. | Alabama—Race relations—History—20th century. | Southern States—Race relations—History—20th century. | Lynching—Alabama—History—20th century. | Lynching—Southern States—History—20th century.
Classification: LCC HX91.A2 S73 2019 | DDC 324.2761/07509043—dc23
LC record available at https://lccn.loc.gov/2019020543

In memory of Pauline Bonagura Mullaney
My high school English teacher

The mind once stretched by a new idea
never returns to its original dimensions.
—Ralph Waldo Emerson

> Don't you mind being called "Bolsheviki" by the same people who called you nigger.
> —*Crusader*, June 1920

CONTENTS

Acknowledgments xi
Prologue 1
Backstory 7

BOOK 1 ■ BEGINNINGS

1. District 17 Headquarters 13
2. The *Southern Worker* and the Dynamo of Dixie 22
3. Scottsboro 33
4. An All-Purpose Jesus 42
5. The Massacre at Camp Hill 47
6. The National Miners' Union, Southeastern Kentucky 53
7. The Shades Mountain Rape and Murders 62
8. Staying the Course 77
9. Reeltown Radicals 85
10. Reversals and Bombshells 90
11. Justice for Angelo Herndon 100
12. Big Sandy: A Murder and Two Lynchings 107
13. The Lynching of Dennis Cross 117
14. Memphis: Mayhem and Mistaken Identity 123

BOOK 2 ■ THE LATE GREAT DISTRICT 17

15. Reaping the Whirlwind 129
16. A Popular Front 138
17. A Culture of Opposition 152
18. All Things Considered . . . 159
19. The Rest of Life 164

Notes 173
Bibliography 187
Index 201

ACKNOWLEDGMENTS

A good beginning includes acknowledging indebtedness to the hardworking staffs of major research institutions, libraries and archives who made identifying, studying, and understanding district 17 and its operation possible. They include the following:

>Schomburg Center for Research in Black Culture
>Manuscripts, Archives and Rare Book Division
>New York Public Library
>Harlem, New York City

>Tamiment Library and Robert F. Wagner Labor Archives
>New York University
>Washington Square, New York City

>Southern Historical Collection and Southern
>   Oral History Program Collection
>University of North Carolina
>Wilson Library
>Chapel Hill, North Carolina

>Clark Atlanta University
>Woodruff Library
>Archives Research Center
>Atlanta, Georgia

>Alabama Department of Archives and History
>624 Washington Avenue
>Montgomery, Alabama

>Birmingham Public Library—Central Division
>Archives and Special Collections
>Birmingham, Alabama

Birmingham Civil Rights Institute
520 16th Street North
Birmingham, Alabama

New York Public Library
Research Division—Stephen A. Schwartzman Building
New York City

RED ■ BLACK ■ WHITE

PROLOGUE

> There are only two or three human stories, and they go on repeating themselves as fiercely as if they had never happened.
> —Willa Cather, *O Pioneers!*

At eight o'clock Wednesday morning, June 24, 1964, I was one of a thousand high school seniors lined up outside the Brooklyn Fox Theater waiting for the doors to open and our graduation ceremony to begin. I had *spilkes*—anxiety, agitation, apprehension—all of it. Everything was happening too fast, it was all too big, too soon, and too much. I couldn't shake a nagging feeling of dread—this was supposed to be a happy day.

It had nothing to do with the Fox. I'd been inside that massive Art Deco movie palace many times. By the mid-sixties it was home to disc jockey Murray the K's Swingin' Soirees—red, hot, and blues all the way! . . . He'd brought Marvin Gaye, Stevie Wonder, and the Ronettes to Flatbush Avenue. No, it wasn't the Fox . . .

Although Franklin K. Lane High School was one of the largest in the city, the gym and auditorium together couldn't accommodate all of us, but the four-thousand-seat Fox could, so that's where we would "commence" our futures. A generational tsunami, we were the first wave of baby boomers—born in 1946, one year after the soldiers came home.

As it turned out, my dread that morning wasn't entirely misplaced. The legacy of the biggest and brightest—at least best-educated generation of the twentieth century—would be three white male presidents: Bill Clinton, George W. Bush, and Donald Trump (all 1964 graduates), who, to be fair, represented the full gamut of our attitudes, ideals, and ambitions—the ones we would continue to either champion or challenge through five succeeding decades of culture war.

The world is growing sick and tired of us. It was not always so. Once we were the ones designated to carry the ball into the end zone. We can't complain that our country didn't pay enough attention to us—or certainly that we didn't pay enough attention to each other!

I gravitated to the political left—something that would have been hard to predict in my sophomore or junior years. In November 1963, three months into our first term as seniors, President Kennedy was assassinated. In January 1964, Lyndon Johnson declared war on poverty. Freedom Summer was launched that June, and three days before our graduation, three civil rights workers—two from New York City—were reported missing in Mississippi. Their decomposed bodies would turn up in August.

By the end of that year there were twenty thousand U.S. military advisors in Vietnam, and by 1965 draft cards were beginning to burn. Suddenly there was a good deal to fight about. I admired the courage of those who protested the draft, the war, and segregation, and who championed voting rights, feminism, and fair housing. I was, in fact, all admiration and no action. Strong opinions didn't get white girls like me invitations to the prom. Besides, Franklin K. Lane sat on Jamaica Avenue exactly and often uncomfortably on the White Queens–Black Brooklyn border. That made for a lot of strong opinions.

Several years ago, I was asked to develop a Black History Month presentation to commemorate the eightieth anniversary of the Scottsboro Boys' arrests—a tribute both to them and to the case that became the Rosetta stone for civil rights justice claims. In the course of my research, I discovered the *Southern Worker*, a 1930s weekly written by communists—many from New York City—who were working to save the lives of these nine black young men, wrongly accused of raping two white women. Their passion stirred memories of some of my former classmates who I'd idolized as a journalist-in-training on the *Lane Reporter* back in Brooklyn. They were three smart guys, all on their way to bigger lives.

Juan Gonzalez, who would go to Columbia and organize a campus strike in protest of the Vietnam War, was our fiery editor. Tall, wiry, and intense, he became a successful investigative reporter and *New York Daily News* columnist for twenty-nine years. Our sports editor, Steve Handelman, a rumpled, sandy-haired guy with a broad grin, served with the Peace Corps and became an investigative journalist with *Time* magazine and the *Toronto Star*. He went on to direct the Center on Media, Crime and Justice at John Jay College of Criminal Justice. David Vidal, a beat reporter like me (more approachable but no less passionate than the other two), planned to go to seminary. Instead, he became a political correspondent for the *New York Times* and later served as vice president of the Council on Foreign Relations. These guys, a

Latino, a Jew, and an African American, convinced this white female proto-conservative who grew up in blue-collar Queens that there was a good deal more to life than being rewarded for good behavior. Their energy and drive were contagious. Somehow, memories of them, galvanized by rediscovery of the Scottsboro case and the luxury of retirement, created the perfect storm that set this work in motion.

What follows is a history of a single district of the Communist Party of the United States of America (CPUSA). It covers twenty years of collective experience in the outpost of Birmingham, Alabama, located a thousand miles from party headquarters in New York City. Headquarters did not always understand or appreciate the district's needs or the reasons it failed to tow the party line consistently. District 17 functioned like a firehouse—in a perennial state of emergency, running on adrenalin. Every crisis demanded immediate attention, and crises often overlapped. A small band of organizers triaged, improvised, rushed themselves or others out back doors and into cars to keep them safe, called meetings, planned and led demonstrations, bailed comrades out of jail, and just kept moving. There were no second shifts to hand off the follow-up. The environment was uniformly hostile, and new organizers were continuously transferring in and out.

Red, Black, White documents five lynchings, two riots, and two brutal labor strikes that occurred within district 17's territory. All this in the space of six years. If it was a film, it would be R-rated because the violence is so intense and persistent. Each crisis demonstrates the tenacity of the racial divisiveness of those years and the brutality of the backlash that occurred after even minimal advances.

In sifting through personal testimonies, newspaper accounts, journal articles, biographies, oral histories, collections of personal papers and autobiographies, I was stunned by the number of men and women, black and white who managed to navigate the social, economic, and political riptides of the southern way of life. I revisited that way of life to witness the 1931 Scottsboro case tear the scab off and expose the culture's rawness. Scottsboro blasted district 17 out of its isolation and kept the fate of those nine young black men on page one of the national press.

I studied the pervasiveness of religion—its critical role in every aspect of Southern life at every level. As Karl Marx maintained, it is opium to some, but in the Depression South it was also used to defend and perpetuate a culture that its founder would likely have roundly condemned. But I am getting ahead of myself...

The legacy of CPUSA is a mixed bag. On the one hand, James Allen, former editor of the *Southern Worker*, recalls that "the Communists showed it was possible, despite formidable obstacles to challenge from within the peculiar Southern system with its heritage from slavery. They advocated black freedom and unity of white and black in the citadel of racism... and left a significant imprint on Southern society and its way of life."[1]

That is true. But at the same time, American Reds were widely condemned as puppets of a foreign government and instruments of the Soviet Union's determination to undermine America's democratic traditions. Communist efforts to end racial inequality were ascribed to a plot to overthrow capitalism, which of course they were. The Soviet Union did indeed use America's Jim Crow practices as propaganda, but in doing so they kept the issue of segregation in the forefront of U.S. political life and challenged white America to do something about it.

During the Great Depression, CPUSA called out the fecklessness of gradualism, collaboration, and conciliation in the struggle to end segregation. The Reds mocked "interracial committees" whose apologetic members were unwilling to offend. They demanded immediate economic, political and social equality for African Americans based on constitutional guarantees.[2]

Red organizers defined and exposed the systemic racism flourishing in organizations and institutions that were insular, myopic, and beholden to special interests. Political systems, they maintained, had a propensity to operate in ways more hostile or deviant than any of their component parts. These systems included law enforcement, legislatures, and the judiciary.

They also raised awareness of a phenomena that the International Labor Defense (ILD) attorneys called "legal lynching." Jurors who practiced legal lynching were those willing to accept any evidence, or none at all, as justification for sending black defendants to the electric chair. These were mirror images of jury nullifiers who disregarded any and all evidence submitted by the defense in cases of white-on-black crime and who refused to indict or convict.

Historians have grappled for decades with the question of whether American communism was just an expression of the nation's radical traditions or a subversive movement that subordinated itself to the will of Soviet Russia. Could these assessments be any further apart? Nevertheless, historian Theodore Draper, who comes down on the side of Russian manipulation, maintains that "it is possible to say many true things about the American Communist movement and yet not the whole truth. It is possible to be right about a part and yet wrong about the whole. The most contradictory things can be true—at different times and in different places."[3] That is the territory where I have chosen to stake my claim.

For nearly ten years it was my business (and passion) to learn about what went on in one CPUSA district in the Deep South. I followed these young Reds as they interacted with Klansmen, black sharecroppers, poor white tenant farmers, preachers, politicians, planters, industrial workers, the unemployed, judges, law enforcement officers, and corporate executives—a chorus to rival Aida's. What emerged was a window on two decades of interface, exchange and struggle—through a depression, another world war, a cold war, a red scare, and rising indigenous social justice movements.

The seeds of Black liberation, of the Student Non-Violent Coordinating Committee, Black Power, the Black Panthers, and Black Lives Matter can all be traced directly to the legacy of the Southern Negro Youth Congress whose members included young black communists, and to the legal tactics of the ILD and the ideals of the League of Struggle for Negro Rights, the National Negro Congress, and the Civil Rights Congress. As these forerunner organizations are rediscovered and their objectives reenvisioned, momentum builds, albeit in fits and starts. Subsequent generations are required to respond to new, more subtle challenges and modern freedom movements demand more focused tactics and defense strategies in order to navigate what continues to be experienced by many Americans as a hostile, resentful, and unjust society.

There are three camps of U.S. historians whose specialty is CPUSA. Traditionalists tend to focus on national party leadership and by and large they maintain that CPUSA never acted independently of the Soviet Union. They include (among others) Theodore Draper, Irving Howe in the 1950s and 1960s, and Harvey Klehr and John Earl Haynes who focused on espionage and crime in the 1980s and 1990s.[4]

Revisionist historians, on the other hand, place the party within the nation's broad radical democratic traditions. They tend to focus on the Depression and Popular Front eras, times when the party championed civil liberties and social justice and they include (again, among others) Maurice Isserman, Robin D. G. Kelley, and Mark Solomon.[5]

Finally, when the Soviet Union collapsed in 1991 and some Moscow archives were made available to researchers, Red scholarship entered a period of reassessment. Historians took a closer look at the interplay between the internationalist orientation of party officials and the narrower focuses of the local units. In 1995 Isserman commented in the *Nation* that "the story of the CPUSA is full of contradictions and it is past time for all concerned to acknowledge them and learn to live with them." Michael Kazin's *American Dreamers: How the Left Changed the Nation*, written in 2010, also subscribes to this perspective.[6]

I am indebted to all these historians for guiding me through the very dense forest of scholarship. Especially to Isserman, Kelley, Solomon, and Kazin, from whose work I have drawn many conclusions.

Like any good story, district 17's is rich and complex, with twists and turns, with villains and heroes, and many mysteries and contradictions. It is a southern story, and as southern novelist Flannery O'Connor maintained, "there is something in us, as story tellers and as listeners to stories, that demands the redemptive act, that demands that what falls at least be offered the chance to be restored."[7]

BACKSTORY

> The adventure of American life today is in the South.
> —Walter Lippmann, 1932

The story of the Communist Party of the United States of America (CPUSA) starts with Russian Bolsheviks overthrowing Tsar Nicholas II on November 7, 1917, issuing the Declaration of the Rights of the People, and establishing a Union of Soviet Socialist Republics.

Two years later, Vladimir Lenin, chair of the Council of Peoples' Commissars, called a worldwide conference to launch a Communist International (Comintern) group. On March 2, 1919, fifty-two delegates from Europe, Asia, Africa, and the United States met in Moscow and adopted twenty-one objectives, including a pledge to colonial peoples of Africa and Asia that "the hour of proletarian dictatorship in Europe will be the hour of [your] liberation."[1]

In the United States, two parties—the Communist Party and the Communist Labor Party—were organized. They merged in 1921 to become CPUSA. At the Third Comintern Congress that year, Chairman Lenin criticized the Americans for failing to recruit African Americans. He subsequently appointed a Negro Commission, chaired by William Patterson, a black U.S. lawyer (and future director of the International Labor Defense) to study the problem. The commission recommended that a plan for addressing U.S. and South African oppression of blacks be added to the Comintern's plan for world revolution. In their own country, the Bolsheviks had granted self-determination to all the nations of the old tsarist empire.

When, in 1926, five years after the Third Comintern Congress, the United States still had fewer than fifty black members, Chairman Patterson appointed Harry Haywood the first African American to study at Moscow's International Lenin School, to the Negro Commission. The young and energetic Haywood subsequently drafted a resolution to establish a "Negro Soviet Socialist Republic in the America South," modeled on the Bolshevik self-determination policy.[2] Haywood reasoned that since U.S. blacks were also a subjugated people, they were also entitled to self-determination—to either remain part of the United States or to secede and create an independent republic.

By that time, Vladimir Lenin had died and Josef Stalin presided at the Third International's Sixth World Congress (1928), where the Black Belt self-determination policy was introduced and adopted. CPUSA, which had been engaged in factional infighting since the 1921 merger (portrayed in Warren Beatty's 1981 epic film, *Reds*), was finally settling down and focusing. For eight years its mission had been limited to labor organizing in the (predominantly white) industrial North. Now, as the Great Depression loomed, the U.S. party would enter uncharted territory in the South, where suffering had come earlier and gone deeper.

In recognition of the widespread economic devastation, two southern districts were created: in Birmingham, Alabama, district 17 had responsibility for interracial organizing of industrial workers, miners, and sharecroppers in Alabama, Tennessee, and Georgia; district 16, headquartered in Charlotte, North Carolina, was responsible for organizing textile and tobacco workers in the Carolinas and Virginia. Both districts were situated close to the Black Belt, that rich wide band of southern farmland that was home to the largest concentration of black people in the nation.

Birmingham, a city of immigrants and laborers was the industrial hub of the South. Organizing coal miners and steel workers was relatively simple—the challenge was to organize them across racial lines. With the highest percentage of blacks of any U.S. city, Birmingham would become a testing ground for the party's Black Belt policy.

In 1930, CPUSA established the League of Struggle for Negro Rights to champion and defend the new policy and to wage an aggressive campaign against lynching. Harry Haywood, who'd returned to the States by then, was appointed the league's first general secretary. It didn't take long, however, for the party's southern field organizers to discover that blacks, by and large, had no interest in becoming "a nation within a nation" or in claiming any right to secession. They wanted to opt into the American dream, to participate in the nation's prosperity, to claim constitutional guarantees, and to assume a rightful place in society. Self-determination sounded too much like segregation. While this complicated the mission, it did not derail it. The Great Depression would present other challenges. Within six months district 17 would be shifting gears to address the overwhelming needs of unemployed workers and sharecroppers who were flooding into Birmingham, Chattanooga, and Atlanta.

Although the growing worldwide economic depression was consistent with Marxist theory that capitalism was in its last days, district 17 didn't have the luxury of waiting for the revolution to start. These comrades had their hands full dealing with emerging issues and pressing needs on top of ongoing violence against blacks, industrial workers, and Reds perpetrated by law enforcement and abetted by local justice systems. Mind-numbing fear became the constant companion of organizers who were "breaking ground in the South." Tours of duty were often short and brutal. Those who'd never been south before couldn't fathom how blacks were able to withstand the everlasting Jim Crow racism, and they often asked themselves what so few of them could hope to do to make a difference. The pace was always two steps forward and at least one back. Some days even that much progress was impossible. It was not what they'd envisioned.

BOOK ONE
BEGINNINGS

1 ▎ DISTRICT 17 HEADQUARTERS

> I must admit that we were subversives, as so often charged. We did conspire to change the Southern social order, to uproot its remnants of slavery, to improve the life conditions of Blacks and whites as well—and to humanize, to civilize relations between them.
>
> —Jim Allen, *Organizing in the Depression South*

If you were a communist traveling across the United States in 1929, your best chance for long-term survival was anonymity. Nineteen-year-old Tom Johnson understood that. Newly released from the city jail in Cleveland, Ohio, this tall, white, muscular young man with high cheekbones and piercing blue eyes was on his way to Birmingham to accept a new assignment. He'd been arrested for organizing black and white miners with the Industrial Workers of the World (IWW), the Wobblies, and charged with criminal syndicalism, which meant "advocating firing the bosses and putting the workers in charge." Yes. That was his goal all right. Johnson was tried and convicted as "James Leyton," not his real name—but then, "Johnson" wasn't, either. He'd been released on the condition that he leave the city and never return. No problem. When you got lucky, you didn't ask questions.

At the same time, another white IWW organizer, a little older than Johnson and known as Harry Jackson, was also making his way to Birmingham. Tough and confident with a rich, often irreverent, sense of humor, Jackson had been organizing on the San Francisco docks. He was short, dark and belligerent, and he'd volunteered (like Johnson) to help launch the party's new Southern District. Neither had been to the South before.

While Johnson was good at motivating and inspiring groups of people, Jackson was a more street-smart one-on-one organizer. The only attributes these young men shared were party loyalty and fearlessness, and it is likely that neither fully understood what he'd signed on for.

The Birmingham of 1929 was a full-fledged city with a bustling downtown business district. Paved streets running north and south crossed wide avenues to form an east/west grid. It was nothing like the backwater that Jackson had imagined, but Birmingham's geology had determined its fate long ago. After the Civil War, rich veins of coal, iron ore, and limestone were discovered running side by side in the Jones Valley. They were the building blocks of steel, and they made Birmingham "the Pittsburgh of the South."

Founded in 1871, the city was developed by absentee landlords, speculators, and northern businessmen who held title to its mines, mills, and railroad lines. Their enterprises, spilling over into new company towns like Ensley, Fairfield, and Bessemer, required hundreds of thousands of workers. And they came—black and white—from the farms and small towns of the Deep South—most without skills. The Tennessee Coal, Iron and Railroad Company (TCI), a subsidiary of Pennsylvania-based U.S. Steel, became Birmingham's largest employer. The Magic City (because it had sprung up virtually overnight) had a large black population spread over several neighborhoods with its own business district four blocks west of city hall.

District 17 headquarters was established at 2117½ Second Avenue North, near the Terminal Railroad Station. Johnson was appointed district secretary and given responsibility for overseeing operations in Alabama, Georgia, and Tennessee. Jackson became southern director for Trade Union Unity League (TUUL) development and he was charged with organizing industrial laborers, and later unemployed workers. They were joined by Frank Burns, a white twenty-four-year-old New York City native who'd just returned from a year's training in Russia. Burns, an energetic organizer, quickly connected with James Giglio (also white) of the Metal Workers Industrial League, who introduced him to Walter Lewis, a black leader among the foundry workers. As they helped the new comrades make inroads into the TCI workforce, they cautioned them to move slowly. Organizing across racial lines was dangerous.

Giglio and Lewis brought Johnson to a black dance hall where his message was warmly welcomed, but repercussions quickly followed. Within a week, Giglio's home was firebombed. The men were being watched. Birmingham's big industries were already feeling the growing economic squeeze and the bosses' tempers were short. By 1929 TCI had shut down two of its Bessemer blast furnaces, and the Woodward Steel and Sloss-Sheffield plants were beginning to lay off.

On March 6, 1930, Harry Jackson organized a rally to celebrate the International Unemployment Day. Simultaneous marches and demonstrations were scheduled across the nation as workers and the unemployed demanded passage of a federal unemployment insurance bill. Less than six months into his assignment, Jackson found himself organizing jobless men. In Birmingham,

Chattanooga, and Atlanta the need to establish unemployed worker councils rose to the top of the district's agenda.

On March 23, Jackson delegated the responsibility for Birmingham's unemployed worker council movement to Frank Burns. Burns got busy taking demonstrators to city hall to protest bank foreclosures, home evictions, and utility shutoffs. He, Jackson, and Johnson put unemployed miners to work reconnecting municipal pipes and telephone and electrical lines faster than the utilities could shut them down. By midsummer, fifty new organizers were flooding the city with flyers encouraging the unemployed:

> FIGHT—DON'T STARVE
>
> White and Negro workers of Birmingham organize and fight back against unemployment. Demand work or wages for the unemployed. Demand the immediate enactment of the bill for social insurance proposed by the Communist Party to provide every unemployed worker with a minimum of $25 per week unemployment insurance. Unemployed workers and those still at work, attend the mass demonstration of the unemployed in Capitol Park on Labor Day.
>
> Force Congress to pass the worker's social insurance bill.
>
> Demand "work or wages."[1]

Johnson explained to a Labor Day crowd of nearly five hundred, mostly black men, that a workers' unemployment social insurance bill could be funded by transferring federal allocations for warships to an insurance fund and increasing taxes on industry. Angelo Herndon, a seventeen-year-old black TCI miner in the crowd that day, joined the Young Communist League. Within a few months he would be organizing for the National Miners' Union alongside Jackson.[2]

As the crowd made its way toward the Community Chest Headquarters to demand cash relief, Herndon watched as city police officers, assisted by TCI security guards, dispersed them. Tom Johnson and Frank Burns were arrested. Johnson was taken outside the city, stripped, beaten, burned with cigarettes, and warned that if he stayed in Birmingham he was a dead man.

Birmingham's black middle class was appalled by the demonstrations. Oscar Adams, black editor of the *Birmingham Reporter*, "the voice of Black Birmingham," described the district 17 organizers as "a bunch of foreigners paid by Moscow and Jewish gold to stir up trouble among the Negroes." He assured his readers that their only real friends were "the rich white people of the South."³

Tom Johnson alerted John Williamson at Central Committee headquarters back in New York City that "we are entirely illegal here. We are followed. We will no doubt be picked up regularly on one charge or another in an effort to disrupt the work.... Our forces, although all good comrades and hard workers, are hardly experienced enough for the tasks set to them."⁴

Johnson wasn't exaggerating. They were regularly arrested and charged with vagrancy. While the Communist Party was not illegal in Birmingham (and would not be until 1951), the Reds were targeted as the enemies of the southern way of life. Their labor organizing imperiled the South's cheap labor advantage, and their demands for labor reform and integrated unions tore at the region's social fabric. The joint efforts of the police, corporate security squads, and the Ku Klux Klan, supported by industrialists and planters, would ultimately drive the Reds underground.

In October 1930, Jackson organized a mass demonstration outside Bessemer's Pullman Plant after two thousand workers were laid off there. Twenty-five hundred men and women assembled but were disbursed by the police before they got started; Jackson was arrested.⁵

Congressman Fish

As the Reds grew increasingly disruptive, Birmingham welcomed New York Congressman Hamilton Fish III and his Special Committee to Investigate Communist Activities, also known as the Fish Committee. The House committee arrived in November 1930 as part of its national tour of large cities. Congressman Fish believed that communism threatened the nation's economic, political, and religious institutions. He maintained that the Reds encouraged a climate of unrest by organizing the disaffected to demonstrate, protest and make demands. This, he said, constituted un-American radicalism and a first step toward establishing a communist regime to overthrow the U.S. government. Most white southerners agreed, giving Fish and his committee a warm welcome.

Chief of Police Fred McDuff provided Congressman Fish with copies of the literature that his men had confiscated when they raided Red headquarters. McDuff estimated that there were between two and three thousand communists in the city. How Johnson and Jackson wished that were true! J. C.

Murphy, a local American Federation of Labor (AFL) official (and a Klansman), bragged about Birmingham's successful corporate spy program, and he delivered to the committee the names of fifty people who he believed to be communists.

In his final report to the House of Representatives, Hamilton Fish would recommend that the Communist Party be suppressed, that alien communists be deported, and that the federal government ban communist literature from being distributed through the U.S. Postal Service.

Despite numerous setbacks that first year (the Fish Committee being a relatively minor one), Johnson and Jackson went ahead with a planned Farm Relief Council meeting in rural Whitney, forty miles north of the city. Seaten Worthy, who was black and the party's candidate for U.S. senator from Alabama, addressed the 125 sharecroppers in attendance. These Relief Councils were the district's earliest attempts to organize black sharecroppers. Roy Colley, a black tenant farmer, chaired the meeting and afterward offered a training session on organizing.[6] Seven months later, Johnson reported to New York City headquarters that four organizers were working with cells of thirty croppers each in Camp Hill, Tallapoosa County. They were laying the groundwork for an agricultural workers' union.

Sharecroppers

In 1931, white southern sociologist Arthur Raper posed what he called a Black Belt riddle. "To whom does the cotton belong?" he asked. "To the tenant farmer who grew it? To the landlord who furnished the tenant? Or, to the banker who financed the landlord?"[7] Sharecropping and farm tenancy were systems fraught with difficulty.

The practice of sharecropping began as a free labor arrangement after slavery ended.[8] It was an attempt by the defeated planters to create a permanent servile labor force. In the antebellum era, cash-poor landlords offered landless farmers—freed blacks and poor whites alike—the opportunity of working for a share of the harvest. In the end, of course, it was the landlords, cotton buyers, and a new breed of "merchants" who would benefit most from the arrangement. Merchants extended credit to planters who in turn advanced credit to sharecroppers to cover the costs of their shelter, provisions, seed, and tools. Croppers were compelled to buy these things from the landlords (and later from plantation commissaries, run by the merchants).

Commissaries became profit centers, since the prices they charged for basic provisions were substantially higher than anywhere else. Acting as agents of the planters, merchants also brokered the harvest sales. Any negative balances owed by croppers at the end of one season were carried to the next. Written contracts were not available.

Inevitably, sharecroppers slid into debt over time. Once caught in that web, they could not, according to state law, leave a plantation until their finances were settled. If they left, they were subject to arrest. One might wonder how this differed from chattel slavery.

Croppers often mortgaged as much as half their share of the harvest to cover commissary expenses. Most years they broke even, but in bad times they had to put a lien on the following year's crop. These "crop liens" guaranteed that they would be trapped in an ongoing cycle of debt. Many lived in two-room shacks without electricity or plumbing, with their children suffering from malnutrition, hookworm, and pellagra. Their lives followed the cycle of planting from March to midsummer and picking from September to December. Credit was advanced from March through July at the rate of one dollar per month for each acre they cultivated, and it was suspended over the summer when all work stopped. Croppers used the downtime to tend their own crops and vegetable gardens. Accounts were settled at the end of the year.

If a cropper challenged a merchant's calculations, he and his family could be evicted, and the cropper would be unemployable. There was no mechanism to file a complaint and no appeal process. Even if a black cropper could save the money (which he could not), it was virtually impossible for him to buy land because of long-standing "gentlemen's agreements" among the white landowners not to sell it to him.[9]

Well into the twentieth century, croppers in the Deep South were still struggling to become independent farmers.

Miners

By 1931, Birmingham's largest employers: TCI, Woodward Iron, and Sloss-Sheffield Steel and Iron, had cut wages by 25 percent. Miners, steel workers, and mill workers, however, were still required to pay rent on their company housing and interest on their commissary accounts. Debt controlled them almost as completely as it did the sharecroppers. Thefts, assaults, and robberies began to increase throughout the city, and the Reds continued to organize protests, demonstrations, hunger marches, and unemployed worker rallies. In the meantime, young Angelo Herndon of the Young Communist League was promoted to organizer. Fearless, he tended to call too much attention to himself and he was becoming a special target of the police.

On January 3, 1931, he, Tom Johnson, Harry Jackson, Joe Carr (a white organizer for the Mine, Mill and Smelter union), and Frank Burns were all arrested for vagrancy. The crime of not being able to prove that you were employed was selectively enforced in Birmingham. All these men were, in fact, employed. Some, like Herndon, still worked for TCI, while others were being paid (if nominally) by CPUSA. Police Chief Fred McDuff had vowed that he and his men would keep arresting them until they either left the city or were sentenced to a chain gang.

At their arraignment Judge H. S. Abernathy counseled that if they were convicted this time they would indeed face a year on a chain gang. Despite this, they opted to defend themselves.

At trial on January 12, Johnson explained to Judge J. P. McCoy that he and his codefendants were not vagrants. They were being tried, he said, for "organizing half-starved white and colored workers in the struggle against the capitalist hunger system. And to this charge," Johnson said, "we are proud to answer, 'Guilty.'"[10]

Several Klansmen were sitting at the prosecutor's table while others were stationed in the hallways to threaten jurors as they passed. One juror was warned that "if you fail to convict those red bastards we'll convict them with a gun."[11]

The all-white, all-male jury included foundry workers and miners, some of whom were unemployed. After deliberating for twenty hours, they reported that they could not reach a decision. Police Chief McDuff became furious when the judge dismissed the charges. He vowed that Johnson would pay.

During February and March, Johnson wrote a series of articles for the *Southern Worker* asking working-class blacks and whites to consider joining forces since they shared a common enemy. By keeping the races fighting with each other bosses were able to avoid strikes. They brought in black scabs when whites struck and if blacks struck they were fired.

Johnson also encouraged black croppers to grasp their opportunity as the majority population in the Black Belt to demand self-determination.

As the Reds attracted larger crowds, more Klansmen volunteered to assist the police. They were happy to beat, flog, and kidnap organizers and to terrorize their followers as a public service. After a mass demonstration in August 1931, Klansmen singled out Herndon and Jackson for a beating. When the police finally arrived, they arrested Jackson for bond forfeiture and charged Herndon with vagrancy. It was apparently only a warning, since both were freed within a few days.

Jackson subsequently sent Herndon to New Orleans on loan to the Trade Union Unity League to assist striking longshoremen on the city docks. Seven thousand black and white men had walked off the job after the announcement of a 20 percent wage cut, and the steamship companies were hiring scabs to replace them. During the inevitable riot, 118 strikers were shot, some with machine guns, and many died. Herndon was arrested and charged with inciting to riot, distributing circulars without a permit and having no visible means of support.[12] After four days, he was released, and Jackson subsequently sent him to Chattanooga to assist with the first All Southern Conference for the Scottsboro defense.

By summer's end, there were more black than white communists in Birmingham, a situation that infuriated Magic City officials. Everyone knew that the Reds practiced social and racial equality in their ranks, and Hiram Evans, the Klan's Imperial Wizard, writing in his *Kourier* newsletter, maintained that they were "dangling before the ignorant lustful and brutish negroes . . . a tempting bait . . . that negro men should take white women and live with them, declaring this is their God-given right under a communist regime." Several Birmingham Klansmen became so incensed after reading Evans's editorial that they burned Tom Johnson in effigy.[13]

White citizens either supported or simply ignored the brutality of the Klan and the police. Little evidence of criticism survives. Angelo Herndon recalled that the police often goaded demonstrators to provoke reactions that would lead to their arrests. White Knights confidently paraded through Negro neighborhoods warning people to keep away from the communists. They distributed flyers cautioning that "Alabama Is a Good Place for Good Negroes but a Bad Place for Negroes Who Want Social Equality."[14]

Although Jefferson County sheriff James Hawkins and Birmingham police chief Fred McDuff sent officers to disrupt demonstrations and arrest agitators, they couldn't slow the Reds down. TCI hired thugs to rough them up, but even that didn't work. Mayor Jimmie Jones often stood between a uniformed police officer and a robed Klansman to watch as demonstrators were arrested in Capitol Park. But despite harassing and jailing them (sometimes every ten days), and despite raids on their offices and their homes, the communists just kept coming back. City officials were also incensed by the growing number of unemployed white men who were attending the rallies. The Reds were instigating that, too.

Birmingham whites tended to either detest the Reds or to dismiss them as integration-preaching atheists. On the other hand, blacks (whose unemployment rate was 50 percent higher than whites) were more likely to accept them. Since the onset of the Depression, whites had been pushing blacks out of positions for elevator operators, sanitation workers, and laborers—work that whites once considered beneath their dignity. The Reds, on the other hand, opposed segregation because they said it destroyed worker solidarity. Young black men like Herndon, Marcus "Al" Murphy, and Hosea Hudson took them at their word and joined the party. All began as organizers and were groomed for leadership roles. Herndon recalled that "we were called comrades without condescension or patronage. Better yet, we were treated like equals and brothers."[15]

A significant number of black women became involved in the unemployed worker council movement, where they were especially effective in confronting relief agencies. Domestic worker Helen Long and bookkeeper Addie Adkins organized protests outside the city's Welfare Board, the Community Chest, and Red Cross headquarters—organizations that were renowned for their disrespectful treatment of black clients.[16] After one rally, the police arrested Long and beat her into unconsciousness.

New York's *Daily Worker* took issue with NAACP national secretary Walter White's comments about these women "running with the Reds." White called them "ignorant and uncouth victims being led to the slaughter by bold radicals."[17] That was a big mistake.

Even blacks who never officially joined the party admired the Reds for their courage and their commitment to social justice. They took the struggle for equal rights into the economic arena by demanding "equal pay for equal work," and they were first to clearly articulate a theory of "institutional racism."[18] Accounts of their audacity traveled from the coal mines through blast furnaces, foundries, and steel mills to the rural communities of Cotton Country.

2 ▌ THE *SOUTHERN WORKER* AND THE DYNAMO OF DIXIE

> Those who cannot change their minds cannot change anything.
> —George Bernard Shaw, *Everybody's Political*

In mid-July 1930, James Allen, a white twenty-four-year-old, two-hundred-pound, tall and scholarly journalist with a jutting jaw, arrived in Birmingham looking for Tom Johnson. They'd met in Cleveland a year earlier when Allen was writing an article about the IWW organizers for the party's *Labor Defender*. He'd developed a deep respect for the decisive, soft-spoken Johnson. Allen planned to stay in Birmingham just long enough to determine whether or not to relocate there.

Allen had accepted an assignment to publish a biweekly district 17 newspaper, the *Southern Worker*, and he was looking for a safe place to set up his press. He had his doubts about Birmingham after learning that the Klan had recently burned Tom in effigy. Comrade Frank Burns warned him that he, Tom and Harry Jackson had to move constantly—they might live in as many as three different rented rooms in one month's time. Sheriff McDuff's men followed them everywhere and repeatedly arrested them for vagrancy.

Born Solomon Auerbach in 1906, Jim Allen was raised in a Philadelphia Jewish immigrant neighborhood. He'd been teaching philosophy at the University of Pennsylvania when the party called on him. Ida Kleinman, his journalist wife, would join him as Isabelle Allen once he got settled. Johnson suggested that he check out Chattanooga, which was a bit more progressive—at least less violently antilabor. That city had a substantial Jewish population, many of whom were members of the International Workers' Order (IWO), a party-affiliated group that had recently split from the Workmen's Circle. The IWO offered inexpensive medical and dental clinics and life and disability insurance for workers of all races and occupations. It advocated for government-sponsored unemployment insurance and old-age pensions and supported industrial unions. Chattanooga was also home to the Adolph Ochs family, publishers of both the *New York Times* and the widely respected *Chattanooga Times*.

In the end, Allen decided on Chattanooga, but he datelined the *Southern Worker* in Birmingham to keep the police at bay. After the first issue was released on August 16, 1930, the Birmingham police raided every known Red hangout looking for "Jim Allen." His inaugural editorial, "What Do We Stand For?," listed "full social, economic and political equality for Negro workers and farmers." That enraged Chief McDuff.[1]

Despite the nation's rising unemployment rate, Chattanooga was still the Dynamo of Dixie. It sat on the Tennessee River 147 miles northeast of Birmingham, and Harry Jackson came to know every one of its mills, foundries, low-rise brick factories, and warehouses. The city had few industrial unions beyond the United Mine Workers, and the hard-driving Jackson intended to change that.

Chattanooga manufactured everything from locomotives and textiles to furniture, steel, snuff, and coffins, but no single industry dominated the city the way that TCI dominated Birmingham. Insurance companies, banks, law offices, restaurants, and hotels sat cheek by jowl along Market Street in the city's commercial district, and because Chattanooga was the Hamilton County seat, a few government buildings, and a courthouse. The Southern Railway yards, just east of downtown, included a hobo jungle, an expanse of broken-down shelters, dashed hopes, rusted equipment, and trash. It was a dangerous place to be after the sun went down.

Jackson trained organizers for TUUL's industrial chapters and delegated responsibility for the unemployed worker movement to Amy Licht, a white Chicago native. Licht planned her first mass demonstration for March 6 to celebrate the International Day of Protest Against Government Inaction Regarding Unemployment and to support the party's workers' social insurance bill. The Workers International Relief organization paid for veteran Amy Schechter, the white heroine of the 1929 Loray Textile Mill strike in Gastonia, North Carolina, to come to Chattanooga and help out. Amy Licht asked Schechter to speak at the rally, but Schechter, always the renegade, could not wait that long. She immediately called her own meeting to praise TUUL's efforts to organize "negro and white workers alike." Schechter characterized TUUL as "an avenging angel sent to strike down the bosses and heal the wounds of working men." In her dramatic forty-five-minute speech (which the press called a "harangue"), she damned the AFL and called its president, William Green, "a tool of the bosses . . . who lolls in Florida with his Executive Council while three million workers are unemployed."[2]

Schechter's "help" was definitely a two-edged sword. While she could turn out and whip up a crowd like no one else, she was white Chattanooga's worst nightmare—a crazy white Red radical. Raised in London, Schechter had organized coal miners and mill workers for years and was substantially older than most of her comrades. Although well educated, she affected a cockney accent and generally appeared rumpled and unkempt. She was loud and sloppy but also fearless and passionate for the cause.[3]

On March 6, Amy Licht's International Day of Protest attracted nearly twenty-five hundred unemployed workers. But the actual march never got underway because the police disbursed the crowd and arrested veteran Amy Schechter for sedition. Although she hadn't said one word that morning, the police had been watching her. Judge Martin Fleming fined her $50 and warned that if she remained in the city she would face a charge of lunacy. In any event, the heroine of Gastonia was sent packing.

Three TUUL organizers arrested for vagrancy that morning weren't so lucky. They were detained for two months pending trial. George W. Chamlee, a white former Hamilton County attorney general who was generally sympathetic to TUUL's mission, agreed to represent them. Chamlee had a reputation for defending black and white clients, especially radicals.

Mary Dalton, Elsa Lawson, and Hy Gordon were the first Reds to be prosecuted in Chattanooga. Their trial lasted four days. All three were charged with advocating the overthrow the government. The tall, balding affable Chamlee rose from the defense table to remind the jury that their relatives (and his) had committed armed insurrection against the federal government less than a hundred years earlier.[4] The three were subsequently acquitted on the inciting to riot charge but declared guilty of vagrancy, for which they paid a fine.

By this time, Jim and Isabelle Allen were living in a small Chattanooga apartment that also served as the *Southern Worker*'s press room. Isabelle handled circulation and correspondence and wrote under the byline Helen Marcy. Tom Johnson contributed articles and editorials, and Allen gathered the kinds of news that the regional and national papers often ignored. TUUL organizers, unemployed worker council leaders and representatives from the Young Communist League and the League of Struggle for Negro Rights, became his earliest and best sources. He covered lynchings; industrial accidents; worker exploitation; the Arkansas sharecropper uprising; coal, steel, and textile strikes; the radical midwestern farm movement; and police brutality. On his "From Mills, Mines & Farms" page, Allen published letters to the editor, and his "Lynch Law at Work" column reprinted articles from other southern papers. His editorials encouraged collective action and interracial cooperation and supported federal antilynching legislation.

When Allen covered Congressman Hamilton Fish's hearings in Birmingham (calling them "open forums for fascism"), he described how the "heads of the Chambers of Commerce, police chiefs, company stools and leading exploiters" fell over each other to get close to Fish. He reported, with obvious relish, that the chagrined Police Chief McDuff was forced to admit that he'd been unable to locate the *Southern Worker* press.[5]

The *Southern Worker* helped to extend the party's underground network. Considered subversive literature in many parts of the South, those who had copies were careful not to get caught with them. Back issues circulated and recirculated through black communities and were often read aloud to illiterate mill workers, miners and farmers. Chattanooga's Trade Union Unity League offered a Reading and Writing Club that met weekly in their union hall and volunteer tutors often used the *Southern Worker* as their text.

With a miniscule and constantly changing staff, Allen still managed to address all the major social, political, and economic concerns of his time while covering in some depth local matters that were often more harrowing. The 1930 riot in the town of Emelle, Alabama, is a case in point. It served as the district's wake-up call to the depth of the rage that was bubbling just beneath the surface of the sleepy towns and farmlands of the Black Belt.

The Robinsons of Emelle

Emelle is a tiny Sumter County, Alabama, farm community located at the crossroads of Highway 17 and Country Road 24, near the Mississippi border. Before 1971, the Alabama, Tennessee and Northern Railroad ran nearby on its way to Mobile, but it did not stop.

On the Fourth of July, 1930, Esau Robinson, a black farmer, and Clarence Boyd, the white owner of an auto parts store in town, allegedly argued over payment for a secondhand battery that Robinson had purchased three months earlier. Boyd claimed that Robinson still owed him $3.50 on the sale.

Robinson left Boyd's store that day allegedly promising to return with the money. Instead, he brought his father, two brothers, and a cousin back with him. During a heated debate, someone threw a punch that led to a brawl that ended with Robinson's father being wounded and Boyd's uncle dead. That was one of three rumors that circulated throughout the white community.

Another version of the incident described Boyd as going to the Jones Chapel, where the Robinson family was having a Fourth of July picnic and confronting Esau, who again refused to pay. Boyd then allegedly pulled the battery out of Esau's car and told him that he could have it back when he paid for it.

In the third account, Esau, his father Tom, brothers Ollis and King, and cousin Dock got drunk, armed themselves, and went to Boyd's store to retrieve the battery. In this explanation, when Robinson hit Boyd over the head with a bottle, Boyd's uncle Grover opened fire. The Robinsons returned the fire and fled. All escaped except Esau, who was captured and tied to a tree. All that can actually be confirmed is that when Sumter County sheriff Will Scales arrived, several eye witnesses maintained that Esau was not the one who'd shot Grover Boyd. The sheriff told them that he would release Esau after the others were captured.[6]

Sheriff Scales then apparently recruited a posse, requested the Meridian, Mississippi, police bloodhounds, and dispatched volunteers to follow what was alleged to be a bloody trail leading away from the store. Putting aside the difficulty of imagining how a wounded man fleeing by car could leave a bloody trail of some miles, the trail supposedly led to Preacher John Robinson's cabin. Esau's uncle, Preacher John pastored the Jones Chapel where the family picnic took place and he was not involved in the shootings.[7]

Charlie Marrs, a white plantation overseer, who led the band of volunteers was reportedly drunk. The posse found the preacher sitting on his front porch with a rifle balanced across his knees. When he objected to having his home searched, Marrs ordered the men to rush the cabin. The preacher held them off long enough for his wife, son, sister-in-law, and nephew to escape out the back door, but two other family members reportedly remained inside.[8]

During the attack, both John Robinson and Charlie Marrs were shot, the latter accidently by a fellow volunteer. By the time Sheriff Scales arrived, both had died. Scales ordered the preacher's home torched despite the fact that two family members might have been inside.[9] As fire engulfed the cabin, it exploded, the result of stockpiled weapons and ammunition.

As the volunteer posse made its way back to town, they discovered Esau's body hanging from a tree in the woods. Nobody could say how it had gotten there.[10]

Like many lynch narratives, these raise more questions than they answer. Why, for example, would a white southern merchant humiliate himself by repeatedly requesting settlement of a debt from a black customer? Why didn't Boyd repossess the battery sooner? On the other hand, if the Robinsons were such violent men, why didn't they attack Boyd when he showed up at their picnic? Why would they risk going to his store in the middle of town to argue over a battery? And what kind of anger or fear could have motivated the Robinsons to stockpile guns and ammunition in the pastor's home? Finally, although $3.50 was not an insubstantial sum, the Robinsons could well have afforded it. They were landowning farmers who paid their debts. Might the real issue have been their daring to question a white man's bill?

The story that ran in *Our Southern Home* describing thirty-eight-year-old Grover Boyd's death offers a clue. The writer noted that "the Robinson family that started the trouble over the small debt for a motor car battery is composed of blue-eyed mulattoes, a class that do not have the sympathy and cooperation of the full-blooded Negroes. One of the Robinsons recently took a trip to Chicago where he became acquainted with gangster operations, and later returned home with the evident intention of putting them in practice."[11]

Tom Robinson and his sons were not sharecroppers. He, his wife, and fourteen children all worked on family-owned land. All had completed elementary school—a rare accomplishment at the time. Preacher John, Tom's brother, was also an independent farmer. None of his children had ever been in trouble with the law, and no member of the Robinson clan had ever been to Chicago. Apparently, there was a good deal more to the story than the $3.50 debt.

Dragnet

After destroying Preacher Robinson's cabin, Sheriff Scales's posse searched the Flat Woods for Grover Boyd's killer. When they found nothing, the sheriff ordered them to fan out. The first group reached Marchetta, Mississippi, an hour later and volunteer Clarence Bush chased Winston Jones, a local black man, into a railway station and killed him. Jones had not been anywhere near Emelle that day.

Several miles away, at a checkpoint in Narkeeta, Mississippi, Viola Dial, a pregnant black woman riding in a car with her husband, Jesse, was shot and killed when Jesse attempted to run the roadblock. Despite an all-night search, no Robinsons were found. When Governor Bibb Graves offered a three-hundred-dollar reward for their capture, the *Southern Worker* charged the state with "putting its official stamp on the lynch law policy of the Southern White ruling class [as it] officially approves and conducts the extermination of a whole negro family. The white ruling class shows its intention of ruthlessly suppressing any attempt of negroes to defend themselves."[12]

Seven other Robinsons—Jacob (Esau's twin brother), Jordan, J. W., James, Elbert, Andrew, and Frank were eventually captured, taken to Kilby State Prison, near Montgomery, and put into protective custody. Other family members had fled the state.

When, on July 7, a coroner's inquest determined that all the dead had been killed by persons unknown Governor Graves sent Chief Walter McAdoo of the Alabama State Law Enforcement Office to Emelle to investigate. A week later, McAdoo reported that a mob of about forty-five men, including the sheriff, his deputies, and several members of the Boyd family, were responsible for the murders of Esau and John Robinson, Winston Jones, and Viola Dial.[13]

The governor subsequently ordered a grand jury inquest and appointed Justice Bart Chamberlain of Mobile to preside. When Emelle's white citizens objected, claiming that he was interfering in a local matter, Graves made it clear that Sheriff Will Scales and the circuit solicitor would be required to explain their failure to perform their duties. Fearful of being impeached (and therefore ineligible to run for their offices in the future) both men resigned.[14]

Late in July, state enforcement officers arrested Tom Robinson and his sons King and Ollis. The seven Robinson men in protective custody were released. On August 20, a Sumter County Grand Jury indicted Tom, Ollis, and King for Grover Boyd's murder. No other charges were filed despite the fact that most people in Emelle knew exactly who'd ridden with the posse. The foreman explained that the jury was unable to determine which individuals had shot John Robinson and lynched his nephew or which of the volunteers had killed Winston Jones and Viola Dial.[15]

The *Southern Worker* denounced this "failure to indict anyone for the deaths of four black people" while both Robinson and his sons had been indicted for Grover Boyd's murder. James Allen appealed to the workers in Birmingham and Chattanooga to rally to the Robinsons' defense and to demand "the immediate recall of all officials from Governor Graves on down who participated in the brutal attack on the fundamental rights of the Negro workers to protect their lives."[16]

The Lynching Committee Report

In July 1930 the Commission on Interracial Cooperation (a biracial organization established to address post–World War I urban race riots) funded the Southern Commission on the Study of Lynching. National lynching statistics had spiked in 1929. Sociologist Arthur Raper, the new director, came to Emelle to investigate the Robinson matter. He was assisted by Walter Chivers, a black Morehouse College sociology professor who interviewed the black witnesses. Chivers had a gift for putting people at ease. His manner was low-key, he was a good listener, and he had a wry sense of humor.[17] Family members, neighbors, and friends of the Robinsons assured him that while a car battery may have been the immediate cause of the argument, it was not what provoked the violence. They claimed that "the trouble grew out of the insistence of certain white men upon running with the Robinson and other Negro women."[18] Apparently, there'd been a long-standing feud over the Boyd males' pursuit of mulatto women.

On October 8, 1930, Tom Robinson was tried, convicted, and sentenced to be executed on January 2, 1931. Ollis Robinson was sentenced to ten years at hard labor, but King Robinson was released.[19] The murderers of Esau Robinson, John Robinson, Winston Jones, and Viola Dial were never apprehended.

Raper noted that "no white person [who he'd interviewed] seemed to feel that anything very bad had happened other than the deaths of Grover Boyd and Charlie Maars" and there was no evidence of "any effort to keep Esau Robinson from being lynched."[20]

In his final report, Raper drew three broad conclusions. First, in the Black Belt, "any crime which occurs among the property-less Negroes is considered a labor matter to be handled by the white landlord or his overseer." Second, "the minority white element considers it imperative that the Negro be kept in his place, . . . he must accept the white man's unqualified right to arbitrate any question which arises between Negro and white. No movement will be tolerated among the Negroes which remotely threatens to disrupt the present system." Finally, ending on what he apparently believed to be a positive note, Raper wrote that "lynching can and will be eliminated in proportion as all elements of the population are provided opportunities for development and are accorded fundamental human rights."[21] That stuck in Walter Chivers's throat.

While Chivers was proud to contribute to the lynching study, he had little faith in the efficacy of liberal interracial organizations. Director Raper apparently believed that if and when the South became urbanized and industrialized and the level of education was raised, civic organizations would grow stronger and respect for law and order would increase and Negroes would benefit. Chivers considered that a very long time to wait—more than a few lifetimes. To his mind, gradualism actually contributed to riots and lynchings. Chivers did not believe that educated, cultured, civic-minded, and thoughtful black leaders would bring about change. They had too much to lose by rocking the boat. In his experience, change was the product of struggle. Effective leadership arose out of conflict and crisis. In the mid-1940s, undergraduate Martin Luther King Jr. enrolled in several of Professor Chivers's courses at Morehouse College, and he was deeply influenced by Chivers's philosophy.[22]

Chattanooga's All-Southern Anti-Lynching Conference

On November 9, 1930, the Trade Union Unity Leagues, the *Southern Worker* and the League of Struggle for Negro Rights cosponsored the All-Southern Anti-Lynching Conference in Chattanooga. Amy Licht, leader of Chattanooga's unemployed worker councils, and Birmingham organizer Angelo Herndon worked on the conference committee. That day, Chattanooga's Black Odd Fellows Hall on East Ninth Street welcomed fifty-four delegates—thirty-five of them were black, and nineteen white.

Tom Johnson, still stumping for self-determination in the Black Belt, assured the delegates that "lynching will only be driven away in the South after the Negro masses have won for themselves the right to set up an independent Negro state in the South where Negroes are in the majority."[23] He remained a believer, although many of his comrades had lost faith. A year in the Black Belt had convinced them that rural blacks had little interest in becoming "a nation within a nation" or in claiming any right to secession. It was actually the opposite. They wanted to participate in national prosperity (if it ever returned), to own their own land, and to claim their constitutional rights. Nevertheless, on November 9, the assembled delegates lined up behind their respected leader and endorsed the self-determination policy.

Every speaker addressed lynching in one way or another. Since 1918, legislation requiring the federal government to prosecute lynchers if the individual states refused to do so had been annually introduced in Congress. Several bills had passed the House, but none ever came to a vote in the Senate. Powerful southern senators argued that murder was a state crime. For them, federal antilynching legislation raised the specter of federal officials snooping into their affairs, which was unacceptable. The Chattanooga delegates recommitted themselves to working harder, demonstrating and protesting more widely, and keeping the antilynching movement alive in the press.

In her closing remarks, Licht reported that a telegram had been sent to Tom Robinson on behalf of the conference. He was awaiting execution in Kilby State Prison, and she'd assured him that the white and Negro workers of the South would never forget him and that "the fight against lynching would be carried on."[24]

In 1931, the Executive Committee of the League of Struggle for Negro Rights, chaired by Harry Haywood, denounced the Southern Commission on the Study of Lynching for reporting only twenty-one lynchings for 1930. Haywood had taken exception to Arthur Raper's claim that after much-needed economic and educational reforms were enacted "courts will convict Negroes and therefore they need not be lynched." Haywood considered that "a cold-blooded proposal to regularize lynching under legal forms."[25]

Haywood charged Raper's commission with failing to include "open lynchings" (riots), "legal" (courtroom) lynchings, and the murders of black men and women by local police departments in their statistics.[26] The league's executive committee argued that local sheriffs regularly assured lynch mobs that if they gave up the victim, a swift conviction would follow—a legal lynching. When that inevitably happened, Raper's committee failed to recognize it as a lynching.

Haywood challenged Raper to present his findings in any large northern city and to agree to a debate. If that was not acceptable, Haywood expressed his willingness to meet in a southern city, suggesting Chattanooga, despite the fact that the South would be more intimidating to the league's board members. No debate was ever scheduled.

Enter the ILD

Although Tom Johnson and Harry Jackson were gratified by the steady growth of the unemployed worker councils in Birmingham, Atlanta, and

Chattanooga, Johnson was deeply troubled about the violence that the organizers still confronted. Police brutality was especially vicious in Memphis and Birmingham. Johnson repeatedly (and increasingly frantically) petitioned New York headquarters for assistance. Birmingham organizers were arrested on a daily basis, and the only legal resource they had was Albert Rosenthal of the local Rosenthal and Rosenthal law firm. No other attorney in the city would represent Reds.

As violence escalated and headquarters continued to hedge, Johnson, a man famous for his equanimity, demanded a response. Ultimately the International Labor Defense (ILD)—the party's legal arm—announced its intention to open a southern district office in Chattanooga.

Founded in 1925 to represent labor organizers, political prisoners, and immigrants, the ILD would expand its mission in the South to include a campaign against "legal lynching," which is what occurred when white jurors inevitably assumed that every black defendant was guilty as charged.

In February 1931, white journalist Lowell Wakefield and his wife, Jesse, who was an organizer, arrived in Chattanooga to open the ILD office at 20 West Main Street. With the assistance of black organizer Doug McKenzie and black activist Sherman Bell of the League of Struggle for Negro Rights, they would arrange legal representation for Red organizers, investigate incidents of legal lynching, and seek out high-profile cases to demonstrate the party's commitment to African Americans.[27] Wakefield's office triaged calls to make the best use of available attorneys, and he traveled constantly in order to arrange bail. He was just getting acquainted with the Birmingham staff when a Chattanooga radio station broke the blockbuster story of 1931—the arrest of nine black teenagers near Scottsboro, Alabama, for allegedly raping two white women. With that announcement, the center of gravity for district 17 immediately shifted from Birmingham to Chattanooga.

3 ▮ SCOTTSBORO

> I believe the spotlight the Reds put on Alabama saved all our lives.
> —Clarence Norris, *The Last of the Scottsboro Boys*

On March 25, 1931, seven months after Esau Robinson's lynching in Emelle, four black teens, riding on a Memphis-bound freight train, were jumped by seven white boys who declared that "this is a white man's car." During the ensuing struggle, most of the whites either jumped or were pushed off the train. One ran to the Stevenson depot to report the fight, despite the fact that he too was illegally hoboing. The station master wired the Jackson County sheriff's office, and two deputies and a posse met the train in Paint Rock.

The four black teens involved in the fight, along with five others discovered riding in other cars, were arrested for assault and vagrancy. Several white males and two white females, Ruby Bates, age eighteen, and Victoria Price, age twenty-three, were also questioned.

When the young women were asked if the black boys had "bothered them," Victoria Price made a fateful decision. Already on probation for prostitution, she knew that if she was charged with vagrancy she would go to jail. In a similar fix, Ruby was ready to agree with whatever Price decided. Yes, they'd been "bothered."

All nine black teens were brought to the Jackson County Jail in Scottsboro. Word of their arrests spread quickly, and more than one hundred locals gathered on the court square. Newly elected sheriff Matt Wann threatened to shoot any one who attempted to take his prisoners. He wired the new governor, Benjamin Meek Miller, to send national guardsmen to prevent nine lynchings. The guard arrived at four in the morning and took the prisoners to a secure facility in Gadsden: Charlie Weems (nineteen), Ozie Powell (sixteen), Olen Montgomery (seventeen), Clarence Norris (eighteen), Willie Roberson (seventeen), Haywood Patterson (eighteen), Eugene Williams (fourteen), and brothers Andy Wright (nineteen) and Roy Wright (thirteen). Olin Montgomery was legally blind, and Willie Roberson was likely developmentally disabled. Ruby Bates and Victoria Price were detained as material witnesses.

Judge Alfred E. Hawkins asked the Scottsboro Bar Association to provide a public defender. Seven of its eight members refused, leaving only the semi-retired Milo Mooney, who'd never handled a capital case.¹ If anyone needed good legal advice, it was these young men. The late edition of the *Huntsville Times* reported that they'd "deliberately tossed the white occupants out of the [freight] car and held the girls prisoner."²

Lowell Wakefield, Doug McKenzie, and Isabelle Allen all headed to Scottsboro. While James Allen was a seasoned editor and political analyst, Isabelle was the journalist. Writing as Helen Marcy, she covered the story for the *Southern Worker*. As the white southern press referred to the defendants as monsters and animals, she humanized them through her interviews with their parents. Her articles were reprinted in the *Daily Worker*, published in New York City, and her first-person perspective reached a wide audience. Marcy was one of the first journalists to publicly question the veracity of the rape charges. Her partner, Doug McKenzie, broke the news that the teens' accusers had been engaging in prostitution.

Haywood Patterson, Eugene Williams, and the Wright brothers all lived in Chattanooga, and that city's Colored Ministers' Alliance petitioned the NAACP for more experienced counsel. Ada Wright (Roy and Andy's mother) hired Stephen Roddy, a white lawyer rumored to have Klan connections and known to have a drinking problem. He was the only white attorney who would take the case.³ Roddy wasn't licensed to practice in Alabama, so he could only assist the bungling Milo Mooney. When the young men were returned from Gadsden for their arraignments, Mooney was given half an hour to prepare them.

Moody appeared confused as the teens were being charged with "forcefully ravaging and debasing Victoria Price and Ruby Bates." Roddy counseled them to plead guilty, explaining that it would put him in a better position to negotiate life sentences. But they refused to plead guilty.

Neither Moody nor Roddy requested a postponement, nor did they attempt to locate any character witnesses. Lowell Wakefield wired New York to send a legal team. Allan Taub, a white ILD attorney representing striking miners in Kentucky, immediately drove to Chattanooga.

Four Trials

Beginning on April 6, 1931, the Scottsboro defendants (only four of whom had ever previously met) appeared before Judge Hawkins two at a time. Since it was the first Monday of the month—fair day—Scottsboro's downtown was crowded with farmers buying supplies and provisions, looking at farm equipment, trading horses, and generally seeking a good time. They found it on the town square. As the prisoners were marched back and forth between the jail and the Jackson County Courthouse, Isabelle Allen reported that security was so lax that, if the National Guard had not been visible, lynchers might have had their way.

Prosecutor H. G. Bailey began with Clarence Norris and Charlie Weems, the two oldest defendants at age nineteen. Four trials were subsequently held in as many days. Defense attorney Roddy finally moved for a change of venue, pointing out the number of national guardsmen required to protect his clients. He looked to Major Joe Starnes and to Sheriff Matt Wann for support, but neither offered it. Incredibly, Sheriff Wann swore under oath that he could not recall any attempts to take his prisoners by force—the very reason he'd requested the guard. Both he and Major Starnes testified that they had no reason to believe that the defendants could not get fair trials in Jackson County.[4] When Sheriff Wann was murdered a year later (May 3, 1932), many said it was because he'd initially snubbed Judge Lynch.

After Roddy's request for a change of venue was denied, everything fell apart. On cross-examination Clarence Norris and Charlie Weems accused each other of raping the women. Neither Roddy nor Moody addressed this, nor did they provide closing arguments.[5] In the end, eight of the nine defendants were convicted of rape and sentenced to death. Thirteen-year-old Roy Wright was sentenced to life in prison. The executions were scheduled for July 10, 1931, at Kilby State Prison, where "Yellow Mama," the electric chair, was housed.

Lowell Wakefield wired Governor Miller requesting a stay of execution so he could prepare for an appeal. He asked for Allan Taub to be approved as defense counsel and be granted the right to interview the defendants. After the governor authorized the stay, Taub traveled to Kilby, met with the teens and offered to represent them. By April 10 most had signed on with him.

In the meantime, the ILD, under the leadership of William Patterson, who was black, began a massive national campaign to expose "the Alabama frame-up." Patterson's team organized demonstrations and rallies in major cities to protest the death sentences. Wakefield arranged for the mothers of Andy and Roy Wright, Eugene Williams, Olin Montgomery, and Haywood Patterson to appear at several of these rallies, to speak in their sons' defense, and to raise funds for their legal expenses. The "Scottsboro Mothers tours" proved to be one of the most effective ways of publicizing the case. Janie Patterson, Ada Wright, Mamie Williams Wilcox, Viola Montgomery, and Ida Norris kept the nation apprised of how their sons were faring.

William Patterson, a successful attorney, operated from Harlem. A member of its renaissance jet set, he socialized with artists, writers, musicians, and activists. He'd joined the party in 1926 after the execution of the anarchists Sacco and Vanzetti. Recognizing his potential, CPUSA sent him to the International Lenin School in Moscow in 1927, where he met Harry Haywood and James Ford. When he returned to the States in December 1929, he was dispatched to Pittsburgh to organize. In April 1931 he was called back to Harlem to lead the ILD's Scottsboro campaign.

The NAACP national secretary, Walter White, was also new to his assignment and unlike Patterson was unsure about how to proceed. Should he try to wrest control of the appeal from the ILD? It would be difficult, as many of the members of his biracial executive board were not comfortable supporting young black men accused of raping white women.[6] What if they were guilty? Even the radical W. E. B. Du Bois, editor of the organization's *Crisis*, urged the condemned teens to put their faith in the "fairness and justice" of the court, to ignore the ILD campaigns, and to tie themselves to "intelligent whites."[7]

When the NAACP Executive Board finally voted to pursue the Scottsboro appeal, White became locked in a battle with William Patterson that lasted the rest of 1931. His initial delay had proved costly—the Scottsboro teens chose to stay with their ILD attorneys.

Chief Counsel Joseph Brodsky replaced Stephen Roddy with Allan Taub, and Milo Moody with George Chamlee, the white former Hamilton County attorney general who'd recently defended three TUUL organizers in Chattanooga. Lastly, Brodsky reached out to Clarence Darrow, the nation's most celebrated defense attorney, but, disapproving of the ILD's mass defense tactics, Darrow refused to join the team.

Brodsky appealed to the Alabama Supreme Court for a new trial, citing incompetent counsel, a hostile courtroom environment, and the state's practice of excluding Negroes from juries as factors in the teens' inability to receive fair hearings. His filing automatically triggered eight stays of execution.[8]

The ILD's mass campaign focused national and international attention on Scottsboro, and Patterson insured that every major U.S. radio station and daily newspaper carried the story. Blacks followed it in the *Chicago Defender*, the *Pittsburgh (PA) Courier*, the *Baltimore Afro American*, and the *Southern Worker*. Only the *Courier* counseled the teens to break with the communists and put their trust in the NAACP.[9]

In the meantime, the white *Birmingham Age Herald* assured its readers that "no reasonable fault can be found with the fairness or the legality of the trials," and the *Montgomery Advertiser* maintained that "Jackson County . . . as a citizenry composed of people who hold inviolate its women, offers no apology to the rest of the country for the penalty imposed upon the blacks who would, according to the evidence, be a dangerous menace to any section of any country in the world."[10]

White southerners were by and large convinced that the young men were guilty and lucky to have escaped lynching. The *Advertiser* dismissed the ILD attorneys as "buzzards and carpet baggers seeking publicity and political power." Even Arthur Raper, director of the Southern Commission on the Study of Lynching, concluded that, although the teens were "likely innocent," the ILD was exploiting them as "pawns in a propaganda war."[11]

The Reds, for their part, acknowledged that nine physical lynchings had been averted, but that the four sham trials conducted at the Jackson County Courthouse amounted to legal lynchings.[12] They made this distinction in the April 10, 1931, issue of the *Daily Worker*.

On May Day, an occasion usually reserved for celebrating workers' rights, Scottsboro demonstrations were coordinated in 110 cities from coast to coast. After photos of the teens ran in both the national and international newspapers (courtesy of the ILD), Alabama governor Benjamin Meek Miller received two thousand letters protesting the eight impending executions. The overwhelming success of Patterson's massive protest enraged white Alabamians who bitterly resented his outside interference in what they considered to be a local matter.

On June 22, 1931, ILD attorneys Chamlee and Brodsky brought their appeal before the Alabama Supreme Court. Attorney General Thomas E. Knight Jr., who three months earlier had introduced a bill to the Alabama Legislature outlawing the Communist Party, represented the state before a panel of judges that included his father, Justice Thomas E. Knight Sr.

As the teens awaited the court's decision, the NAACP pressed them to break with the ILD "before the Reds' antics send all of you to the electric chair." Walter White offered the services of Clarence Darrow, a NAACP board member, but the teens understandably chose to remain with the Reds who'd stopped their executions and who had not, as some NAACP officials had, referred to them and their parents as "ignorant and stupid." Walter White had made a major, and apparently irreparable blunder on that account.[13] Six months later, when the Alabama Supreme Court Justices had still not announced their decision, Brodsky approached Darrow a second time. But they could not agree on the terms for working together, and in January 1932 both Darrow and the NAACP withdrew their interest in the case.

Victoria and Ruby

A bit of Old White South folklore alleges that "only white men and black women have sexual freedom." Victoria Price and Ruby Bates knew better. Hollace Ransdell, a young midwestern journalist, would soon discover why.

In April 1931, Ransdell, an American Civil Liberties Union (ACLU) southern field agent, was asked by the organization's national executive, Roger Baldwin, to look into the case. Baldwin had been called on to mediate between the NAACP and the ILD attorneys over representation of the Scottsboro teens. While he was a personal friend of Walter White, Baldwin also respected William Patterson. He asked Ransdell to provide more background information.

Ransdell initially delved into the "fundamental differences over principles and tactics" of these organizations. Whereas the NAACP shunned publicity in order to avoid antagonizing southern white prejudices, the ILD appealed bluntly and directly to the public, agitating on the streets and in the press. In Ransdell's opinion, there was no basis on which to expect that they could ever work together.

She visited the young men in Kilby Prison, spoke at length with both sets of attorneys, with law enforcement officers, judges, residents of Scottsboro, Chattanooga, and Huntsville, politicians, and members of the clergy—anyone who would agree to meet with her, even briefly. She was determined to collect as much information for Baldwin as possible. George Chamlee told Ransdell that Bates and Price had not accused the teens of raping them until they were detained as material witnesses themselves. He claimed that the Scottsboro police had "swept up" the young women into making their accusations. After interviewing the women herself, Ransdell concluded that there was a good chance that Chamlee was right. She described Victoria Price as "the type who welcomes attention and publicity at any price."[14]

Finally, she met with Victoria and Ruby together with their mothers—not once, but several times. Ransdell understood that, under ordinary circumstances, the word of either Price or Bates would not have counted for much. Hardly flowers of white southern womanhood, both had failed to measure up to female standards of honesty, virtue, honor and chastity—but in 1931, they would have to do. Their testimonies were crucial to the execution of eight black rapists.

Both women lived in Huntsville and alleged that they had been riding home in the freight car that afternoon after several unsuccessful attempts to find work. Their shifts at Huntsville's Margaret Spinning Mill had been cut back to every other week, and their pay was averaging only about $1.20 a day. Victoria had worked in the mills since she was ten; Ruby, who was from a sharecropping family, started at sixteen. Both fathers had left the families, and Ruby and Victoria helped to support their mothers and younger siblings. They subsidized their limited incomes with irregular support from local charities, by volunteering for extra shifts whenever possible, and by taking in boarders. Male borders were sometimes willing to pay for special favors, and mill families headed by single women often accommodated them.[15]

Prostitution was a fact of life—one of the few avenues available for women abandoned by their husbands to provide for their children. The coming of the Depression had made it even more necessary.

Ransdell wrote that Ruby Bates "lived in a bare but clean unpainted shack in the Negro section of Huntsville and mixed with [blacks]"; she was what respectable whites described as "the lowest of the low, that is, a white woman whom economic insecurity has forced across the great color barrier."[16]

Victoria Price, older, tougher, and more resilient, had a far worse reputation. She ran a speakeasy in Huntsville and engaged in prostitution there and in Chattanooga. Ruby, while also known to be of uneasy virtue, was more reserved. She took her cues from Victoria, which led authorities to initially assume that she was slow—an assessment that Ruby deeply resented.

The *Daily Worker*, the *Southern Worker*, and the *Labor Defender* expressed little sympathy for Price and Bates. They described them as cheap hookers and portrayed the Scottsboro teens as victims of an unjust social and economic system.

The white *Montgomery Advertiser*, *Huntsville Times*, and *Birmingham News*, on the other hand, viewed the two as poor, fatherless, defenseless victims of nine black predators who'd thrown six white boys from a train in order to have their way with them. Price and Bates were white women, and more to the point, southern white women who were entitled to male protection. It was their misfortune to have been abandoned by their men.[17]

Ransdell described Victoria and Ruby as "victims themselves," who in turn were "mercilessly cruel to other victims." The young journalist produced a comprehensive study of the Scottsboro case for her boss in just a few weeks. In the end, however, she could not get the twenty-two-page report published, not even by the commissioning ACLU. It was judged to be too volatile and too provocative. Ransdell had come to the incendiary conclusion that "if the nine youths on that freight car had been white there would be no Scottsboro Case. The issue at stake was the inviolable separation of black men from white women."[18]

She and Roger Baldwin distributed the report widely, but only the *New York Graphic* and the *Daily Worker* published it, and the NAACP's Walter White repeatedly quoted from it. Ransdell had asked: "How could anyone look at the eight terrified, bewildered young Negroes in their death cells, and these two girls, enjoying excellent health and delighting in their fame—and still maintain that the boys deserved to die?"[19]

Forty years later, Anne Braden, a white Alabama journalist, provided a bit of insight. In a 1972 brochure that she prepared for the Southern Conference Education Fund, Braden offered the following observation:

> For me the awareness began in 1946 in a courtroom in Birmingham, Alabama. I was 22, a young newspaper reporter, covering the courthouse. That day a young black man was being tried—not for rape, but for something called "assault with intent to ravish." A young white woman testified that he passed her on the opposite side of a country road and looked at her in an "insulting" way. He was sentenced to twenty years.
>
> I was appalled by the case. Torn by what was happening to the black man. But torn too, as I watched the white woman. She appeared to be very poor, but she had obviously dressed in her best—and for that day she was queen in the courtroom. The judge, the prosecutor, her father who told of her fright when she came in from that walk—all rallied round to defend her honor.... I realized the horror of what she was doing to herself. Tomorrow, after her day as a queen, she would go back to a life of poverty and boredom; waiting on her father, on her brothers, and

someday on a husband—paying with a lifetime of drudgery for those magic moments when she could achieve the status of a wronged white woman.[20]

Driven by their own fear of arrest and seduced by the attention they received, Bates and Price unwittingly became celebrities. After Scottsboro, the same people who'd ignored them all their lives began listening to them, protecting them, and even fawning over them. It was too good to last, and of course it didn't.

Ruby recanted her testimony in 1933 and was vilified throughout Alabama. She was accused of accepting a bribe from the communists. The *Huntsville Times* referred to her as Harlem's Darling and petitioned the state attorney general to charge "the former Huntsville guttersnipe" with perjury. After Ruby left Huntsville, she toured with the Scottsboro Mothers and campaigned on behalf of the ILD for the teens' release. In 1940, she married Elmer Shut, moved to Yakima, Washington, and lived out her life as Lucille Shut.

Victoria, who never recanted, bitterly resented the fact that Ruby had done so. In later years Victoria no doubt convinced herself that she had been raped. After several divorces, she married sharecropper Walter Street when she was fifty. They lived on a tobacco farm in Flintville, Tennessee, for twenty-seven years, where she was known as Katharine Street.

In 1976 when NBC-TV released the docudrama *Judge Horton and the Scottsboro Case*, Victoria brought a $6 million libel suit for her portrayal in the film. The producers believed that both she and Ruby had long since died. After NBC settled with Victoria, she was able to buy her first home. Ruby subsequently filed a lawsuit but didn't live long enough to see it through. She died on October 27, 1976, in Yakima at the age of sixty-three. Victoria died in Flintville on October 19, 1982, at the age of seventy-seven. Neither ever had children.

4 ■ AN ALL-PURPOSE JESUS

> I think it is safe to say that while the South is hardly Christ centered, it is most certainly Christ haunted.
> —Flannery O'Connor, *Mystery and Manners*

Most of the young Reds who found their way to Birmingham in the 1930s knew a lot about economics, philosophy, and political theory, but not much about organized religion, which Karl Marx defined as "the sigh of the oppressed creatures, the heart of a heartless world, and the soul of soulless conditions."[1]

While he distrusted religion, Marx never advocated abolishing it. He hoped to structure a society in which people would simply no longer need it. While he believed that religion did not change anything, Marx understood that it could be used to manipulate people, to invest their hopes in some imaginary future in order to relieve present suffering. Communism, on the other hand, offered a rational path to solving the problems of this world.

The district 17 Reds would quickly learn, however, just how central a role religion, specifically Christianity, played in the southern way of life. It resonated with sharecroppers—black and white—and was equally essential to middle-class and affluent whites who often shaped it to justify and defend white supremacy. Southern religion, so rife with contradiction and paradox, served needs at all levels of southern society, and had to be accommodated.

Black sharecroppers and tenant farmers who had no political or economic power and very little education often found consolation in Bible stories about Hebrew slaves escaping their captors; in the social justice tirades of Old Testament prophets, and in the Beatitudes of Jesus. The prophet Amos assured them that God's first concern was justice, and Jesus spoke of a time when the social order would be upended, when "the first will be last and many who are last shall be first."[2]

Their Jesus was not the red-haired, blue-eyed Son of God that the planters worshipped on Sunday mornings. That one didn't offer consolation, but then the planters didn't need it: they were already masters of the temporal world.

The teachings of their "gentle Jesus meek and mild" seemed, even to them, more relevant to Sunday school students. They preferred the more robust Saint Paul and his practical advice concerning social equality, beginning with his instructions to slaves to obey their masters.

But this white planters' Jesus, like the Jesus of the black cropper, delivered eternal salvation through the grace of God, and that was serious. Whites believed that while God determined a person's station at birth, making some blessed (like themselves) and others not so much, the gift of salvation evened everything out in the end. Anyone's soul could be saved at any time. In God's kingdom, God made things right. This became the first level of defense of segregation from a Christian point of view.

Croppers, black and white, were generally evangelicals who believed that the Bible was the literal word of God and that salvation was His gift through the sacrifice of His son, Jesus Christ. Black evangelicals tended to understand salvation as both a future event and as the working out of God's Kingdom—through collective action. White evangelicals, however, stressed salvation's individual benefit: the saving of one's soul.

Both black and white evangelicals recognized "baptism by the Holy Spirit." This manifested whenever a believer became so filled with God's Spirit that he or she received gifts of ministry such as understanding "tongues," interpreting prophecy, and healing the sick. Evangelical worship services, black or white, were lively energetic testaments to God's goodness.

The Jesus of the poor white farmer—hardly meek and mild—was a working man, a carpenter with faith so strong that he could drive out demons. He promised that, with enough faith, others could do the same. But first, one had to be saved. Unless you were born again (spiritually transformed), you were not eligible to receive the gifts of the Holy Spirit. Thankfully, being saved (giving your life over to Jesus), was a once-and-for-all-time event.

The image of Jesus in the South (and likely elsewhere) was often a projection of the believer's own heart and mind. As white southern Christians strained to align the Gospel with the southern way of life, black Christians, reflecting on the same texts, found encouragement, if not deliverance.

Black croppers worshipped in small congregations led by men or women who'd been "called to preach," rather than ordained. Like white croppers, they looked forward to visits by itinerant preachers who conducted outdoor revival meetings, where many neighbors, family members, and friends recommitted themselves to the Lord.

In the minds of many black croppers, Jesus was akin to a trickster who defied convention by challenging and destabilizing authority. He could be counted on to "make a way where there was no way." This Jesus walked beside folks every day helping them stay one step ahead of the boss, the landlord or the sheriff.[3] He never promised that God would remove the inequities of life, only that He would provide strength to cope with them. That hopeful spirit often spilled over into sharecropper union meetings to create a revival-like atmosphere.

The Social Gospel

The progressives' social Gospel tradition was revived during the Depression, largely by white ministers whose radical visions of Jesus had cost them their pulpits. These men envisioned Jesus as a prophet who was just as concerned with justice for the living as he was with caring for the souls of the dead. Because they recognized many of Jesus's teachings as compatible with socialism, they called themselves Christian socialists.

Howard Kester, a white ex-Presbyterian minister who worked for the pacifist Fellowship of Reconciliation, was radicalized in 1933 during a relief operation with striking coal miners in Wilder, Tennessee. His decision to align with those miners who in their desperation began to fight violence with violence cost him his job. But Kester concluded that "to attempt to emancipate the mass of white and negro workers in the South employed in mine, mill, farm and factory only through the methods of goodwill, moral suasion and education is to invite continued exploitation, misery and sufferings of generations yet unknown."[4] Kester's change of heart literally changed the course of his life. He later became chaplain of the Southern Tenant Farmers' Union.

Kester's experience was not unique. Preachers, black and white, made some of the most effective leaders of the sharecropper and tenant farmer movements. Both the Southern Tenant Farmers' Union and the Alabama Share Croppers' Union held their meetings in churches and used Bible readings, prayer and hymn singing to celebrate their solidarity. Every meeting opened with prayer and closed with a blessing.

Well-educated Protestant clergymen—seminary-trained Baptists, Methodists, Presbyterians, and Episcopalians—were not immune to the temptation to manipulate the image of Jesus in defense of "Christian segregation." In 1966, Kyle Haselden, editor of *Christian Century*, accused them of preaching an "ethics-less gospel . . . to preserve their religion while making it serve the basest interests."[5]

"They eliminated the hard, judgmental imperatives of the faith," Haselden wrote. "Truth and justice were pushed out but the lesser merits of church-going, Bible reading, courtesy and hospitality remained. . . . They kept evangelistic and mission fervor, ritualistic religious acts and sentiments—and this gave them a warm glow of personal righteousness."[6] They were, for all intents and purposes, cultural Christians.

While some clergymen disdained "Christian segregation" as an oxymoron that was impossible to accept, let alone explain, others more easily incorporated it into their religious experience. It tended to make their lives easier and often enhanced their careers.

Not to be outdone, the Ku Klux Klan also exploited Jesus's elasticity. Church membership was required of all the Knights of the Invisible Empire, and in 1924 Imperial Wizard H. W. Evans, a former Methodist minister, wrote, "as the Star of Bethlehem guided the wise men to Christ, so it is that the Klan is expected to guide men to the right life under Christ's banner."[7]

Jesus the Klansman was the New Testament Jesus who'd outwitted and humiliated the high priests and Pharisees.[8] Klansmen W. C. Wright, writing for the *Imperial Night Hawk*, glorified him as "the model Klansmen" because he "sought, first of all, to deliver the people of his own race, blood and religion . . . and [he] emerged from the Jewish clan to create his own."[9]

While all Christians put their faith in Jesus and in the hope of eternal salvation, it was sometimes difficult for outsiders to determine which Jesus they were talking about and what kind of salvation they were referring to. Klansmen were only the most obvious among those who conflated salvation and white privilege.

Many white Christians despised the Reds for their atheism or simply for being Jewish. The term *communist* covered both bases. The communists' rejection of Jesus compounded by their radical politics was an affront to the southern way of life.[10]

To their credit, the Reds accepted that there were needs that only religion could satisfy. Christianity was indispensable in the South, whether in its evangelical, Pentecostal, conservative, or liberal manifestation. It held rich, poor, and middle-class blacks, whites, segregationists, and Klansmen all in thrall. Jesus spoke to all of them, albeit in different contexts and in different ways.

Many Reds, if they had to identify, would probably consider themselves cultural Jews. Most were children of Eastern European immigrants who worked at blue-collar jobs, or taught school, labored in factories, or ran small businesses. Some of their parents had emigrated because of their own unpopular political beliefs. They'd learned Torah and Talmud traditions at home, including the concept of *tikkun olam*—a requirement to make an effort to repair the world. For them, action would always be more important than belief.

Many were drawn to the Communist Party because of its moral toughness—because of its "negro work" and antiracist commitment. As journalist Daniel Oppenheimer notes, "Belief is complicated, contingent, multi-determined.... It is hard to be a person in the world, period, and how much more confusing that task can become when you take on responsibility for repairing or redeeming it."[11]

5 ▌ THE MASSACRE AT CAMP HILL

> One may die of too much endurance as well as too little.
> —Joseph Conrad, *Chance*

In April 1931, just weeks after the Scottsboro teens were arraigned, Tallapoosa County planters suspended sharecropper and tenant credit at their commissaries. The price of cotton had dropped significantly in 1930, and croppers were encouraged to look for part-time work at the new Russell Saw Mill near Alexander City.

Sharecroppers from adjoining plantations met in small groups to discuss the crisis. Estelle Milner, a black twenty-one-year-old Birmingham schoolteacher, party member, and daughter of a Tallapoosa cropper, brought a copy of the *Southern Worker* to one of these meetings and read aloud about how the Reds were organizing Farm Relief Councils up in Whitney.[1]

Two brothers, Ralph and Tommy Gray, said they would contact district 17. When Ralph did, Tom Johnson sent Mack Coad, a black Chattanooga TUUL organizer to Camp Hill. Coad brought along Harry Simms, a white Young Communist League organizer.[2]

The Grays were grandsons of Alfred Gray, a black Perry County Reconstruction senator. Ralph, a World War I veteran, had a reputation as a troublemaker because he'd refused to chop Sheriff Kyle Young's cotton. The sheriff wouldn't pay him more than fifty cents a day. Infuriated by Gray's refusal, Young warned him that "white folks aren't going to stand for Negroes setting the price of labor in Tallapoosa."[3] Neither ever forgot the incident.

The Grays brought Coad and Simms around to meet the croppers and arranged for meetings to discuss "credit suspension strategy"—union organizing. Coad also updated them about the Scottsboro case, which by then was before the Alabama Supreme Court. Several of the Scottsboro teens came from sharecropping families.

The longer Coad and Simms remained in Camp Hill, the longer the croppers' list of demands grew. They wanted to market their own cotton instead of selling it to the plantation commissary merchants, generally called furnish merchants because they furnished supplies to croppers, often at double the price elsewhere—and croppers were not permitted to trade elsewhere. The furnish merchants stored the croppers' cotton until the prices rose. It wasn't fair. Day laborers wanted cash payment for picking cotton, and everybody wanted written contracts.[4]

After an informer betrayed Coad to the planters, croppers were warned that anyone caught associating with him or with the Gray brothers would be evicted. Despite these threats, in April the croppers chose four delegates to represent them at an All-Southern Scottsboro Defense Conference, cosponsored by the ILD and the League of Struggle for Negro Rights, to be held in Chattanooga on May 24, 1931.

Neither the white nor the black Chattanooga preachers welcomed these delegates or the others who came from all over Alabama and Tennessee. The police arrested many of them for loitering. Bessie Ball, a local white woman who tried to attend, was beaten by her husband. Their daughter had him arrested, but at trial the judge congratulated him and suggested that next time he use a shotgun on the Reds.[5] All the Camp Hill delegates were arrested when they tried to enter the Black Odd Fellows Hall and were detained long enough to miss the event. B. D. Amis of the League of Struggle for Negro Rights and Tom Johnson were also jailed. The two hundred delegates who managed to get inside, however, voted to establish an ongoing Southern Scottsboro Defense Committee.[6] At the same time, the planters made good on their threats to evict any cropper who associated with the Grays. Union organizing threatened their cheap labor advantage—and that was unacceptable.

By July 1, the fledging Croppers' and Farm Workers' Union counted eight hundred members. That summer the price of cotton dropped to six cents a pound—one-third what it had been in 1929. The planters announced that they could not extend credit on six-cent cotton—it didn't even cover the cost of fertilizer. They were furious with the Reds who they believed were encouraging the croppers to make all these demands, and they called on Tallapoosa County sheriff J. Kyle Young to do something about it. He didn't waste any time.

Union Busting

On Wednesday evening, July 15, 1931, Sheriff Young, acting on a tip from a black informer, took a few deputies to an abandoned building seven miles south of Dadeville, where a union meeting was allegedly in session. Eight croppers were inside, with Mack Coad drafting a petition to Governor Miller to demand the Scottsboro teens' release. When Young and his men burst in, the croppers created a diversion and pushed Coad out the back door. Young was livid. This was worse than he expected. These niggers were not only making demands but passing judgment on white man's justice in the Scottsboro affair. He and his deputies roughed some of them up to teach them a lesson.

The following day, the same informer sent Young to the Mary Church outside Dadeville. This time the sheriff brought a posse and surprised 150 croppers in the act of electing delegates to an upcoming Scottsboro Defense Committee meeting in Birmingham. Ralph Gray, the sheriff's nemesis, was standing guard outside.[7] Young decided to make an example of this black man who considered his labor worth more than fifty cents a day. They argued, and as Gray reached for his gun, the sheriff shot him. As he fell, Gray also fired, hitting Young in the stomach. As his deputies rushed him to an Alexander City hospital, Camp Hill Police Chief Matt Wilson ran to a nearby revival meeting shouting, "the niggers have shot the sheriff all to pieces." The fiery preacher ordered him to "keep quiet," and assured the congregation that "somebody's just trying to bring Chicago down here." Most of the men left however, to get their guns.[8]

Despite his wounds, Ralph Gray survived long enough to return to his cabin. Chief Wilson's men tracked him there, killed him, fractured his wife's skull, and wounded several of his friends. Then Wilson went looking for that black Birmingham schoolteacher, Estelle Milner, who thought she was so smart. When he found her, he beat her so violently that he ruptured several of her vertebrae.[9] His deputies arrested thirty-three croppers, including her father, and threw them in the Dadeville jail. Five others were reported missing and assumed dead. Gray's body was dumped on the Tallapoosa County Courthouse steps in Dadeville and used for target practice—a lesson to would-be organizers.[10] One month later, on August 6, fifty-five Croppers' and Farm Workers' Union members regrouped to form the Alabama Share Croppers' Union (ASCU), and divided up into five Tallapoosa County locals. They would never meet again in large numbers under a single roof.

The Reds were to blame, the planters said. They not only pumped up the blacks to make demands, but they told them that the Scottsboro trials proved that white justice was corrupt.[11] White men couldn't allow this to go on.

Chief Wilson told reporters that his deputies found literature in Gray's cabin encouraging blacks to "demand wages of $2 a day and urging them to intermarry with the white race." He hadn't thought it necessary to intervene when members of his posse shot croppers as they tried to escape, and yes, he'd ordered Gray's cabin and the Mary Church torched.[12] Wilson's deputies searched in vain for Mack Coad, who by that time was well on his way to Atlanta.

Local whites did not consider the police chief's methods excessive since they believed that black insurrection was being encouraged by these outside agitators who were taking full advantage of the Scottsboro situation. Most whites never imagined how completely Scottsboro changed the calculus. That single case came to represent every injustice that blacks had ever suffered. Scottsboro called up issues of disenfranchisement, racial and labor discrimination, lynching, violence, poverty, and the white obsession with female purity. The Scottsboro teens' defense came to be nearly as important to the croppers as their own demands for labor reform and financial equity. And while the Scottsboro case might be considered in some ways an issue worthy of black self-determination, it had nothing to do with seceding from the United States or with forming a separate nation. Blacks had decided to stay and fight back, and white Alabama was terrified.

An Ongoing Battle

Throughout the summer of 1931, as blood flowed in Camp Hill, the ILD was vying with the NAACP over the Scottsboro Boys' defense. The NAACP's persistent warnings about the Reds' deviousness had backfired in July when Eugene Davidson, editor of the black *Washington World*, wrote that "if [the NAACP] now feels that fighting the spread of communism is more important than fighting white Southerners who will lynch, massacre and slaughter and expect to get away with it then it has outlived its usefulness."[13]

At the same time, headlines in the *Montgomery Advertiser* were screaming "Race Riots and Red Violence" and editor Grover Hall was insisting that "the simple ignorant Negroes have been duped by wily pied piper Communists who came in solely to stir up trouble and to fleece the poor sharecroppers of their earnings." Hall did not acknowledge the hunger, poverty, and oppression that croppers had been enduring for decades, but he did publish unsubstantiated rumors about croppers stockpiling machine guns and dynamite in preparation for race war.[14]

When the white *Birmingham Herald* erroneously reported that eight carloads of black communists were coming from Chattanooga to Dadeville to break their comrades out of jail, whites organized vigilante patrols.[15] By the time the white *Birmingham News* reported that the eight cars were actually a black funeral procession, it was too late—the damage was done. One Tallapoosa resident had already appealed to the Klan in an open letter in the *Dadeville Record*, asking the Knights to take action to "quiet disturbances among our Negroes in Tallapoosa County and to stop the flow of outside influences."[16]

Whites rejected the possibility that blacks might be fighting back on their own initiative. Ben Cothran, white president of Alabama's Commission on Interracial Cooperation, appealed to Tuskegee Institute superintendent Robert Moton to take a delegation of "prominent and respectable Negroes" to Dadeville and discourage the croppers from "going Red." Moton did as he was asked, but he and the "respectable Negroes" were completely ignored.[17] The croppers had finally found an organization willing to fight alongside them as comrades, and they were not interested in speaking with emissaries from the Commission on Interracial Cooperation (CIC), the NAACP, or Tuskegee. Where had they been when the Scottsboro Boys were facing the electric chair?

On July 18, 1931, ILD's white Southern Counsel George Chamlee represented the forty-seven Camp Hill croppers who'd been arrested and charged with everything from assault to conspiracy to commit murder. The following day the *New York Times* reported that J. Louis Engdahl, ILD national secretary, held Sheriff Young responsible for Ralph Gray's murder.

"The Negroes of this county have been organizing against miserable starvation wages," he said. "The plantation owners planned to cut the sharecroppers off from all food advances, giving a small number of them the alternative of working in the fields or in saw mills at wages of 60 to 90 cents a day. The lynchers went after the members and leaders of the union. . . . The Sheriff's posse is now hunting and shooting down Negroes in several towns in that section, as well as raiding and shooting tenant farmers in their homes. This is a deliberate slaughter."[18]

Engdahl demanded "immediate cessation of the terror let loose by the landowners and the police against the sharecroppers."[19]

White Alabamians, still smarting over the national sense of outrage that Scottsboro provoked, were incensed. Their rage would have had no bounds had they read a black *Chicago Defender* editorial opining that "the Negro in Alabama has no vote and can have no voice except in protest by motion or petition. If a Negro turns communist in Alabama . . . he is driven to his new alliance by a despair he can hardly control."[20]

A few weeks later, George Chamlee and his ILD white cocounsel Irving Schwab won reprieves for thirty-three of the Camp Hill prisoners due to insufficient evidence.[21] One of these men was Estelle Milner's father. The charges were never refiled. By September 1931, the last fourteen croppers were released and all charges against them dropped. Dadeville had decided not to invite the kind of scrutiny Scottsboro had.[22]

In August, the NAACP hired Howard Kester, then southern secretary for the Fellowship of Reconciliation, to investigate the Camp Hill Massacre. Local white farmers told him that the five croppers reported missing were dead, and one of Sheriff Young's deputies explained to him that "the Sheriff heard the niggers were having a Communist meeting and we went with him to break it up." When Kester asked why, the deputy said, "the Communists want to take peoples' property away and divide it up," assuring Kester that "[everything] was fine down here until the Chattanooga Reds came and told the Dadeville niggers that everything in the South was made with nigger labor and that they ought to get some of it back."[23]

John Henry Calhoun, a journalist with the Associated Negro Press, reflected: "Most Southern whites who want to be fair concede that the Scottsboro Boys are victims of a condition brought about by race feeling [i.e. discrimination]. But the methods of the communists have made the Southern white close his eyes to justice. The same is true for the croppers . . . the Southern white will interpret any organization among the Negroes which implies force—even that of collective bargaining, as a threat against whites."[24]

6 ❙ THE NATIONAL MINERS' UNION, SOUTHEASTERN KENTUCKY

> The miners lost because they had only the Constitution. The other side had bayonets and in the end bayonets always win.
> —Mother Jones, speech at the Battle of Blair Mountain, August 1921

In February 1931, district 17 sent Angelo Herndon to Wilcox County, Alabama, to assist sharecroppers in Alberta organize a sharecroppers' union chapter. Raised outside Cincinnati, Ohio, Herndon knew a great deal about miners and mining but virtually nothing about sharecropping.

At first things went well. He was warmly welcomed by a black preacher known as Rev. Hamilton who offered his church as a meeting place. The gatherings were well attended, but unfortunately, most of the young men were only interested in hearing about job opportunities in Birmingham. Herndon told them honestly that there weren't any. Still, he forced himself to stay positive. Finally when some white croppers began to attend he believed that he was finally making progress. Years later when he reflected on this he would describe himself as becoming so elated that he "flung all caution to the wind and spoke [my] mind . . . I assured them that the only possible solution to their problem was complete unity between black and white sharecroppers, in short, a militant union which would fight for the improvement of their lot."[1]

Herndon kept meeting with croppers in small groups across Wilcox County and planning for a mass meeting on March 10. A few days before the big event, however, and without warning, Rev. Hamilton, who'd so warmly welcomed him, betrayed him to the landlords. The preacher had either gotten cold feet or was a pawn of the planters all along. One panicked white cropper warned Herndon that a lynch mob was forming and drove him into Camden as fast as his broken-down truck would take them so he could board a train to Selma. Herndon barely made it.[2] A few days later, a banner headline in the *Selma Times Journal* screamed, "Mulatto Negro Stirs Up Trouble Between Whites and Blacks in Governor Miller's Hometown."[3] Herndon seemed fated to live on the edge.

★ ★ ★

Because district 17 couldn't afford the luxury of specialists, every comrade had to be ready to become an organizer, protest leader, mass meeting speaker, or *Southern Worker* reporter on short notice. In his memoir, *Organizing in the Depression South*, James Allen recalled that "it was not unusual then for young and inexperienced Party members to undertake tasks that appeared beyond their reach."[4] One could expect to be sent, like Herndon, wherever the need was greatest. Jesse Wakefield, for example, left Chattanooga in May 1931 for an assignment in Harlan County, Kentucky, to assist striking miners and their families.

Bloody Harlan

The Great Depression counted some of its paramount achievements in the southeastern Kentucky coal fields. After World War I, a surplus of coal, like the steel surplus in Birmingham and the cotton surplus in the Black Belt, glutted a once-robust market. Miners in Harlan, Bell, Knox, Breathitt, and Perry Counties all suffered wage and hours cutbacks. On February 16, 1931, after the Black Star Mountain Coal Company announced yet another reduction, miners took home less than a dollar a day. In May, the miners of Bell and Harlan Counties walked off the job and shut the mines down. Even when the United Mine Workers (UMW) refused to support their wildcat strike or to provide financial relief, the men would not return to work.

When three deputy sheriffs and a miner were killed in a clash over a mine shutdown in Evarts, Kentucky, thirty-four miners, four of them black, were charged with murder. At that point, the UMW abandoned the Evarts local. A month later that strike failed. The miners who'd struck were blacklisted and would likely never work again. The Battle of Evarts marked the beginning of the Kentucky Coal Wars that raged for another six years.[5]

Unemployed and blacklisted miners and their families were starving by the summer of 1931. Many were homeless. On June 15, a delegation of Harlan County miners led by Jim Garland and Jim Grace drove to Pittsburgh to attend a National Miners' Union (NMU) conference there. They'd heard that this Red union was organizing in West Virginia, eastern Ohio, and western Pennsylvania. When Garland and Grace were invited to speak, they voiced their grievances, requested assistance, and apparently pledged their unreserved support for the NMU. "The name of Reds," Garland said, "doesn't scare us at all."[6]

The NMU sent white organizer Dan Brooks (Dan Slinger) to Harlan on June

19, and district 17 dispatched Jesse Wakefield a week later. The North Carolina Workers International Relief sent supplies and volunteers.

Wakefield arranged bail for thirty-four miners, provided defense counsel for those awaiting trial, and distributed food and supplies to their families. Brooks spent that summer recruiting and training organizers, and Workers International Relief volunteers opened five soup kitchens. The local Red Cross had declared its neutrality and offered no assistance whatsoever. By the end of July, a Harlan chapter of the NMU was up and running with twenty trained organizers.

Finley Donaldson, a Holiness preacher who was also a miner, emerged as a leader. At a meeting in Wallins Creek, he assured his fellow workers: "The NMU stands for the principles that our forefathers fought for at Bunker Hill. ... I love America, but I hate the men running the country and working hardships on the workers. The men who made the laws against us are corrupt. The coal operators call us 'Red Russians,' but when you take away the means of furnishing food and raiment for this body of mine then you certainly are injecting red blood into my system."[7]

All summer long Jesse Wakefield was followed wherever she went. On July 23, 1931, the car she used to bring supplies to the miners' families was dynamited, and on August 1 she was finally arrested and charged with criminal syndicalism. She was released the following day but rearrested before the week ended. Wakefield would spend a total of five weeks in the Harlan County jail.

Despite these setbacks, union membership steadily increased. No other union—not the UMW nor even the IWW—had cared for the miners and their families like the NMU. The ILD released a national publicity campaign exposing the coal operators' reign of terror; Wakefield's situation was featured so prominently that Sheriff Blair threatened to move her to a jail in the remote community of Hyden. He later changed his mind and released her on her sworn promise to leave the community and not return.[8]

Since the soup kitchens functioned as union organizing centers, they became special targets of the Harlan County Coal Operators security force. Miners and other volunteers who kept the kitchens running were routinely arrested and food delivery trucks were sabotaged. The Evarts kitchen, which fed four hundred people every day, was dynamited, and on August 30, two Clover Fork volunteers, Joe Moore and Julius Baldwin, were murdered. Baldwin had recently been elected president of the Evarts local.

That same night, Deputy Lee Fleenor, second in command to Harlan's high sheriff John Henry Blair, drove to the Evarts kitchen, saw Baldwin and Moore standing in the doorway, and opened fire. Mrs. Moore maintained that her husband was killed simply "because he was the relief chairman."[9]

Although Fleenor claimed self-defense, he'd shot Baldwin through the back of his head. Neither were Baldwin's wife nor his brother, who'd witnessed the shooting, called by the grand jury. Judge D. C. Jones, whose wife was a member of the Harlan County Coal Operators' Association, told the jurors how it was going to be: "I'm anxious to protect the miners and to prevent the preaching in these mountains of the Soviet doctrine that seeks to destroy the Government and the Church. . . . If you don't have enough backbone to enforce the law, I'll get [people] who will."[10] Two hours later, they acquitted Fleenor.

A year later, when members of Senator Bob LaFollette's Senate Education Subcommittee held hearings in Harlan and Bell Counties, they would discover Lee Fleenor's name on the Harlan County Coal Operators' Association payroll.[11]

In August, Blaine Owen (Boris Israel), a white twenty-one-year-old district 17 organizer and journalist for the Federated Press, came to Harlan to cover the trials. He was in the courtroom when Judge Jones called the NMU organizers and the ILD Reds "radicals who have no right to look to this court or to any other court in this country for justice." By that time the NMU had four thousand members and the Harlan Coal Operators' Association had posted a $2,000 reward for the capture of chief organizer Dan Brooks, dead or alive.[12]

As Owen left the courthouse, two men grabbed him from behind and pushed him into a car, where two of their friends were waiting. One of them was Deputy Sheriff Marion Allen. They "took him for a ride" to the top of Pine Mountain, where they beat him unconscious. Left for dead, Owen woke up hours later and crawled and stumbled his way down the mountain. He passed out several times and was ultimately found and cared for by a couple who took him into their small cabin at the bottom of the mountain.[13] When he was able to travel, they drove him back to Harlan.

In September, the Federated Press replaced Owen with Helen O'Connor, who found a special delivery letter waiting for her. "Madam," it read, "You have been here long enough already. Remember, the other Red reporter got what was coming to him, so don't let the sun go down on you here." It was signed "Hundred percent Americans." O'Connor didn't even unpack. Two weeks later, Jim Grace, leader of the delegation that brought the NMU to Harlan, was arrested, released, ambushed, kidnapped, and nearly beaten to death. By the end of October, all the soup kitchens had closed.[14]

In November, the National Committee for the Defense of Political Prisoners, an ILD affiliate of journalists, came to Harlan, scheduled public hearings, took depositions from the miners, and published their findings. Sensational reporting by Theodore Dreiser and John Dos Passos, among others, kept the bloody coalfield struggle alive in the national press.[15]

Despite this public exposure, attacks by the coal operators' security forces continued. The local police ignored them. Subsequently the NMU moved its headquarters from Harlan to Pineville, the Bell County seat. On December 13, 263 delegates attended a district meeting there and voted to strike on January 1, 1932.[16] Three days later, the new headquarters was raided and nine reps—five women and four men—were arrested for criminal syndicalism. White ILD attorney Allan Taub, who'd been working on the Scottsboro appeals, traveled to Pineville to represent them.

On January 10, 1932, Taub met novelist Waldo Frank, who'd led an independent group of volunteers to distribute food and clothing. Both Frank and Taub were arrested at the Pineville Hotel that evening, driven to Cumberland Gap, and severely beaten. Frank was released, but Taub was arrested for "plotting to overthrow the Government of the United States of America and the State of Kentucky." When the judge suspended his clients' trials, the ILD threatened to send the National Committee for the Defense of Political Prisoners to Bell County to investigate. In addition, five thousand NMU miners were already protesting in nearby Pineville. The trial dates were subsequently (and quietly) returned to the docket.[17] Taub and all nine of his clients were released on bail on January 14.

The day Taub and Waldo Frank met, Harry Simms (Harry Hersch) a white organizer who'd been working with Mack Coad and the Camp Hill sharecroppers, arrived in Bell County. A nineteen-year-old native of Springfield, Massachusetts, Simms had learned organizing in New England's textile mills and he'd volunteered to come to Kentucky.

On February 10, at a Workers International Relief rally in Pineville, Simms spoke to the crowd. The following day, Green Lawson, a young section strike organizer who'd attended the rally, offered to take him to meet with miners in nearby Bush Creek. As they walked along the Louisville and Nashville railroad tracks, two deputized mine guards, Arlie Miller and Red Davis, came up behind them on a hand truck. Coal fields were private property, and owners often hired guards to keep strangers out. When the young men stepped aside to let them pass, Miller, according to Lawson, recognized Simms from the rally, shot him in the stomach, and kept going.

As Simms lay bleeding, Lawson ran for help. A local farmer took Simms to the Knox County Hospital in Barbourville. When Deputy Red Davis told his father what had happened, the elder Davis rushed to the hospital to guarantee Simms's expenses so that he would be admitted. Simms died the following day.[18]

Malcolm Cowley, who'd been working with Waldo Frank, reported Simms's death in the *New Republic*. He included one Pineville coal operator's response to the young man's death: "They shot one of those Bolsheviks up in Knox County this morning.... Harry Simms his name was.... That deputy knew his business. He didn't give the Red a chance to talk, he just plugged him in the stomach. We need some shooting like that down here in Pineville."[19]

Thomas Bethell, formerly an official of the UMW, described Simms as

> the kind of outsider that the mine owners particularly and especially despised. They didn't have any reason to be afraid of him, exactly ... but there was something unspeakably arrogant about him. It wasn't his personality—he was remembered as cheerful, quiet, good humored, patient and a good listener.... He was good at organizing meetings even when people were tired of meetings, or afraid to go to them. When he talked to miners about political theory and economics, he did not condescend. ... He believed in what he was doing, there was no bravado about it, and miners who had never before had any help at all from outsiders admired him greatly.[20]

Deputy Arlie Miller apparently recognized in Simms several things that he despised: an outside agitating meddler—a self-righteous, smooth-talking, rich atheist Jew.

A memorial service for Simms was scheduled for February 14, 1932, in Barbourville, but the local police with the aid of fifty volunteer deputies and thirty-five national guardsmen prevented the miners from attending.

Later that week, Deputy Arlie Miller testified to a grand jury that Simms had pulled a gun on him, but eyewitness Green Lawson swore that Simms was unarmed. After considering all the testimony, Judge Frank Baker dismissed the murder charge and ruled that the available evidence pointed to Miller either acting in his own defense or protecting Deputy Davis.

In March 1932, Rob Hall, white president of Columbia University's National Students League, brought three busloads of student volunteers to Harlan County, Kentucky, to distribute food, clothing, and supplies. They were sponsored by the IWO.

The Kentucky State Police stopped their caravan at the Bell County line and refused them entry. When Hall objected, one officer called him a "Russian born Jewish communist." Hall was actually a native Alabamian and a Presbyterian.[21] When he returned to Columbia, he joined the Communist Party and after graduation accepted an assignment with the Nebraska farm movement. In 1935, Rob Hall would be appointed director of district 17.

Despite the determination of the NMU and the ILD's exposure of the collusion between the coal operators, law enforcement, and the judicial system, the strike in Bell and Harlan Counties ended after three months. The coal operators were successful in shifting the focus from the miners' grievances to their "atheistic subversive Red leadership."

Jesus of the Cumberlands

Mistrust bore its way into the heart of the NMU around the time that Harry Simms died. Several of the organizers returned from a training course at the Chicago Workers' School later that week and were horrified by what they'd seen and heard there. They wondered aloud if they'd really understood what the Reds were promising when they'd offered help. In Chicago the miners heard lots of praise for Russia, contempt for Christianity and patriotism, and endorsement of adultery, atheism, and interracial marriage—the very things that the coal operators, the sheriff, the judges, and the preachers had warned them about. The arrogance of a few Chicago Reds who'd never worked among religious fundamentalists would deal the death blow to one solid year of union building.

Rev. Finley Donaldson, now president of the Harlan County local, advised his union comrades to withdraw their membership. He'd learned, he said, that the Reds were bent on "destruction of government, religion and family life."[22]

Christianity was front and center in coal country. Section crews often began their shifts with prayer. The Holiness sect, the largest denomination in the Appalachian Mountains, was led by preachers like Donaldson who'd been called by the Holy Spirit. They preached a literal interpretation of the Scriptures and maintained that every idea, action, or reaction in life was either right or wrong, true or false, black or white. The devil hid in shades of meaning, in compromise, in subtlety, and in all half measures.

Religion for these independent people was an individual affair. If one did not agree with a particular preacher, it was perfectly acceptable to move on until they found a more compatible one. They were not "church people"—not "joiners." UMW president John L. Lewis had found them to be too independent and too undisciplined to work with, and he'd given up on them in 1931.

Mountain people acknowledged the soul-saving power of Jesus and the gifts of the Holy Spirit: healing, wisdom, prophecy, and speaking in tongues—but they did not see how religion had any claim to social responsibility. Jack Weller, a minister with the United Presbyterian Church in eastern Kentucky in the 1960s, observed that "the church in Appalachia is beyond doubt the most reactionary force in the Mountains."[23]

"The Holiness sect," he wrote, "relies on sentiment, tradition, superstition and personal feelings, all reinforcing the patterns of the culture. It is self-centered . . . prayer [is] a tool to serve my needs and to help me. [Its] main purpose is to reiterate the accepted religious ideas and to satisfy personal ego needs and not to bear witness to or to do work for God."[24] Mountain religion tended to feed fatalism and passivity—the idea that it "ain't no use" to try to change things.

It is not difficult, therefore, to understand how the miners' disappointment with the Reds might dampen their fighting spirit. When Finley Donaldson could no longer reconcile the NMU's philosophy with his religious beliefs, he resigned the union presidency. In mid-February 1932, he assured his fellow union members: "The teachings of the Communist Party [will] destroy our religious beliefs, our government, and our homes. In teachings they demand their members there is no God (sic); no Jesus; no Hereafter; no resurrection of the dead; all there is for anybody is what they got in this world. I heard them in a mass meeting and in a big demonstration in Chicago denounce our government and our flag and our religion." And then he slammed the door on all of it: "I feel at this time that the great capitalists and officials of this great nation of ours in some way will give relief and assistance to our poor starving humanity which is now suffering in America."[25]

On February 28, two hundred Knox County, Kentucky, ministers, teachers, and private citizens, many of them miners, attended a mass meeting in Barbourville to pledge to "fight communism and create more respect for laws." They called themselves the Christian Patriotic League. Former Kentucky governor Flem Sampson agreed to serve as president.[26]

At the end of March 1932, the coal operators declared victory, the miners of Bell and Knox Counties returned to work, and the NMU left the mountains. The following year saw passage of the National Industrial Recovery Act, and the UMW returned to southeastern Kentucky to try again. The Kentucky Coal Wars continued.

On September 12, 1932, a banner headline in the *Kentucky Advocate* screamed "Acquitted Mine Guard Shot through the Heart." Seven months after he'd been cleared of the murder of Harry Simms, twenty-five-year-old Arlie Miller was found in rural Flat Lick in Knox County shot through the heart and his throat cut. Four men who'd allegedly gone there with him were questioned and released. His murder was never solved.

7 ▌ THE SHADES MOUNTAIN RAPE AND MURDERS

> We always need someone to blame. We cannot bear our
> anguish if we know that it springs from our own hearts.
> —Lillian Smith, *Killers of the Dream*

A few weeks after the Camp Hill Massacre, a dragnet was underway in Birmingham to find the black suspect in the rape and murders of two white society women. On the Sunday evening of August 4, 1931, Mountain Brook police officer Charles Nollner had responded to a frantic call from a young woman reporting a shooting in a picnic area on Shades Mountain. Nineteen-year-old Nell Williams stated that she, her sister Augusta, who was twenty-three, and their friend Jennie Wood, twenty-seven, were driving back to Mountain Brook after seeing a movie in Birmingham. As they entered the Leeds Highway, a black man allegedly jumped on the running board of Jennie's car and ordered her at gunpoint to turn into a side road that led to a secluded area. He robbed them and then, holding them at gunpoint, lectured the three women for two hours on "the mistreatment of negroes and other communistic ideas."[1]

Subsequently, Nell explained: "When the Negro started getting fresh with my sister, I tried to grab his gun." During the struggle, he shot all of them, ripped the keys out of the ignition, shot out one of the front tires, and fled. Augusta, who had a stomach wound and Jennie, shot in the neck, were seriously injured, but Nell, who'd been shot in the left arm, was able to drive back to the highway to get help. It is unclear how she managed to do that since the assailant had taken Jennie's car keys. Nevertheless, all three were admitted to St. Vincent's Hospital at about 8:00 p.m. Augusta died within hours and Jennie within days, leaving Nell Williams the only eyewitness.

Nell described the rapist as "a stout light-skinned well-educated black man from the North, about thirty-five years old." However, before Jennie Wood died, she'd described him to her father, Wade Wood Sr., as a "soot black man" with several gold teeth. These discrepancies, the lack of any physical evidence of rape, and Nell's shifting recollections stalled the investigation. After an unproductive search of the woods, the police fanned out into Birmingham.

For the next six weeks the city teetered on the edge of a race riot. Black men were randomly arrested and beaten in futile attempts to obtain a confession. White vigilantes burned black businesses. Hardware stores reported an increase in the sale of guns and ammunition, and Mayor Jimmie Jones imposed a ten o'clock curfew. The *Southern Worker* called it a "reign of terror."

Nell's mystifying account of her attacker's two-hour lecture on "communistic ideas" linked the Reds to the crime and fed hysteria about communists manipulating blacks into a race war. Camp Hill was still very much on everyone's mind. An August 6 *Birmingham News* editorial titled "On What Hateful Bread does Communism Feed?" declared that "if this [murder and rape of white women] is the aim of the [Communist] propaganda . . . then Southerners and all Americans who understand the inequalities of the races . . . must by every possible means lance out of the social body these infamous and unnatural teachings."[2]

Maintaining that the Birmingham Reds were likely harboring the black rapist, Mountain Brook deputy sheriff R. E. Smith issued warrants for the arrest of all known communist organizers. Smith believed that at least two men were involved. Someone must have picked the rapist up afterward.

Angelo Herndon, back from a near-lynching in Wilcox County, was among those arrested. He was subsequently taken from his jail cell in handcuffs at sunset, dragged down a flight of stairs, thrown into a car, and driven into the woods. When the car stopped, three officers pulled him out.

"We don't care anything about your Communist Party," one told him, "we want to know who shot Nell Williams and the other girls."[3] When Herndon said he didn't know, they beat him with rubber hoses.

"If you didn't do it you know who did," another growled. "If you don't tell us you won't leave here alive." When Herndon did not respond, they beat him again and continued to demand the names of the white communists he ran with. They took turns flogging him until he couldn't walk. The ranking officer taunted that if he complained no one would believe him.[4]

When they finally dragged him back to the jail, Nell Williams was there looking at four black men in a holding cell. Herndon was thrown in with them. Although he heard someone tell her to "say yes," she shook her head.[5]

On August 15, the *Southern Worker* published Lowell Wakefield's telegram to Police Chief Fred McDuff:

> We hold you responsible for the safety of all those arrested in connection with the Williams shooting. We demand the immediate cessation of the reign of terror against Negroes in Birmingham and the immediate withdrawal of the lynch posses. We demand the right of the Birmingham workers to defend themselves against lynch mobs and against the shooting up of Negro neighborhoods.
>
> We warn you against any attempt to smash the Communist Party or other working-class organizations by framing militant workers, using the Williams shooting as an excuse. This is the same as the terror in the Scottsboro and Camp Hill cases against which there has been world-wide protest.[6]

A furious McDuff redoubled his efforts. Things got even worse after the Negro Businessmen's League offered a $3,000 reward for information leading to the arrest of the murderer. Herndon later wrote that "many negroes in Birmingham can still recall with rising anger the price in bruises, in mauling and in mental anguish as arrests increased in the pursuit of that reward."[7] Herndon was charged with vagrancy. After Wakefield got him released, he jumped bail and Harry Jackson sent him to Atlanta to organize unemployed workers there.

The Suspect

On September 23, six weeks after the Shades Mountain attack, Nell Williams was driving through Birmingham with her mother and her boyfriend, Edward "Buck" Streit, when she thought she recognized her attacker. She screamed, "there!" and pointed him out. As Buck called to him, the man walked toward their car. Buck jumped out, drew his gun, and forced him into the back seat. He told Nell to find a phone and call the police. She ran into the nearest store while he held the gaunt, dark, skinny, sickly, barely literate Willie Peterson at gunpoint.

Peterson was a thirty-seven-year-old World War I veteran, a former coal miner who hadn't worked in two years because he suffered from tuberculosis. Although he did not fit Nell Williams's description of her attacker in any way (including being able to wax poetic about communist theory), she insisted that he was the man. She'd recognized him, she told the police, by his gray felt hat.[8]

After Peterson's arrest, witnesses came forward to place him in his own home on the Sunday afternoon when the rape was committed. Nevertheless, he was sent to Kilby Prison's hospital ward.

Nell's father, Clark Williams, a prominent Birmingham attorney, desperately wanted to keep the matter out of court. He could not abide his daughter being subjected to questions about what she'd been doing in that secluded stretch of woods off the Leeds Highway.

Apparently, his wife, Helen, agreed, since she'd participated in kidnapping Peterson. Whether that idea was hers, Nell's, Buck's, or Attorney Williams himself makes little difference. In Alabama, a white woman who cried rape could expect white men to close ranks around her.

Nell's brother Dent, also a lawyer, joined their father in meeting with Richard Fries, Peterson's legal counsel, to discuss a settlement. Using a conference room at the Birmingham City Jail, Sheriff James Hawkins brought Peterson up from Kilby Prison so that Nell could make a positive identification. Despite the intense pressure put on him to confess, Peterson insisted that he was innocent. In the end, a grand jury would have to decide whether or not he went to trial.

On October 2, Nell made a third positive identification of Peterson, this time in a courtroom before the grand jury. After Peterson entered a plea of not guilty, her brother Dent leaned over as if to speak with her, then stood up and fired five shots, hitting Peterson three times—twice in the chest. Both Dent and his father had been searched for weapons as they entered the courtroom, but Nell had not. Neither Sheriff James Hawkins nor Police Chief Fred McDuff seemed able to prevent the attempted murder. Assistant Solicitor Jim Long rushed over to the stricken Peterson, told him that he was dying, and urged him to confess, but Peterson shook his head. "I didn't do it," he said before he was rushed to Hillman Hospital.[9]

While he was in the hospital, the grand jury went ahead and indicted Peterson for robbery, for the murders of Augusta Williams and Jennie Wood, and for the attempted murder of Nell Williams. No mention of the rape charge was made. The trial was tentatively scheduled for December 15. That same day, October 2, 1931, Dent Williams, was arrested for assault with intent to kill Willie Peterson.

Speculation

The *Southern Worker* speculated as to why the state seemed so determined to pursue this case.

"There is a double reason why the boss class of Birmingham wants to legally murder Peterson on the framed-up charge of having killed two society women on the night of August 4," James Allen wrote. "One of them is because the bosses want to cover up the fact that the killing was the result of a petting party. The exposure would cause a scandal that would shake up the rotten structure of the 'best society' of Birmingham. The other reason is that the Peterson case has been and will continue to be useful as a means of continuing the terror against the negro workers of Birmingham."[10]

A black *Pittsburgh (PA) Courier* reporter on assignment in Birmingham was more specific. He'd driven to the exclusive Mountain Brook community to interview the housemaids, nannies, cooks, chauffeurs, and yardmen who staffed the local Tudor mansions. They maintained that the police were ignoring persistent rumors that "an outraged white woman had traced her erring husband up the same road that the young ladies had traveled."[11] She apparently surprised them that Sunday afternoon.

It was true that the police found "a lot of cigarette butts" at the scene, but they refused to disclose any information about the fingerprints they'd allegedly lifted off the enamel paint on Jennie's blue LaSalle. The Williams and Wood families, the *Courier* reporter noted, "seemed determined to protect the young white women from any impairment of their social standing."[12]

The Mountain Brook domestics told this reporter (whose story ran without a byline to protect his identity) that they'd been warned to "cast no dispersions [sic] on the virtue and veracity of the young white women involved." They would lose their jobs if they were caught spreading the rumor.[13]

Had a wronged wife shot all of them, he wondered, or just the women? Was there an injured man out there with untreated bullet wounds, or perhaps another dead body? Had more than one man been with the young women that afternoon? If so, who were they and where were they now? If the story was true, an angry white woman was getting away with the two murders and the attempted murder that Peterson was on trial for.

"Dent Williams," the *Courier* reporter explained, "knew when he shot the Negro picked out by his sister that in death Peterson could not further deny guilt and that his sister, vindicated and revenged, would have no more questions asked."[14] That had been the family's goal from the beginning—to stop speculation.

Angelo Herndon, like James Allen, was convinced that the Wood-Williams murder cover-up was also an attempt to end interracial organizing in the mines. Looking back on the situation, Herndon wrote in 1937: "There was frame-up in the air for weeks before the Peterson case started. The miners were organizing against wage cuts; the white and Negro workers were beginning to get together and demanding relief and jobs and the human rights that had been taken from them. If the bosses could engineer a frame-up against some Negro, a lot of white workers would begin to think about that instead of about bread and jobs."[15]

The Trial

Henrietta Peterson wanted the ILD to represent her husband, who had survived the murder attempt. She believed that they could do for him what they'd done for the Scottsboro teens. At the district 17 office, they'd explained to her that a legal team would be provided for Willie and a national publicity campaign would be organized. They promised to pursue a not-guilty verdict and would not settle for life in prison. All Willie's legal fees would be taken care of. Henrietta was referred to Albert Rosenthal of Rosenthal and Rosenthal, who agreed to take the case.

But Dr. Charles McPherson, secretary of the Birmingham NAACP, who was horrified that his organization might once again be shut out of a case with national consequences, paid a visit to Henrietta Peterson on October 24. Advising her to keep away from the Reds, he offered the services of J. T. Roach and J. R. Johnson, two respectable white Birmingham attorneys. McPherson warned her that if the ILD campaigned as they had in the Scottsboro case, whites would make sure that Willie went to the electric chair. The Reds, he said, were plotting to overthrow the government and the newspapers were already identifying Willie as one of them. McPherson reminded her that Rosenthal was a Jew—didn't she know that powerful whites hated Jews? If she made enough whites angry, one might try to kidnap Willie and lynch him. "It's sure as death," he said, "if you put your husband in the hands of the ILD lawyers the jury, the judge and the solicitor won't even listen to them."[16]

A desperate Henrietta Peterson sat in her living room and cried. She didn't know what to do. She was only twenty-four years old and had never been outside Birmingham. McPherson was a famous black surgeon who headed up the NAACP. Maybe he did know best. Ultimately, she gave him permission to organize a citizens' committee and to raise the $3,000 fee for Johnson and Roach.

In a letter to Walter White, Charles McPherson reported that Peterson had "the sympathy of many high class and intelligent white people."[17] Rumors, he said, were flying all over the city about just what those young women had been doing up on the mountain that Sunday. The Williams family's credibility was badly damaged. A few weeks later McPherson told White that Nell Williams had reportedly made several suicide attempts.

Willie Peterson's trial began on December 7, 1931, with Judge J. Russell McElroy presiding. Defense attorneys Johnson and Roche expressed confidence that Peterson would not be convicted. They anticipated an acquittal or a mistrial. "Johnson believes a white person did it," McPherson told Walter White.[18]

Clark and Helen Williams, Nell's parents, and her boyfriend Buck Streit all testified for the prosecution. Peterson, alive against all odds but still ill, was unable to attend the trial to look Nell Williams in the face when she testified under oath that he was the man who'd shot her and killed Augusta and Jennie. J. T. Roach argued that Peterson fit neither Nell Williams's nor Jennie Wood's description of their attacker. While Peterson was unavailable to demonstrate this to the jury, Roach quoted a journalist who'd recently described him as "a wiry little Negro who resembled Mahatma Gandhi." The defense also provided photos and Roach asked the jury to consider how Peterson, suffering from tuberculosis, managed to attack three young, healthy women.

Peterson had a second-grade education; how could he have lectured for two hours on "communistic ideas"? Roach even got Nell's mother to admit that Peterson had approached their car without fear when Buck Streit called him over. Would a murderer have taken such a chance? Roach asked. Would he have remained so calm?

J. R. Johnson subsequently called twenty-eight witnesses black and white, to establish that Peterson was at home on the afternoon the crime was committed, that he did not fit any of the conflicting descriptions of the assailant, and to substantiate that he was too weak to have either committed the crime or to have fought off the young women.

Johnson also hired, and the NAACP paid for, the services of private investigator H. W. Fuller. He'd learned that the prosecution was planning to call a black man identified as Henry Wilson, who would testify that Peterson had visited his Tuscaloosa barber shop shortly after the murders and bragged about shooting the girls.

Thankfully, one of Fuller's black investigators had interviewed a Tuscaloosa housemaid who told him that Henry Wilson was actually Tom Sheppard, and he wasn't a barber. Word was that he'd gotten ten dollars to lie. Fuller kept digging until he discovered that J. P. Robinson, a Tuscaloosa police officer, had recommended Sheppard to two unidentified white women who were desperate for help. They offered him $25 to testify against Willie Peterson, who'd never been to Tuscaloosa. Sheppard was initially paid $10 and promised the balance after Peterson was convicted. He could earn another $25 if he found someone who would swear that he'd overheard Peterson brag about the crime. Detective Fuller found that man, who agreed to testify against Sheppard. The story reeked of conspiracy and collusion, giving credence to the rumors about Nell Williams being frantic to cover her actions the night of August 4.

Johnson and Roach were prepared to cross-examine "Henry Wilson" and blow the case wide open. But Wilson was never called by the prosecution. Either someone got cold feet, or they'd discovered that the defense knew what they were up to.

On December 10, Johnson and Roach met in Judge McElroy's chambers to request permission to call "Henry Wilson" [Sheppard] themselves and ask if he'd been hired to provide testimony. The judge denied the request, and the trial moved to closing arguments.

The jury deliberated for forty hours—an extraordinarily long time for such a case. In the end, they were deadlocked, and Judge McElroy declared a mistrial. Incredibly, Willie Peterson, a black man accused of attacking a white woman and identified by her under oath, had not been convicted by a white southern jury. Despite the state's intention to retry the case, the defense maintained that it had already made history.

Retrial

One month later, on January 18, 1932, Peterson's second trial began. Judge Harrington P. Heflin, brother of former Alabama senator "Cotton Tom" Heflin, presided. The defense remained confident. Rumors circulated that they had solved the mystery of what had happened on Shades Mountain.

But the subsequent appointment of Roderick Beddow as special prosecutor stunned Walter White. Beddow was also representing Dent Williams, and White knew him well. In 1931 he'd retained him to defend the Scottsboro teens because Ford, Beddow, and Ray was considered the best criminal law firm in Birmingham. At that time, White had been willing to overlook the fact that Roderick Beddow had opined that "some lynchers might be justified in taking the law into their own hands."[19] White was focused on Beddow's batting average in the courtroom. In the end, it hadn't mattered. The Scottsboro teens didn't trust Beddow and didn't want him. They'd opted to stay with the Reds. Now White wrote to ask Beddow how it was possible for him to both represent Williams and to prosecute Peterson.

Beddow replied: "You know Walter how I feel about prosecutions. I am loathed to prosecute anyone. I had rather be on the other side. However, this was one of those crimes that should be punished. If the guilty party were to escape where the evidence is strong, cogent, and convincing, depicting a depravity of mind almost unparalleled in the annals of crime history in this country, this would have, in my judgement, brought about misunderstanding between the white and colored races that only time could bridge."[20]

What evidence? All he had was the gray felt hat that Nell said she'd recognized, the fact that Peterson lived in Birmingham, and what he mystifyingly described as "[Peterson's] height, weight and peculiar appearance."[21] White shook his head.

And there was more. Beddow had reinstated the rape charge initially brought against Peterson but never introduced in the first trial. He knew that a rape accusation would make another acquittal unlikely. A black man charged with raping a white woman was a condemned man. When Henrietta Peterson found this out, she went back to the ILD and begged for their help. They'd been conducting mass publicity campaigns and demonstrations to free Willie since the first trial, despite the fact that she had gone with the NAACP.

Johnson and Roach were unable to get "Henry Wilson" on the stand for the second trial, which closed the door to revealing Nell and Helen Williams's bribe. Johnson was livid, but the more conservative Roach was relieved. He'd feared that outing Wilson might backfire. It would be the testimony of a career criminal and a rogue police officer against the word of two respectable white society women.

The prosecution had nothing new to offer except the rape charge. The defense reiterated that Willie Peterson was physically incapable of raping anyone or fighting off two healthy young women.

In the end, however, despite McPherson's faith in the "changing sentiment of whites," and despite the best efforts of his two "respectable" white attorneys, Willie Peterson was convicted of first-degree murder on January 29, 1932. This time the jury deliberated for only twenty minutes. Judge Heflin sentenced him to die in the electric chair on August 25, 1932.[22]

J. R. Johnson immediately filed a motion for a new trial, which Judge Heflin denied. The Alabama State Supreme Court was his next stop.

The Supreme Court of Alabama

The NAACP hired John Altman, general counsel of the Alabama Federation of Labor, to handle Peterson's appeal. Altman was assisted by his associate Walter Smith and chose not to include either J. R. Johnson or J. T. Roach on the team.

On April 17, 1932, Altman addressed the Alabama Supreme Court, citing prejudicial statements made to the jury by Judge Heflin. Before deliberations began, the judge had allegedly told the panel "it ought to take you but a few minutes to reach a verdict in this case." J. T. Roach had moved for a mistrial at the time, but Judge Heflin denied the motion.

Juror Horace Dugger told the empaneled jury that he believed Peterson was guilty and that he was glad he'd been chosen so that he could "stick him."

Altman argued that Peterson's conviction came down to Nell William's testimony, and she'd repeatedly perjured herself.[23] He noted that no physical evidence was submitted and that the fingerprints lifted by the police at the scene were never produced at trial. Fingerprints, Altman said, would have quickly either damned or exonerated his client, since Nell Williams testified that her attacker had gotten inside the car. Finally, the rape charge against Peterson, originally dropped for lack of evidence, had been reintroduced, only because exonerating a black man accused of raping a white woman, regardless of the lack of evidence, was virtually impossible in Alabama in 1932.

On June 22, 1933, one year after Altman submitted his appeal, the Alabama Supreme Court refused to reverse the lower court's ruling.

A furious Oscar W. Adams Sr., editor of the *Birmingham Reporter* and a longtime NAACP member, wrote that all the parties involved "knew that the young woman had identified the wrong man. And yet they had gone ahead. Rather than humiliate Miss Williams by contradicting her story, the State of Alabama was willing to convict an innocent man. The 'honor' of one white woman was more important than the life's blood of a black man."[24]

The ILD subsequently launched a national publicity campaign to support Willie Peterson and to appeal to the governor for clemency. They criticized the NAACP for mishandling the case and clearly hoped to take over the appeal.

On August 13, 1933, one week after the Alabama Supreme Court announced its decision, Nell Williams married Louie Reese Jr., the son of wealthy Birmingham real estate developer, Louie Reese Sr., in a traditional society wedding.

The U.S. Supreme Court

Willie Peterson had one option left—an appeal to the U.S. Supreme Court. Between the time of the application to the Alabama Supreme Court and the notice of the justices' decision, John Altman had suffered a stroke, and he was angry when the NAACP insisted on hiring Charles Hamilton Houston, the black dean of Howard University Law School, to assist him. Altman resisted until Charles McPherson agreed that he could remain the lead attorney. Houston was notified of this deal in writing. The white attorney was not comfortable working collaboratively with a black attorney. Ironically, Houston was a personal friend of the ILD's William Patterson, who would have welcomed him on any legal team. The situation was critical.

Houston arrived in Birmingham in late August and met with Police Chief Fred McDuff and Sheriff James Hawkins on August 29. Both told him that they'd never believed there was enough evidence to convict Peterson, and they were willing to submit written statements to that effect. Even Jennie Wood's father was not satisfied that the right man had been convicted.[25]

Houston interviewed Willie Peterson in the Birmingham City Jail, his wife Henrietta, and his former attorneys J. R. Johnson and J. T. Roach. He spoke with Assistant Solicitor Jim Long, who'd been present when Dent Williams shot Peterson. Despite representing the prosecution, Long admitted to being impressed by the fact that Peterson refused to confess his guilt even when Long assured him that he was dying. Long offered that a Christian terrified of burning in hell would never have done that.

Finally, Birmingham detectives Virgil Sanders and Luther Holmes spoke about the inconsistencies that had troubled them throughout the case. Jennie Wood described her attacker as having gold teeth. Peterson had none. Nell Williams was unable to explain how although the attacker took her car keys she drove down the mountain to get help. And finally, the detectives were never able to locate anyone who recalled hearing shots or screams from the Leeds Highway, which ran very close to the woods.

No one who Houston interviewed, with the exception of Special Prosecutor Roderick Beddow, believed that Peterson was guilty, and only two white Birmingham clergymen had trouble believing that Nell Williams would lie.

Johnson and Roach were never able to introduce the persistent rumors running through the black and white communities as circumstantial evidence to offer another possible motive for the crime. Houston understood that it would have been suicidal for the Mountain Brook maids to testify to what they'd heard and seen, and he also knew that all the "better families" had closed ranks. If any of them knew the white man or men who'd been on the mountain that day, they weren't going to tell anyone. The police would never find any record of treatment for gunshot wounds at any hospital emergency room or doctors' offices—even if they cared to look, which they did not. Apparently, the man or men had survived. No one was reported missing.

Frustrated, Houston constructed a detailed timeline that he hoped might help uncover any other overlooked motives. He found one. Houston concluded that Willie Peterson had to be convicted to save Dent Williams—not to exonerate Nell Williams.

Augusta Williams and Jennie Wood were murdered on August 4, 1931. Peterson was arrested on September 23 and Dent shot him on October 2. Due to growing skepticism in the white community about the black man's guilt, public sentiment began to turn against Dent. He and Roderick Beddow knew that if Peterson was exonerated, Dent would be tried for the attempted murder of an innocent man. Revenge was one thing, cold-blooded killing another.[26]

On October 9, both Peterson and Williams were indicted. Peterson's trial began on December 7 and ended with a deadlocked jury. Once a mistrial was declared, Beddow requested postponement of Dent's trial.

Peterson was retried on January 18, 1932, with Roderick Beddow reintroducing the rape charge. Dent was acquitted one month later. After all, he was a grieving brother who'd attempted to kill the black man who'd murdered one of his sisters, shot the other, and raped their best friend.[27] In July 1933, a disheartened Houston wrote that "when Dent Williams is acquitted, and Willie Peterson is sentenced to be electrocuted, Alabama clamps the LID on the Negro's hopes for Southern Justice."[28]

Houston prepared a full report and delivered it to Charles McPherson on September 2, 1933. It was included in the appeal to the U.S. Supreme Court but was never considered. In January 1934, the justices refused to review the case. Willie Peterson's execution was set for February 16, 1934.

Loss of two appeals was a major setback for the NAACP. Houston believed that the organization's "leadership of the Negroes in the South" would inevitably pass to the ILD. It did not make him happy to hear that his friend William Patterson was publicly charging "the respectable NAACP leadership" with betraying Peterson by "muffling the sensational evidence."[29] Was that fair? How would "Pat" have managed it? Could he have gotten Willie Peterson exonerated if he and Houston had worked together? It was all moot.

Patterson often quipped to Houston that his clients could be guilty for all he cared. "I'm concerned with rights," he liked to say, "and when the ILD wins a case rights are automatically extended across the board, and not only for Negroes."[30]

After the U.S. Supreme Court declined to hear her husband's appeal, Henrietta Peterson became involved in the ILD's nationwide protests and demonstrations. She would do anything to keep Willie alive. With less than a month before his execution date, the ILD campaigned hard to generate indignation over the death sentence. As in the Scottsboro case, the governor's office was flooded with letters, petitions, resolutions, and telegrams from all over the nation.[31]

At the same time, and against Altman's wishes, Houston recruited a committee of Robert Moton, superintendent of Tuskegee, representatives from Birmingham's Interracial Commission, its Citizens' Committee, and the Alabama Commission on Interracial Cooperation to petition the governor for a stay of execution. They were successful. By the time the committee arrived at his office, a weary Governor Miller was ready to grant it and be done with them. What they didn't know was that he'd received a handwritten letter from Sheriff James Hawkins, who'd been assigned to take Peterson back to Kilby Prison: "I don't believe Willie Peterson is the Negro who committed this offense, and this belief is shared by Chief Fred McDuff, who is even more familiar with the facts than I am.... The young women who suffered outrages at the hands of some Negro are members of our best families and my closest friends. It is embarrassing to me to do or say anything that would displease them, but I am not willing to go through life feeling that my silence might have allowed an innocent person, although a Negro, to die."[32]

The governor granted the stay from February 16 to March 30, 1934.[33] When the NAACP subsequently petitioned for a clemency hearing, Governor Miller scheduled one for March 6. This was John Altman's last hope of saving Peterson's life, and he was not taking any chances.[34] He told Houston, Charles McPherson, and Walter White that he didn't want any blacks attending the hearing, which might make the panel feel coerced. It was unfair, it was disgraceful, he said he knew that, and if it mattered to them, he personally agreed, but a man's life was at stake. Houston, White, and McPherson reluctantly followed his humiliating instructions.

When William Patterson heard about it, he was furious. Clemency was unacceptable to him, to the ILD, to Mrs. Peterson, and to the black people of the state and the nation. Peterson was innocent and should be set free. On March 6, as the clemency hearing began, the ILD demonstrated in front of the governor's office. They demanded Peterson's unconditional release. Henrietta Peterson was with them when they tried to force their way into the hearing room to address the board.[35] All were ushered out. Mrs. Peterson was completely distraught.

Charles Nollner of the Mountain Brook Police Department, the first officer to interview the mortally wounded Jennie Wood, told the board that she'd said the man who shot her had several gold lower front teeth. Peterson, who had no gold teeth, could not have been that man. "I don't think he was given a square deal," Nollner said.[36]

Another deputy testified that black witnesses who could have placed Peterson in Birmingham at the time of the murder refused to testify at his second trial because they'd been threatened with having their homes torched.

Sheriff James Hawkins, as promised, testified that he'd always believed Peterson was innocent.[37] Birmingham Police Chief Fred McDuff, however, withdrew his statement to Houston concerning Peterson's innocence. His change of heart was extremely damaging, and John Altman was furious. But Hawkins was retiring, and since McDuff intended to declare himself a candidate for sheriff in the upcoming 1935 election, any testimony supporting Peterson would hurt his chances.[38] McDuff won that election and served as Jefferson County sheriff until 1939. He died in 1943.

E. S. Cade, who'd served on the grand jury, believed that Peterson never would have been indicted had the jurors been able to see him in person and observe his physical condition. Finally, Lewis Mullinicks, a juror on the second panel, testified that while he believed Peterson was innocent, the other jurors warned him that if he voted for acquittal he would never get home. Charles Hamilton Houston also submitted his report to the clemency board.

After everyone was heard, Clark and Nell Williams, her husband Louie Reese, and Wade Wood Jr. (who was likely Jennie's brother, since her father had already expressed his doubts about Peterson being the man who attacked his daughter), requested that the clemency board allow Peterson's execution to stand.[39] They prevailed.

Charles Hamilton Houston took his delegation back to the governor's office to deliver the clemency board hearing testimony as well as his own report and a copy of the police flyer that had circulated after the crime offering a $3,300 reward for information leading to the arrest of the murderer described as having "gold inlay work on his lower teeth."[40] On March 20, 1934, ten days before the stay expired, Governor Miller commuted Peterson's death sentence to life in prison. Peterson died there in 1940 at the age of forty-six.

Willie Peterson, a deacon in his church and a World War I veteran, had enjoyed the respect of his community and the love of his young wife. Neighbors and friends recalled him as a hardworking miner and a vigorous young man before the mine dust made him sick. But to a rich family on the other side of Shades Mountain, Peterson had simply provided a convenient solution to an inconvenient problem.

8 ▎ STAYING THE COURSE

> If you set out to take Vienna, take Vienna.
> —Napoleon Bonaparte, Ulm-Austerlitz Campaign, 1805

For District 17, 1931 was a difficult year. Tom Johnson and Harry Jackson had spent most of it in jail, and stress took a heavy toll on them. Increasingly, Johnson was edgy, short-tempered, and dispirited. He questioned his ability to hold the operation together. In July, after spending four weeks in a dirty and dangerous cell, he petitioned New York to send guns: "We must get them at once," he wrote. "This is no joke, but it might turn out to be a life or death matter to us.... We might have to leave town ahead of a lynch mob."[1]

In September, two plainclothes policemen attacked Johnson on a Birmingham street, pushed him into a car, and drove to the county line, where they stripped, beat, and abandoned him. They warned him that if he returned to Birmingham he was a dead man.[2] This time he believed them. Johnson subsequently suffered a nervous collapse and was sent back north to recover.

Harry Jackson held things together for the rest of that year, but it was impossible for one man to monitor labor organizing and unemployed council operations for three cities; to keep channels open with the Tallapoosa sharecroppers, who were still without a liaison to headquarters; and to keep track of who'd been arrested and where.

By 1932, so many of Birmingham's mines, mills, and factories had closed and so many businesses had failed, that a hundred thousand people were out of work and another sixty thousand were employed part-time. The situation was no better in the Black Belt. Mack Coad had gone to Russia for training, and Harry Simms, who'd been working with Tommy Gray's daughter Eula, had volunteered to go to Kentucky and had gotten himself killed. Eula Gray was a talented organizer in her own right, but she needed help. After the Camp Hill bloodbath, the croppers were becoming increasingly militant.

New York finally stepped in to restructure district 17. They sent thirty-year-old Nat Ross, a Columbia University graduate, to replace Tom Johnson. Harry Jackson introduced Ross to the staff and promised to stay until Ross got himself settled. In the spring of 1932, Jackson left for Pittsburgh to work with the troubled NMU.

Described by one ILD staffer as "a spell binder," Nat Ross was also a hard worker—he was well organized and a stern disciplinarian.[3] Born in Minnesota, he'd learned community organizing working in the Carolinas. Because of the deteriorating economic conditions across the United States, Ross fully expected the revolution to come in his lifetime. He believed that capitalism was experiencing its final crisis, and he would make sure that district 17 was ready for whatever came next. Ross scheduled regular district meetings and was so intense, one comrade said, that his face muscles twitched. He was a respected, if not a beloved leader.

The more laid-back Sid Benson, a twenty-year-old Marxist doctrine specialist, replaced Harry Jackson. Born in Russia, Benson had grown up in New York City. He loved literature, art, and the theater and had a talent for debate and argumentation. Both he and Ross were secular Jews with a lot to learn about black sharecroppers.[4]

In April 1932 Ross called a one-day conference for Birmingham and Tallapoosa County organizers. He wanted to get the urban and rural comrades talking with one another—some for the very first time. Cropper organizers met with steel and mine worker recruiters, as well as with ILD staff and the unemployed worker council reps. Ross reviewed the district's new table of organization for them and listed the party's priorities: interracial organizing, promoting black voter rights, stressing the right to serve on juries and the right of sharecroppers to sell their crops on the open market, and freeing the Scottsboro nine.[5]

A week later Ross announce formation of an executive committee consisting of himself, Sid Benson, and Lowell Wakefield, and a seven-member operational bureau that included (in addition to the committee members), Hosea Hudson representing the unemployed worker councils and one representative each from the Mine/Mill union, the ore miners, and the steel workers—seven in all: four black and three white comrades. Calling themselves the Political Bureau, they met on Sundays in private homes.[6]

Ross sent black unit leaders like Hosea Hudson, Henry Winston, Henry Mayfield, Frank Williams, and Al Murphy to the party's National Training and Worker Schools in New York. Hudson effectively became Ross's foreman.

On May 1, 1932, the police broke up a crowd preparing to march in the district's annual May Day parade and followed up with a series of raids. White journalist Blaine Owen and five others were beaten severely and arrested for sedition. At the arraignment, when Owen was asked if he believed in social equality, he assured Judge H. S. Abernathy that he not only believed in it, but that he would rather associate with Negroes than with the police thugs who'd beaten him.[7] A spectator in the courtroom shouted "burn them until they turn as black as the niggers they're so crazy about."[8] After Wakefield arrived with bail, all six were released. This was to be Wakefield's last official duty in Birmingham. He and his wife Jesse were being sent to Seattle's district 12 to open an ILD office, and Donald Burke and his wife Alice, who were also white, were coming from Virginia to replace them.

Burke subsequently moved the ILD office to Birmingham to share space. Budgets were tightening. In late May, Ross scheduled another staff meeting to introduce Burke and to review the procedures to follow when comrades got arrested. When Burke returned to his new office, he found it had been trashed. All the files and equipment were destroyed. Don and Alice Burke subsequently sent their infant daughter to stay with Alice's sister in California, where she remained for three years. Within months, Alice and unemployed worker organizer Wirt Taylor were arrested in Fairfield and spent eight weeks in jail.[9] Taylor, a white Alabama native, would later be arrested on an obstructing traffic charge and sentenced to time on a chain gang.

Despite ongoing harassment and violence, Ross, Benson, and Burke kept moving forward. On September 21, they hosted an All Southern Conference on Scottsboro at Birmingham's Prince Hall (Colored) Masonic Temple. Nearly five hundred delegates filed into the auditorium, and as they were about to begin, police officers entered and ordered everyone to either segregate or disburse. The delegates filed out and regrouped in a nearby vacant lot, where, closely observed by the police, they listened to the speakers. The most popular by far was Viola Montgomery, mother of Olen Montgomery, one of the Scottsboro teens.

Attitude

In the spring of 1932, Nat Ross had finally appointed a full-time district liaison to the Tallapoosa County Croppers' and Farm Workers' Union. Although Eula Gray had been holding the operation together since Coad and Simms left, Ross apparently never considered her for the position. She would continue to organize for the Young Communist League and by 1934 could report to the Central Committee that there were seven functioning YCL units in the county.

Ross had chosen Marcus "Al" Murphy, a black organizer at Birmingham's Stockholm Pipe and Fitting Company, who'd recently been fired for his Scottsboro advocacy. A year earlier he'd been arrested during the massive manhunt for the killer of two white society women on Shades Mountain. He'd violated the mayor's curfew and was grilled for hours. When the police demanded the names of his white comrades, Murphy gave up nothing.

He was twenty-five years old, short and stocky, soft-spoken, thoughtful, and very black. Better educated and considerably more militant than Mack Coad, Murphy would work with the Gray family to transform the Croppers' and Farm Workers' Union into an underground resistance movement with a new name: the Alabama Share Croppers' Union (ASCU). This movement would spread beyond Tallapoosa, and by the end of the year locals were operating in Lee, Macon, and Chambers Counties.

Like Harry Haywood, Murphy believed in black self-determination. He divided union members into groups of ten armed men and assigned each unit a coordinating captain. Murphy maintained that he had no problem with eliminating informers. He rationalized that an informer had gotten Ralph Gray killed and others, including a preacher, were responsible for the Camp Hill massacre. There is no evidence, however, that he ever exercised that kind of justice. Merely making his philosophy widely known was apparently effective.[10] Camp Hill had clearly marked a turning point. Afterward, no open protests or demonstrations were ever held in Cotton Country. Resistance became the operative term.

Murphy's greatest challenge was Ross's dictum to recruit across racial lines. He knew it couldn't work in the Black Belt. White croppers and tenant farmers had ridden with Sheriff Young's posse; blacks, not surprisingly, didn't trust any of them.[11] The union's commitment to racial equality repelled whites, and neither Murphy nor the rank and file were willing to mute it. This commitment was, in fact, one of the chief reasons why black croppers were attracted to the union. Murphy would never agree to soft pedal the party's social justice demands just to attract white croppers.

Under his guidance, the ASCU expanded into Dallas and Lowndes Counties, into western Georgia, and ultimately into Louisiana. Murphy moved his headquarters from Tallapoosa to Montgomery—to a barbershop on Monroe Street, in the city's black downtown district. He worked with black party leader John Beans and with Charles Tasker, the black leader of the city's unemployed worker council movement. Tasker's wife, Capitola, chaired the

Women's' Auxiliary. Her "sewing clubs" met over all Montgomery County and built a network for information gathering and distribution.[12]

The Taskers mimeographed flyers and handbills in the back room of "Al Jackson's Barbershop." They updated the black community about the Scottsboro case. Montgomery had been a center for underground organizing ever since the teens' arrests. Raymond Parks, husband of Rosa, raised money for their defense fund and brought food and clothing to them in Kilby Prison. The Parkses also attended district 17 rallies and helped the Taskers raise bail for jailed croppers.[13]

Although he remained active in the NAACP, Raymond Parks moved comfortably among radical black circles in Birmingham and Atlanta. Comrades often spent time at his home on South Union Street.[14] Rosa recalled armed men sitting around her kitchen table, which was piled high with guns. They talked freely because lookouts were posted at the front and back doors and they all called each other "Larry" to protect their identities.[15]

In 1932 the Reds were the only activists, black or white, who were willing to work directly with poor blacks. The NAACP focused on pursuing constitutional guarantees through the court system and so worked on behalf of rather than with poor and working-class people. The organization's initial failure to defend the nine Scottsboro teens had bitterly disappointed Raymond Parks.[16]

The Norman Thomas Study Club

It was likely the Taskers who introduced Al Murphy to the group of white activists in Montgomery who called themselves the Norman Thomas Study Club. It had to be someone who Murphy trusted, and he trusted Charles Tasker. Murphy agreed to meet with them in the summer of 1932 in the basement of Temple Beth Or, across the road from the Montgomery Country Club.

The rabbi, twenty-seven-year-old Benjamin Goldstein, had joined the club in 1931, three years into his tenure at the temple. All the members were pacifists, socialists, or progressives. Bea and Louis Kaufman, who belonged to the Beth Or congregation, led the effort to raise funds for the Scottsboro teens' appeals.

On March 24, 1932, after the Alabama Supreme Court upheld the Scottsboro convictions and the ILD petitioned the U.S. Supreme Court on the teens' behalf, Rabbi Goldstein joined Birmingham's Citizen Scottsboro Aid Committee. Activists coming south to assist the Scottsboro defense found a welcome respite in the homes of the Norman Thomas club members.

They met for weekly discussions ranging from the Scottsboro case and the black sharecroppers' grievances to the nation's economic misery and the rise of fascism in Europe. With family and friends living in Germany, some of the Jewish members were concerned about the growing obsession with who "real Germans" were. New German laws defined an individual with three Jewish grandparents as a non-Aryan, and prohibited intermarriage. This echoed the "one-drop-of-blood" criteria used to categorize mulattoes in the South. Adolf Hitler seemed to mirror the South's obsession with racial purity, its pride in a Lost Cause, and resentment over harsh peace terms.

Those who met with Al Murphy at the temple on March 24 included Louis Kaufman, a wholesale liquor salesman and treasurer of the Schloss and Kahn Grocery Company; Bea Kaufman, president of the local Council of Jewish Women; and Olive Stone, a sociology professor at Montgomery's Huntingdon College. With the exception of Goldstein, all had been raised in the South. Stone was a member of one of Dadeville's "first families." When they asked how they could help, Murphy was clear—he needed bail money.[17] They subsequently devised a plan.

Stone would carry envelopes of donated cash to the downtown post office, leave them on a prearranged counter, and wait for Murphy to retrieve them. This was clearly a risk to Murphy's life and to her continued employment.[18] Invariably, as they worked together, Murphy came to trust the professor, the rabbi, and the Kaufmans.

Two years earlier, the Tennessee Valley Authority had awarded Stone a grant to write a social history of the Tallapoosa County sharecroppers. During a stay in Dadeville, she'd met Sid Benson, who was working with union members there. She was charmed by this young man who shared her passions for literature, theater, and politics. They discussed and debated aspects of southern culture and the role of privileged planters (like her late father) who Benson called colonial exploiters.

After Benson brought Stone to a cropper union meeting, she invited him to a study club session.[19] When he and Nat Ross came to Montgomery to consult with Murphy, they also attended a club meeting. Afterward, Ross returned to Birmingham, but Benson stayed on to speak with the rabbi. Bea and Louis Kaufman provided him room and board.

After Benson left, the rabbi began speaking more forcefully about the plight of the Tallapoosa sharecroppers. Several of Beth Or's trustees reminded him that when he was hired he'd agreed to "leave the Negro question alone." Wasn't it enough that he'd angered so many in the congregation with his loose talk about the Scottsboro affair?

Most temple members contributed generously and faithfully (if anonymously), to Negro uplift, relief, and humanitarian causes, but they worried about their identities being discovered and their generosity being misunderstood as an endorsement of integration. The enthusiastic rabbi was strongly encouraged to be more circumspect.

Radicals

In July 1932, the study club welcomed twenty-two-year-old Jane Speed and her mother, Mary Craik (Darlie) Speed. Rabbi Goldstein likely extended the invitations. His neighbor, Dr. Charles Pollard, was Darlie's brother-in-law. Darlie Speed was a member of Montgomery's white, wealthy, and progressive Baldwin clan. Martin Baldwin, her grandfather, had presided over the Mobile and Montgomery Railroad, the First National Bank, and the Country Club. Her younger sister, Jean Read, was a popular socialite, and Jean's husband, Nash, a freelance journalist, was rumored to be a Red. The Nashes hosted garden parties and held formal teas at Hazel Hedge, their twenty-acre estate in the heart of the Cloverdale district.[20]

Darlie had scandalized the family in 1917 by divorcing her physicist husband, James Buckner Speed, and moving to New York City. Later she took her children Jane and William to live in "Red Vienna."

In 1931 Darlie and Jane returned to Montgomery and became friendly with Rabbi Goldstein, the only white clergyman who regularly visited the Scottsboro teens.[21] He'd managed to convince the warden that he was their spiritual advisor.[22]

Most of the study club members—the Kaufmans, Dorothy and Bernard Lobman, and Sadie Franks (all from Beth Or), Olive Stone, and several high school teachers and social workers—called themselves pacifists, socialists, or Marxists. Many of the women were also active in the local chapter of the Women's International League for Peace and Freedom. The Speeds, however, were Communists and didn't care who knew it.

In September 1932, during Yom Kippur, Rabbi Goldstein assured his congregation that the nine Scottsboro teens were innocent. When his trustees chided him again for introducing politics into the service, especially on the highest of holy days, Goldstein responded that "one could not speak of social justice and then stand on the sidelines when the limits of fairness were being tested."[23] This time they were truly angry, and they weren't going to warn him again.

Montgomery's elite, and those who aspired to breathe their rarified air, defended strict racial etiquette. Grover Hall, white editor of the *Montgomery Advertiser*, while predictably intolerant of disrespect from blacks, made excuses whenever his own black employees lied, stole, or wasted time because he believed that they didn't know any better. Although he despised the KKK and had won a 1928 Pulitzer Prize for his editorials exposing them, he was adamant about keeping blacks out of the voting booths since they vastly outnumbered whites in the Black Belt.[24] Hall was also convinced that the Scottsboro teens had received a fair trial and that sensible white southerners understood that they could take the race issue only so far.

That summer, Hall published letters from readers who were concerned about the persistent rumors that the Tallapoosa croppers were organizing again. Camp Hill apparently hadn't convinced them to give up their demands for written contracts, cash settlements, and marketing their own crops. Hall maintained that they'd been indoctrinated by the Reds. It had to be the Reds because he was convinced—as was most of white Alabama—that, left to their own devices, blacks had neither the desire nor the capacity to be defiant.[25]

Hall published those letters the same week that Janie Patterson, mother of Scottsboro defendant Haywood Patterson, addressed a rally in Harlem, New York: "Many have tried to tell me the ILD was low-down whites and Reds . . . but I have faith that they will free [my son] if we all unite behind them. . . . I don't care whether they are Reds. . . . They are the only ones who put up a fight to save these boys and I am with them to the end."[26]

Sharecropper prayer meeting house, Hale County, Alabama, 1936. Photo by Walker Evans. Library of Congress, Prints & Photographs Division, FSA/OWI Collection, LC-USF342-T01-008149-A.

Sharecropper cabin, Hale County, Alabama, 1936. Photo by Walker Evans. Library of Congress, Prints & Photographs Division, FSA/OWI Collection, LC-USF342-T01-008156-A.

Sharecropper family working near Anniston, Alabama, 1936. Photo by Dorothea Lange. Library of Congress, Prints & Photographs Division, FSA/OWI Collection, LC-USF34-009325-C.

Sharecropper's children, Montgomery County, Alabama, 1937. Photo by Arthur Rothstein. Library of Congress, Prints & Photographs Division, FSA/OWI Collection, LC-USF34-025351-D.

Al Murphy, Sikeston, Missouri, 1977.
Southern Oral History Program Collection,
Southern Historical Collection, Wilson Library,
University of North Carolina at Chapel Hill.

Angelo Herndon with Robert Minor (*front left*) and James Ford (*front right*). From the photo collection held at the Tamiment Library, New York University, by permission of the Communist Party USA.

Bull Connor, Birmingham, Alabama, commissioner of public safety. Courtesy of Birmingham Public Library.

Earl Browder, National Secretary, CPUSA, 1934. From the photo collection held at the Tamiment Library, New York University, by permission of the Communist Party USA.

Alabama Governor Bibb Graves. Alabama Department of Archives and History. Donated by Alabama Media Group.

Grover C. Hall Sr. Editor of the *Montgomery Advertiser*, 1926–1941. Alabama Department of Archives and History. Donated by Alabama Media Group.

Harry Simms, front cover of *Labor Defender*, March 1932. From the collections of the Kheel Center, Cornell University.

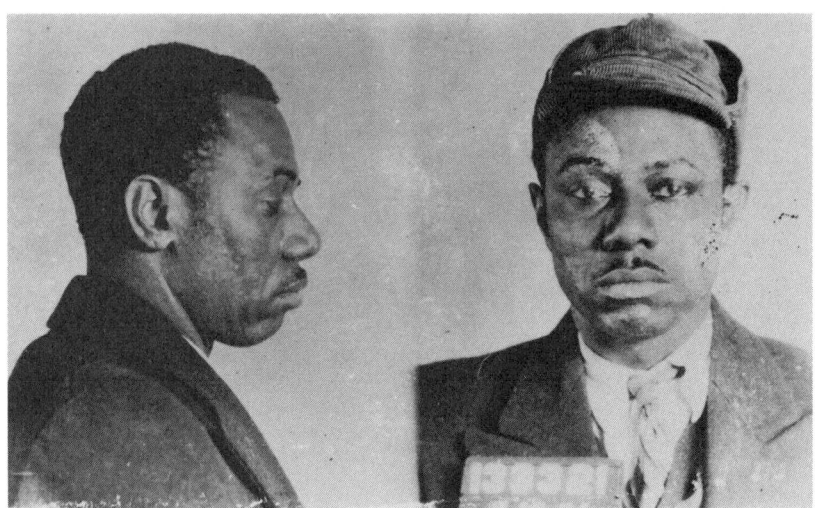

Hosea Hudson, arrested for vagrancy in Birmingham, 1932.
Southern Oral History Program Collection, Southern Historical Collection, Wilson Library, University of North Carolina at Chapel Hill.

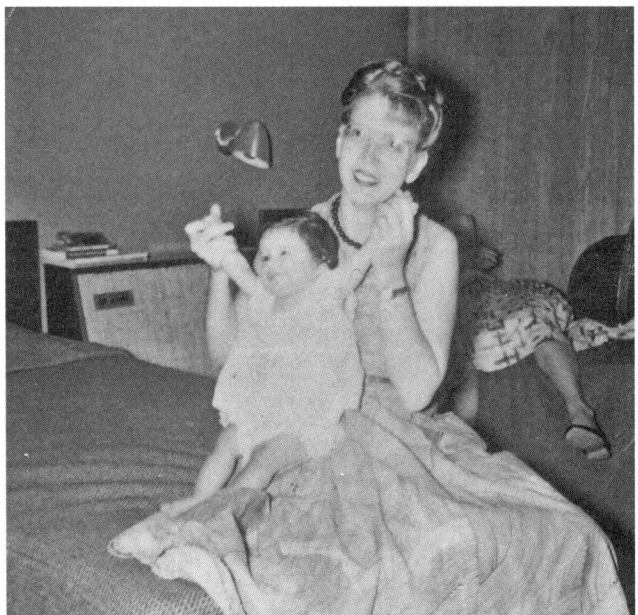

Jane Speed, Puerto Rico, 1954.
Courtesy of Aurora Levins Morales.

Mack Coad, Birmingham, Alabama, 1930. From the Tamiment Library, New York University.

Private James Allen, 1942. Courtesy of Jesse Auerbach.

Rabbi Benjamin Goldstein and daughter Josie, Montgomery, Alabama, 1931. Courtesy of Josie Goldstein Rogers.

Scottsboro Boys and attorney Samuel Leibowitz. Standing from left to right: Olen Montgomery, Clarence Norris, Willie Roberson (front), Andrew Wright, Ozie Powell, Eugene Williams, Charley Weems, and Roy Wright. Haywood Patterson is sitting next to Samuel Liebowitz. Morgan County Archives, Decatur, Alabama.

Ruby Bates testifying at Haywood Patterson trial, March 1933, Decatur, Alabama. Morgan County Archives, Decatur, Alabama.

Victoria Price, Haywood Patterson trial, March 1933, Decatur, Alabama. Morgan County Archives, Decatur, Alabama.

Walter F. White, National Secretary NAACP, 1949. Library of Congress, Prints & Photographs Division, Visual Materials from the NAACP Records, LC-DIG-ds-13132.

Charles Hamilton Houston, NAACP Legal Defense Fund, 1939. Library of Congress, Prints & Photographs Division, Visual Materials from the NAACP Records, LC-DIG-ds-13133.

9 ▮ REELTOWN RADICALS

> Strength is a matter of a made-up mind.
> —John Beecher, "Reflections of a Man Who
>   Once Stood Up for Freedom"

In November 1932, Walter Parker, a white Macon County planter, called in a loan he'd made to his black cropper Cliff James. James had put money down to buy some of Parker's land that he was already working. Parker demanded the $950 remaining balance immediately and refused to grant an extension. After all the trouble the black croppers were causing, and especially after Camp Hill, Parker was through helping any of them buy land. He also suspected that Cliff James was up to no good—likely working with the Reds organizing the croppers around Reeltown. Parker was right. James was working with Al Murphy.

Parker turned the note over to a Dadeville lawyer, who instructed Sheriff Young to serve a writ of attachment on James's two cows and two mules. On December 19, Sheriff Young, who was still recuperating from the bullet he'd taken at Camp Hill, sent Deputy Witt Elder to serve the papers and take the animals. Without his animals, James couldn't farm and he would fall further into debt.

When Deputy Elder arrived, James ran him off the property. Elder swore he would "get some men and come back and kill you niggers in a pile."[1] When Elder returned with reinforcements, James's neighbors were waiting. They were armed and surrounding his livestock pen. It was a standoff until one of the deputies shot and killed cropper Jim McMullen. In the chaos that followed, both Deputy Elder and Cliff James were wounded. Three croppers were also injured, and one of the deputies was dead.

Walter Parker was furious. He told Sheriff Young that he believed James was a ringleader in "that nigger union." Young promised that he would take care of him.

Deputy Elder was taken to a local hospital, but Cliff James traveled eleven miles to Tuskegee's Veterans' Hospital for treatment. Dr. Eugene Dibble, the black medical director, treated his wounds and then called the Macon County sheriff.[2]

Dibble was in the middle of a collaborative study in partnership with the public health service and the state and county health departments to "observe the effects of untreated syphilis on black men." Since Macon County was 82 percent black and had a high incidence of the disease, it was considered a prime research site. Dibble agreed that even if there were no funds to treat syphilis, an "observation study" could determine the disease's natural course. After all, the U.S. Surgeon General had assured Tuskegee superintendent Robert Moton that the results of the study "could have a marked bearing on the treatment, or conversely the non-necessity of treatment, of latent syphilis." Dibble knew that everything would be lost if he was caught assisting black revolutionaries.[3]

Over the next forty years, the Andrew Memorial Veteran's Hospital followed four hundred syphilitic sharecroppers without treating any of them—despite a promise of free medical care for participating in a study to determine if they had "bad blood."

Dibble's call to the sheriff resulted in Cliff James landing in the Montgomery County Jail, where his neighbors Jud Simpson, Milo Bentley (who'd suffered a severe head injury), and Ned Cobb were being held. Fears of race war swept white Tallapoosa. Still, Sheriff Young was apparently unable to raise a local posse of white croppers, so he was forced to recruit from the neighboring counties of Macon, Elmore, and Lee. He deputized nearly five hundred men, directed them to Reeltown, and told them that he'd found a union membership list in James's home. They were ordered to round up the croppers on that list and any other croppers they came across. They understood. Black croppers were beaten and jailed randomly, and four were killed before Young congratulated them for having put down this long-anticipated outbreak of race war.[4]

Sheriff Young and his vigilantes had conducted a three-day reign of terror. Whole families fled into the woods for safety, and W. S. Hanson, a white Tallapoosa physician, reported treating more than a dozen black men for gunshot wounds.

The five croppers who'd tried to protect James's animals were indicted for assault with intent to kill despite the fact that Deputy Elder could not produce the court order directing him to seize James's property. Louis Kaufman (of the Norman Thomas Study Club) posted their bail ($750 each), and Rabbi Goldstein arranged lodging for the ILD attorneys who came to represent them.

Goldstein, Jane Speed, Darlie Speed, and Jane's aunt Jean Read went to Governor Miller's office to demand an investigation. Read summarized that meeting in an open letter to the *Montgomery Advertiser*:

"We pointed out [to the governor] that the attorney for the arrested men was not allowed to see them except in the presence of the sheriff, and that two of them, Judson Simpson and Milo Bentley, were lying seriously wounded in jail. The Governor said that no sheriff had the right to prevent an attorney from conferring with his clients, and that the attorney could appeal for a court order restraining the sheriff from interfering. However, the court order would have to be executed by the sheriff himself."[5]

Disgusted, they drove to Reeltown, where Deputy Elder refused to speak with them and his son threatened to "get them all."[6] By the time they returned to Montgomery, Cliff James had died. Milo Bently died the following day. The rabbi invited the city's black ministers to his home on South Perry Street to organize food and clothing drives for the croppers, and the ILD's Donald Burke organized a double funeral for them on January 2 and a rally in Birmingham's Black Phythian Temple. There, eulogizers blasted Dr. Dibble and Tuskegee superintendent Robert Moton for their betrayal of James.

Their bodies lay in state for a week at the Jordan Funeral Home before three thousand blacks followed their red-flag-draped coffins to Grace Hill Cemetery.[7] This massive turnout agitated, angered, and terrified white Birmingham, who held the Reds responsible.

But this time even some white Alabamians were expressing sympathy for the Reeltown croppers and criticizing the sheriff's brutality. An editorial in the white *Birmingham Post* allowed that "the causes of the trouble are essentially economic. . . . The resistance of the Negroes at Reeltown against officers seeking to attach their livestock on a lien bears a close parallel to battles fought in Iowa and Wisconsin between farmers and sheriff's deputies seeking to serve eviction papers. A good many white farmers, ground down by the same relentless economic pressure from which the Negroes were suffering, expressed sympathy with the Negroes' desperate plot."[8]

In April 1933, the five croppers who'd defended James's property went to trial. Former senator "Cotton Tom" Heflin prosecuted, and ILD attorneys Irving Schwab and George Chamlee represented them. All were found guilty and sentenced to between five and fifteen years in prison. They served, on average, ten years.

The Agricultural Adjustment Act

The agricultural "economic trouble" the *Birmingham Post* article had alluded to steadily worsened in the Black Belt.[9] A great deal of hope was therefore invested in the November 1932 election of Franklin Roosevelt, particularly after he muscled his Agricultural Adjustment Act (AAA) through Congress during his first hundred days. The AAA created the Agricultural Adjustment Administration, charged with solving the farm crisis. Secretary of Agriculture Henry Wallace was given authority to control farm production and to purchase surpluses.

An Iowa native who'd planted corn and raised hogs, Secretary Wallace knew very little about cotton farming. He understood, however, that the laws of supply and demand always worked against farmers—the more they produced, the lower market prices fell. So, he proposed an emergency surplus crop reduction plan to create artificial scarcity and to stimulate a demand for produce.

Under Wallace's direction, cotton, rice, and tobacco farmers who agreed to reduce their acreage by 30 percent were eligible for a federal subsidy of $11 for each acre left fallow. Once markets rallied, the subsidies would end. Farming was a business, Secretary Wallace maintained, and like any business it would respond to production control. The beauty of the plan was its simplicity—or so he thought.

Wallace delegated the plan's administration to state extension service networks, which in Alabama included the farm bureau. Unfortunately, this led to unanticipated and generally disastrous consequences. Because the spring planting had already begun by the time the legislation took effect (and because Wallace was unwilling to hold off payments for another season), planters who applied for subsidy payments for 1933 were required to plow under a quarter of their crops. The AAA paid a total of $161,777,697.00 to destroy ten million acres of cotton, soybeans, and corn.[10] Millions more were spent to destroy perfectly healthy farm animals. Starving Americans were at first stunned, then enraged. Destroying healthy crops and animals in an attempt to restart the stalled economy seemed both a colossal and cruel waste.

Displacement of sharecroppers was a major consequence of the AAA. The land most planters chose to leave fallow was acreage that they leased. Since the crop was the tenants' only asset, when it was removed they had no basis on which to access credit. The controversial decision to mail federal subsidy payments directly to landlords and to assume that they would refund their croppers' losses, based on their percentage of the harvest, created another crisis.

Cully Cobb, the AAA's Cotton Section administrator, a southerner who understood that white planters would never voluntarily participate in a program that paid black croppers directly, insisted that the landlords be compensated and that they provide for their croppers and tenants. Consequentially, most croppers never received any compensation. Many planters considered reimbursing croppers as simply "paying them not to work." Croppers who protested were threatened with eviction.

The ham-handed implementation of the Agricultural Adjustment Act highlighted the administration's ignorance of the farm tenancy system. The crop reduction program actually incentivized landowners to evict croppers and tenants. Planters jumped at the opportunity to free themselves from the demands of these landless farmers. They were only too happy to hire them as hourly cotton choppers and pickers. They'd apparently forgotten that the cumbersome sharecropper arrangement had been engineered and subsequently maintained to protect white privilege.

Walter White of the NAACP petitioned the Roosevelt administration to stop paying subsidies until an equitable distribution process could be designed, but he was ignored. In Alabama, the conservative Farm Bureau and Extension Service continued to administer the program. John P. Davis, a future founder of the National Negro Congress, wrote that the federal government "failed absolutely to protect the equities of the tenant.... Yet the administration in Washington—like Pontius Pilate—washed its hands of the whole matter and left it to the consciences of the white plantation owners of the South to see that justice was done."[11]

10 ▍ REVERSALS AND BOMBSHELLS

> Some circumstantial evidence is very strong—as when you find a trout in the milk.
> —Henry David Thoreau, November 11, 1850, journal entry

In March 1932, the Alabama Supreme Court affirmed the eight Scottsboro teens' convictions, and eight executions were scheduled for May 13. Andy Wright, the youngest, would continue his life sentence. Defense attorney Joseph Brodsky, exercising his last option, appealed to the U.S. Supreme Court. Two months later the high court agreed to review the cases.

On November 7, 1932, all nine convictions (including Andy Wright's) were reversed in *Powell v. Alabama* on the grounds that the defendants had not been provided adequate legal counsel. Nine new trials were ordered, and twelve days later Reeltown, Alabama, exploded in what local authorities described as an outbreak of race war.

News of the new trials reached ILD national secretary J. Louis Engdahl, while he was completing a six-month fund-raising tour of Europe with Scottsboro mother Ada Wright. As delegates to the World Congress of International Red Aid, they were obliged to attend the closing session before they headed home. After the meeting, Engdahl collapsed and subsequently died of pneumonia. He was forty-eight years old, and many of his colleagues believed that Scottsboro had hastened his death.

A radical journalist, Engdahl joined the party in 1925, edited the *Daily Worker* for years, and served a term on the Executive Committee of the Communist International (Comintern). He was a nervous, gloomy man who always seemed distracted and under emotional stress. In 1929 morale was so low at the *Daily Worker* that the staff petitioned to have him removed. Since he was not an attorney his subsequent transfer to the ILD was surprising. Whittaker Chambers, who worked with Engdahl at the *Daily Worker*, categorized it as "kicking Engdahl upstairs."[1] It was Engdahl's misfortune that the Scottsboro case broke on his watch.

William Patterson, one of the party's rising stars, was appointed acting

ILD director during Engdahl's travels. Patterson, who was black, had recently returned from two years on assignment in Russia, Britain, France, and Germany. Harry Haywood succeeded him as chair of the Negro Commission. In May 1932 Patterson took charge of the Scottsboro campaign, and two months later Engdahl was dead.

Within three years of coming to Harlem from San Francisco in 1920, Patterson had established a successful law practice and joined the NAACP. In 1925 he volunteered with the national campaign to free the anarchists Sacco and Vanzetti. After that failure, Patterson apparently lost faith in the NAACP, joined the Communist Party, and began to socialize with some of the luminaries of the Harlem Renaissance, including Langston Hughes and Paul Robeson.

In November 1927, the party sent him to Russia to learn the language and to study Marxist theory. He participated in the 1928 Third Communist International, met fellow African American communists Otto Hall, Claude McKay, James Ford, and Harry Haywood, and was appointed chair of the Negro Commission.

At the December 1932 ILD Convention, one month after Engdahl's death, Earl Browder nominated Patterson for national ILD secretary, and he was appointed by acclamation.

Now, as 1933 began, white Alabama's high rage over the nine new Scottsboro trials was his to deal with. In the upcoming round, Patterson knew that the ILD and its new black director would be on trial. Those nine young men needed the best lawyer they could get. That would be, without a doubt, Samuel Leibowitz of New York City, a successful criminal defense attorney who was neither a radical nor a communist.

Leibowitz was touted as "the next Clarence Darrow," and Patterson considered his independent political stance an asset. At the very least it would demonstrate that the Reds were not trying to make martyrs of the young men to advance a political agenda.[2] Convincing Leibowitz to accept the case, however, wouldn't be easy. Darrow had twice refused it.

Patterson made his proposal in January 1933 and advised Leibowitz that the trial cycle would begin in March. Although the ILD couldn't pay his going rate, his expenses would be covered, and Patterson expressed hope that Leibowitz would consider it an opportunity to "represent not only nine innocent boys but a nation of twelve million oppressed people struggling against dehumanizing inequalities."[3] Finally, Patterson assured Leibowitz that the ILD did not expect him to give up or even to mute any of his social, economic, or political views as a condition of accepting the case.

Leibowitz immediately expressed interest but admitted to being concerned about all the publicity surrounding the case. He told Patterson "some of my friends have advised me to take no part in this case. They fear that the defendants have been prejudged that... they are doomed because their skins are black. I cannot partake of that opinion."[4]

He expressed confidence in the U.S. judicial system and faith in the people of Alabama: "I cannot believe that [they] will be false to their great heritage of honor, and to those brave and chivalrous generations of the past, in whose blood the history of their State is written. If the views I have expressed match yours, then I will accept the task of conducting the defense."[5]

How grand, Patterson thought. He had his own reservations about their ability to work together. Taking a deep breath, he wrote a terse reply. "The views you have expressed do not match ours," he said, "and yet despite the wide gulf that lies between us ideologically we stand ready to accept your services as trial attorney.... The terms you have specified are acceptable to us."[6] Leibowitz was on board.

Decatur

The new Scottsboro trials began in March 1933 with Haywood Patterson, who'd been living on death row for two years. Because he was contentious, the guards often chose him for the despised detail of removing bodies from the electric chair.[7] The young man was tough, he looked mean, and his jailers were determined to break him.

Patterson's defense team—Leibowitz, Joseph Brodsky, and George Chamlee—would focus on Alabama's practice of excluding blacks from juries—a violation of both the Ninth Amendment and the due process clause of the Fourteenth Amendment. At a pretrial hearing on March 27, Chamlee requested a change of venue, hopefully to Birmingham, where he believed Patterson stood a better chance. A change was granted, but it was only to Decatur, the Morgan County seat. A city of sixteen thousand, Decatur was eighty-one miles north of Birmingham and twenty-five miles west of Huntsville. Eighty percent white, the city had once been a manufacturing center humming with tanneries, cotton and lumber mills, but the Depression had ended that. Patterson was housed in the old county jail—a broken-down, vermin-filled facility no longer considered safe for white prisoners.[8]

Leibowitz next requested that Circuit Judge James Horton throw out all the indictments since there were no blacks in Alabama's jury pool. This, he said, precluded his clients receiving a fair trial.[9] Judge Horton agreed to keep the motion under advisement.

Leibowitz subsequently laid a foundation for an appeal by calling a string of black teachers, artisans, small-business owners, and professionals to demonstrate that there were blacks capable of serving on juries and who were willing to do so. While Judge Horton ultimately refused to dismiss the indictment against Patterson, he noted for the record that the defense had made its point: blacks were routinely excluded from Alabama juries.[10]

On April 3, the prosecution called Victoria Price. She identified Patterson as one of her attackers, holding the jurors spellbound with her vivid description of their ride in the freight car. Over the next four days, Leibowitz cross-examined her. Although Price was inconsistent, sarcastic, and repeatedly denied any prior arrests or convictions, the seasoned criminal attorney was unable to shake her story. She was amazingly confident. As Leibowitz cited her arrests for "adultery and fornication," described her notoriety as a streetwalker in Huntsville, and asked her point blank if she'd spent the night before the alleged attack in Chattanooga's hobo jungle, she maintained that she couldn't recall, didn't understand, or simply glared at him.[11]

At several points, seemingly on the verge of losing his temper, Leibowitz had apparently forgotten warnings about straying too far from the strict etiquette regarding a gentleman's interactions with a white southern lady. But he did not consider Price "a lady," and he could not imagine how any of the jurors might. As a result, he made some serious mistakes. Leibowitz hammered home that Price was a liar and a tramp, and he treated her with disdain while referring to his black client as "Mr. Patterson." If that wasn't bad enough, he demanded that the prosecution treat Patterson with the same respect. Both judge and jury were stunned.

It was not until the fourth day, however, when Leibowitz called a surprise witness, that the Decatur trial entered the history books. Ruby Bates testified under oath that neither Haywood Patterson nor any of the Scottsboro teens had attacked her or Victoria Price. There had been no rape . . . there was no case . . . and the defense abruptly rested.

Jonathan Daniels, white editor of the *Raleigh News and Observer*, reported: "[Ruby Bates] declared that she had testified to a whole narrative of falsehood which resulted in the sentencing of eight Negroes to the electric chair." Her recantation "made it clear that the crime was done not by the Negroes but by those who posed as their victims."[12]

"With the confession of Ruby Bates," he concluded, "the honor of the white South is far more on trial in Alabama than it was when it was being defended against nine Negro hoboes. Today the honor of the South must be defended from the attacks of whites who would, with cold blooded ruthlessness, have lied eight Negroes to death."[13]

John Spivak wrote in the *Daily Worker*: "I kept wondering how Ruby's testimony could do anything but end the case. If one of the two complainants who brought these boys to the brink of death confessed that neither she nor her companion had been raped, where was the case? There was the word of only one woman, known as a tramp and contradicted by her own companion. How could twelve men, no matter how prejudiced, now find Patterson guilty?"[14]

Incredibly, Bates's testimony had no effect on the jurors. On April 9, 1933, they found Patterson guilty. For the second time, he was sentenced to death. The defense moved for a new trial.

Montgomery Reacts

Before Haywood Patterson's trial began, Rabbi Goldstein was in Birmingham collecting signatures for a petition to Governor Miller for a change of venue. Someone from Montgomery had apparently seen him, because three days into the trial the *Montgomery Examiner*'s banner headline screamed, "Goldstein Stumps for Scottsboro 7." On April 10, the Capital City's Jewish community also read with horror that, during his summation, Morgan County prosecutor Wade Wright had pointed to Leibowitz and Brodsky and asked the jurors, "Is justice in this case going to be bought and sold with Jew money from New York?"[15] Temple Beth Or's trustees convened in emergency session. Goldstein was putting their entire community at risk.

On April 11, congregation president Ernest Mayer directed Rabbi Goldstein to either sever his ties with the ILD, the Scottsboro teens, the Birmingham communists, the sharecroppers, and the local radicals—or resign.[16] He'd finally crossed the line, and if he didn't agree to go quietly they were prepared send him packing. Louis Kaufman and only one other board member supported him.[17]

Goldstein resigned on April 12 and informed the Jewish Telegraphic Wire Service that "my resignation resulted from my activities not only on behalf of the Scottsboro Negroes for whom I demanded a fair trial and a change of venue, but also on behalf of the Tallapoosa Negro share-croppers for whom I demanded fair treatment." The *Jewish Daily Bulletin* subsequently reported that "Montgomery Rabbi Loses Post in Fight on Behalf of Negroes." A furious Ernest Mayer demanded a retraction. He maintained that the rabbi had not resigned but was fired.[18]

On Easter Sunday, April 16, 1933, Goldstein spoke at a Scottsboro Defense Rally in Birmingham. He had nothing left to lose. Jane Speed, Howard Kester (the white Fellowship of Reconciliation's Southern Representative), Bishop B. G. Shaw of Birmingham's AME Zion Temple, and Scottsboro mother Ada Wright shared the platform with him.

Two weeks later, on May 1, Jane Speed was arrested at another rally and charged with "speaking before a public assembly of mixed races without physical barriers of separation." She told a *Birmingham News* reporter that "the police's chivalrous attitude toward white Southern womanhood was thoroughly exposed as they brutally twisted my arms, cursing me in the vilest and most foul language. . . . It seems very strange to one of my upbringing that the men who came forward to protect me were Negroes." When she chose to remain in jail rather than pay the $50 fine, her story made the front page of the *Montgomery Advertiser*. When she returned to Hazel Hedge, her aunt Jean informed her that she and her mother had to leave—the sooner the better.[19]

Before he left on May 25, Goldstein told a reporter for the *Montgomery Advertiser* that "anyone who tries to take an impartial attitude toward the conduct of the Scottsboro case is immediately branded a Communist and a nigger lover." The Beth Or trustees countered with a press release asserting that they "repudiated outside interference in Southern affairs and pledged their unequivocal support for segregation."[20]

Darlie and Jane Speed subsequently went to New York City. Speaking at a League of Struggle for Negro Rights rally in Harlem, Darlie maintained that she'd once been confident that the "good people of Alabama would come to the aid of the young black men" (i.e., the nine Scottsboro teens), but she'd become convinced that "you cannot defend a black man in the South. . . . We heard the best citizens of the South say, 'Oh, the Scottsboro boys are innocent, alright, but if we let Negroes get by with this case no white woman will be safe in the South.' It became apparent that the ILD was the only group in America that would defend a black.... The South pushed me right into the arms of the ILD and the revolutionary movement," she said.[21]

Less than a year later, in May 1934, Professor Olive Stone of the Norman Thomas Study Club was notified that her contract with Huntingdon College would not be renewed. She lost her position as both dean of students and professor of sociology and social work and moved to Atlanta.

First Bombshell

On June 22, 1933, ten weeks after Haywood Patterson's second conviction, Judge James Horton announced that Samuel Leibowitz's destructive and very public posttrial statements to the press made it impossible to assemble an impartial jury for the sentencing phase. He suspended the eight upcoming trials, set aside the Patterson verdict, and granted the defense its motion for a new trial. The citizens of Alabama, black and white, could not believe it. Neither could Leibowitz. Attorney General Thomas Knight Jr., who during the trial had referred Patterson as "that thing over there," nearly choked on his rage as he announced the state's intention to retry the case.[22]

Unlike the jurors, Judge Horton apparently was unable to ignore the testimonies of Ruby Bates and Dr. R. R. Bridges, one of two physicians who'd initially examined Bates and Price. While the women claimed to have been raped, Dr. Bridges testified that their pulse rates were normal, their clothes were intact, and there was no evidence of blood. Although they said they'd fought off their attackers, neither had any scratches or bruises. In addition, Dr. Marvin Lynch, who'd assisted Dr. Bridges (but did not testify), told Horton that when he confronted the women with his doubts about the attack, they laughed at him.[23] Horton also wondered aloud why none of the white boys involved in the fight had been called to testify.

Judge Horton could have thrown out all the indictments (as Leibowitz had petitioned at the pretrial hearing) because of the state's practice of excluding blacks from jury service—arguably a violation of the Ninth and Fourteenth Amendments. He chose instead to focus on the lack of evidence and the unreliability of the witnesses.

Attorney Joseph Brodsky, while not wanting to look a gift horse in the mouth, was not completely satisfied. "Judge Horton is fair according to his lights," he granted, "but those lights are the lights of a 'Southern Gentlemen' which means that he accepts and takes for granted . . . the necessity of white supremacy in the South."[24]

Isadore Schneider, writing for the ILD's *Labor Defender*, disparaged "all the kudos that liberals were strewing the Judge's way," and challenged them to think more carefully. "Judge Horton in his decision granting a new trial shies off from the important issues and industriously whacks away at Victoria Price's testimony. Not a word about the lynch atmosphere, the baiting by the State's attorneys, the exclusion of Negroes from the jury. . . . These were the issues to be met. But it was easier and safer to call Victoria Price a liar. . . . Liberals always have the wrong reasons for renewing their faith in mankind."[25]

Still, Judge Horton's order for a new trial was enough to cost him reelection in 1934. He'd always run unopposed, and many believed that he was on his way to becoming Alabama's next governor. All that changed overnight. He was accused of disloyalty, cowardice, and of being "bought off by the Communists."

Haywood Patterson's third trial began in November 1933, once again in Decatur. Governor Miller, at the request of newly elected lieutenant governor Thomas Knight Jr., moved the remaining Scottsboro teens' trials from Judge Horton's jurisdiction to Judge William Washington Callahan's docket. Callahan, who'd never attended college or law school, overruled nearly every objection the defense team made, sustained the majority of objections brought by the prosecution, made several himself, and reprimanded Leibowitz continually.[26] Callahan also made it as difficult as possible for reporters to cover the trial.

Once again Leibowitz stressed that the unconstitutional practice of excluding blacks from jury service in Alabama kept Patterson from receiving a fair trial. Incredibly, in his instructions to the jury Judge Callahan counseled that they "should very strongly presume that no white woman would voluntarily have sex with a black man."[27] The jury deliberated for three days before returning a guilty verdict on December 4, 1933.

By year's end, Clarence Norris had also been retried, reconvicted of rape, and again sentenced to death. The Leibowitz team appealed his conviction to the Alabama Supreme Court as well. Six months later, in June 1934, Alabama's high court affirmed both the Patterson and Norris convictions, and Leibowitz and Brodsky were on their way back to the U.S. Supreme Court.

Second Bombshell

Residents of Tennessee would recall the summer of 1934 as exceptionally muggy. Samuel Leibowitz and his wife were fortunate in being able to get away for a ten-week cruise and would not return until late September.

In June, J. T. Pearson of Birmingham, who used the name Charles Price, traveled to Huntsville to find Victoria Price, who he claimed as a distant cousin. When he found her, he asked Victoria if she might be interested in signing a piece of paper that would get her out of testifying in any more trials and make her $500 richer. Victoria said she would think it over. She then discussed it with Huntsville police chief H. C. Blakemore, who told her to play along.

Two months later, Victoria's "cousin" returned with a man who he said was a New York lawyer. When Victoria asked for $1,000 and the lawyer agreed, she said she was ready to sign his paper. Cousin Charles then allegedly contacted the ILD and told "someone" that Victoria Price was willing to recant her testimony for $1,000.

On October 1, Sol Kone and Daniel Schriftman, two white attorneys who worked with Joseph Brodsky, met Victoria and her "cousin" in Nashville. The Nashville police arrested them on the spot and they were extradited to Alabama to face bribery charges. Kone and Schriftman insisted that they'd been set up, but by whom? Victoria? The prosecution? The press? All of them in league with the police? Had Cousin Charles and/or the police manipulated Victoria? Or, had Kone and Schriftman simply been caught trying to bribe her? At the November 1934 inquest, Victoria admitted that it was her "cousin" who'd offered the money, not the attorneys. There was also some confusion about whether or not Kone and Schriftman had a suitcase filled with $1,500 in small bills in their possession or whether Deputy Sheriff Corcoran had "planted it." Schriftman insisted he'd brought a briefcase, not a suitcase, and there was no money in it. The briefcase was never found. Ultimately, both men were indicted along with Cousin Charles.

When Kone and Schriftman failed to appear on their trial date, the Alabama authorities decided not to prosecute either of them or Pearson (Cousin Charles).[28] Victoria Price, who'd been underestimated by the defense attorneys before, was ecstatic. She considered it payback for Leibowitz's shabby treatment of her during Patterson's second trial.

When Leibowitz returned from Europe, he was furious. He accused Brodsky of destroying everything. The bribe, he said, made Ruby Bates's recantation worthless as well. Even if the U.S. Supreme Court granted the teens another trial, even if they got a change of venue, where would they find an impartial jury? He then very publicly broke with the ILD.

"I cannot continue as counsel in the Scottsboro case until all secret maneuverings, ballyhoo, mass pressure and Communist methods are removed," Leibowitz told reporters. Brodsky subsequently fired him. Their feud played out in the press for months. Leibowitz charged the ILD with misusing Scottsboro Defense Funds and putting the nine teens at risk by their "inflexible demands, extra-legal strategies, and protest marches that inflamed public opinion across the South."[29]

Brodsky countered that Leibowitz had never raised any objections about these methods during their three-year collaboration. He charged Leibowitz with losing the second Patterson trial because of his attacks on Victoria Price, despite being forewarned that an all-white male jury would never stand for a character assassination of a white woman.[30] Finally, he said that Leibowitz had done irreparable damage to the defendants by entertaining the New York City press corps with his imitations of the Decatur jurors—describing them as "bigots whose mouths are slits in their faces, whose eyes popped out at you like frogs, whose chins dripped with tobacco juice, bewhiskered and filthy."[31] When this mismatched alliance finally imploded, there was more than enough culpability to go around.

11 ▮ JUSTICE FOR ANGELO HERNDON

> Where justice is denied, where poverty is enforced, where ignorance prevails and where any one class is made to feel that society is an organized conspiracy to oppress, rob and degrade them, neither person nor property will be safe.
> —Frederick Douglass, speech on the twenty-fourth anniversary of Emancipation, 1886, Washington, D.C.

On January 16, 1933, two months before Haywood Patterson's second trial, nineteen-year-old Angelo Herndon stood before Judge Lee B. Wyatt in Atlanta's Fulton County Courthouse to answer charges of inciting insurrection. This was a capital offense in Georgia.[1] Herndon's attorney, Ben Davis Jr., who was black, had been recruited by the ILD's William Patterson. Davis was a recent Harvard Law School graduate and the son of "Big Ben" Davis, editor of the *Atlanta Independent*. John H. Greer, his associate and also black, maintained a small Atlanta practice. Like Leibowitz, neither of them was a communist. Unlike Leibowitz, they were young and inexperienced.

For nine months Herndon had been organizing unemployed workers in Atlanta and demanding rent relief on their behalf. He'd led demonstrations and protests throughout the city, and while his brashness had endeared him to his constituency, he'd been targeted by the local authorities.

On June 30, 1932, the Fulton County Emergency Relief Center ran out of funds. Herndon subsequently led an integrated hunger march of nearly a thousand people to the courthouse to demand that it be reopened. On July 11, he was arrested and charged with inciting insurrection. Under an 1861 Georgia slave statute, advocating unity between blacks and whites for any reason was punishable by death. Herndon was taken to the overcrowded Fulton Tower Prison, where he remained for six months awaiting trial. He and his fellow prisoners were often compelled to sleep on top of each other for lack of floor space. In August, when an elderly prisoner died there, his body was left for three days in a hot airless holding cell with six other prisoners.[2] In December, Herndon's attorney Ben Davis finally got him released on bail.

Herndon's trial began on January 16, 1933, with County Judge Lee B. Wyatt presiding and the tall, lanky Assistant State Solicitor John H. Hudson, a

National Guard colonel and Methodist minister, prosecuting. Herndon later reflected that Hudson represented "not only the majesty of the law, but the might of the army, and the sanctity of the church."[3]

Tension between the black defense team on one hand and Solicitor Hudson and Judge Wyatt on the other was palpable. When Davis moved for dismissal, citing the defense that the ILD used in the Scottsboro appeals—that Negroes were excluded from jury service in Georgia—his motion was denied. When he questioned the validity of the anti-insurrection statue used to charge Herndon, Hudson objected and was sustained.

Assistant prosecutor L. Walter Le Craw read the indictment to the jury: "Pamphlets found in [Herndon's] possession indicated that the [Communist] party urged confiscation of the land of southern capitalists for the benefit of Negro tenant farmers, replacement of artificial state boundaries with a unified Black Belt, and self-determination for the Negro majority including the right to secession."[4]

When the jurors appeared confused, Hudson clarified: "Blacks and whites should unite for the purpose of setting up a Nigger Soviet Republic in the Black Belt," he said bluntly.[5] Davis's objection was overruled.

The defense called several Emory University professors to testify that the literature found in Herndon's room and placed into evidence was not insurrectionary. In his cross-examination, Prosecutor Hudson questioned the professors' patriotism and dismissed the university as "a hotbed of iniquity." Davis countered that the KKK, not the Communist Party, was insurrectionary.[6]

Taking the stand, Angelo Herndon explained that the unemployed councils in Atlanta "organized both black and white workers together on the same basis of common problems and interests," and he urged both races to put "this question of the white skin and the black skin behind them because both are starving and the capitalist class will continue to prey on this tune of racial discrimination . . . in order to keep the negro and white divided."[7]

A more experienced defense attorney might have attempted to limit Herndon's rhetoric, but Davis allowed him to continue. "Workers," Herndon maintained, "have built up this country and are therefore entitled to some of the things that they have produced."[8]

A broad-shouldered former college all-American football player, Davis patiently informed the jury that membership in the Communist Party was not illegal. Unfortunately, he failed to press the issue of the unconstitutionality of the Georgia statute, and that would become a problem later on.

The trial dragged on for three days, with Davis's and Greer's motions being overruled continuously. Most of the defense evidence submitted was dismissed as irrelevant and/or immaterial. Hudson and Le Craw's objections, on the other hand, were uniformly sustained.

On the last day, Solicitor Hudson summarized the state's case against Herndon. "Gentlemen of the jury," he said, "you have heard the defendant lay down his defy to the State of Georgia. He is a confirmed revolutionist, with an unbreakable soul. But we accept his challenge. Gentlemen, when you go into the box, I expect you to arrive at a verdict that will automatically send this damnable anarchistic Bolsheviki to his death by electrocution, and God will be satisfied that justice has been done and the daughters of the state officials can walk the streets safely. Stamp this thing out now with a conviction."[9]

In his 1937 autobiography, *Let Me Live*, Herndon recalled that, "as I listened to [Hudson], it struck me with full force that he had made a sensational impression upon both judge and jury. It became very clear to me why that was so. He spoke their language. He interlarded his lynch frenzy with goodly sprinklings from Holy Writ. Blood and piety, these are the two principle ingredients of boasted Southern civilization. Murder is perfumed with the altar incense of religion to hide its rotten stench."[10]

In his summation, Ben Davis pointed to the irony of a justice system that would condemn a peaceful interracial protest as insurrectionary while refusing to prosecute lynchers. The judge glared at him as he continued:

> The Rev. Hudson says Herndon is stirring up racial hatred by advocating the doctrines of workers organizations, but I ask since when did it become racial strife for Negro and white workers to organize together for the betterment of their conditions? Is it not because young Herndon sat before you today and told you in the words of a man and not those of a cringing coward that he would never give up his principle of fighting for the workers and Negroes, that he sits framed? Gentlemen, this very case is a blot upon American civilization which boasts of liberty, democracy, freedom of speech and press.[11]

On January 18, 1933, the all-white, all-male jury found Herndon guilty but recommended mercy. He was sentenced to from eighteen to twenty years at hard labor. Davis and Greer immediately filed an appeal to the Georgia State Supreme Court.

On May 23, 1934, the state's high court affirmed Herndon's conviction without hearing the case. The justices reasoned that, while his integrated hunger march never actually became violent, it had the potential to do so. And why? Because the literature describing the "Black Belt Self Determination Theory" found in his room described a mission they believed to be unachievable without the use of violence. The only good news was that their refusal to hear the case cleared the way for an appeal to the U.S. Supreme Court.

Clyde Johnson, a white twenty-three-year-old National Student Union organizer working in nearby Rome, Georgia, was dispatched to Atlanta to replace Herndon as coordinator of the unemployed worker movement. In July, Nat Ross also sent Hosea Hudson.

On July 4, 1934, ILD reps Donald Burke and Alice Burke took a replica of a Georgia "convict cage" to a number of northern, western, and border-state cities. They embarked on a ten-thousand-mile tour to publicize the Herndon case and to focus attention on the barbaric practices of southern prisons. This ominous-looking black van, outfitted with bunks, bars, and chains, was identical to vans used to transport convicts to and from worksites. Prisoners worked ten-hour shifts on road construction and maintenance projects chained together in groups of five with eight feet of space between them. No toilet facilities were provided, nor was there any shelter from the boiling sun.

The Burkes displayed this cage in major U.S. cities to demonstrate the fate that awaited Herndon. It drew huge crowds, and many people signed petitions demanding that Georgia governor Eugene Talmadge release the prisoner. In nearly every city, however, the rolling exhibit encountered problems with local police, most seriously in Denver and Chicago.[12]

In September, the Provisional Committee to Defend Angelo Herndon was organized in Atlanta to assist Ben Davis and to raise funds for Herndon's defense. This alliance of community organizations, black clergy and professionals, students, and white liberals was underwritten by the ACLU.

The Supreme Court

Herndon's trial became a turning point in Ben Davis's life. During trial preparations when he'd discussed Marxist theory with his client, the young attorney realized that he had more in common with Herndon than he'd imagined. After Herndon's conviction, Davis joined the party. Later, he reflected on that decision: "Credit for recruiting me goes not to the communists but to the savage white supremacy assaults of trial Judge Lee B. Wyatt.... It required only a moment to join [the party], but my whole lifetime as an American Negro prepared me for that moment."[13]

In 1935, after receiving numerous death threats, Davis moved to New York City and organized for the party's Harlem branch. He also edited the *Negro Liberator* and later the *Daily Worker*. Herndon, freed on bail pending appeal, also moved to New York City. The NAACP offered to underwrite his appeal, but Herndon chose to stay with his ILD team, now led by Whitney North Seymour, a New York appeal litigation specialist and a former assistant solicitor general with the Justice Department. Seymour's petition to the U.S. Supreme Court maintained that Georgia's insurrection statute violated the Fourteenth Amendment. Disappointingly, the justices ruled that they had no jurisdiction over the case because Davis had not raised that constitutional issue earlier. Herndon was ordered back to prison on October 28, 1935.

Seymour, a civil libertarian, but not a communist, refused to be discouraged. He chose to continue attacking the constitutionality of the statute rather than challenge the all-white jury system.[14] To that end, he served Fulton County sheriff James Lowry with a writ of habeas corpus declaring that Herndon had been illegally imprisoned. In December 1935, former governor Hugh M. Dorsey, lately appointed to the State Superior Court, unexpectedly ruled that the insurrection statute indeed violated the Fourteenth Amendment.

In January 1936, Georgia officials appealed Dorsey's decision to the Georgia Supreme Court. Solicitor General John A. Boykin contended that "the doctrine of violence is in the mind of every communist."[15] When that court reaffirmed Herndon's conviction, Seymour remained undaunted. The justices had provided him with a path back to the U.S. Supreme Court. In the meantime, Herndon was again freed on bail pending appeal.

The ILD subsequently arranged two coast-to-coast Free Angelo Herndon fund-raising tours. A powerful speaker with a compelling story, the young bespectacled and always dapperly dressed Herndon attracted large crowds. He often appeared on stage with the Scottsboro mothers and a very penitent Ruby Bates, and he was subsequently invited to the White House to meet with First Lady Eleanor Roosevelt.

In February 1937, in *Herndon v. Lowry*, the U.S. Supreme Court finally addressed the Fourteenth Amendment issue. On April 26, in a five-to-four decision, the justices struck down Georgia's insurrection law as an "unwarranted invasion of free speech." That ruling not only voided Herndon's conviction, but for the first time in U.S. history, a state law had been overruled to protect Fourteenth Amendment rights. The Herndon decision extended federal protection to free speech.

After serving almost four years in prison, Angelo Herndon was freed in May 1937. When he returned to Harlem, he was elected national vice president of the Young Communist League and appointed to both CPUSA's National Committee and the Executive Committee of the National Negro Congress' Youth Division. Random House released his autobiography *Let Me Live* on January 1, 1937.

In his review for the April 1937 issue of the *Communist*, James Ford called it "the story not of one young man but of a whole people."[16]

Herndon was also gratified when the *Saturday Review* called it "a significant case study in the evolution of political radicalism in America." But *Herald Tribune* critic Rose C. Field upset him terribly with her comment that "it is clear that while the material is his, the writing was done by another hand." [*New York Herald Tribune*, March 14, 1937] Herndon subsequently composed a three-page letter of protest to the *Tribune*'s editor, Stanley Walker.[17]

On February 26, 1938, Herndon married Joyce Chellis, a stenographer from Gadsden, Alabama, and brought her to New York City. From 1942 to 1943 he coedited the *Negro Quarterly: A Review of Negro Life and Culture* with novelist Ralph Ellison. They published social commentary, essays, and reviews by Langston Hughes, Sterling Brown, L. D. Reddick, Richard Wright, and Doxy Wilkerson, among others, and were partially supported by party funds.

During World War II, when Herndon took exception to CPUSA's decision to mute its racial justice campaign, he alienated many party supporters. When he championed the Double V Campaign and came out squarely against the war, National Party Secretary Earl Browder turned on him and withdrew support for the *Negro Quarterly*. Herndon subsequently moved to San Francisco where he published the *People's Advocate*. In 1944, the party expelled him for his continued outspoken opposition to the war.

By 1946, Herndon was in Chicago in business for himself. No longer a celebrity, he was trying to adjust to private life, something he'd never really experienced. That fall he returned to Harlem to visit his former publishing partner, Ralph Ellison. According to Ellison, "Herndon regaled [me and my] wife Fanny with his success as an insurance broker and merchandiser. He was selling furs to black women on the installment plan."[18]

Two years later, Herndon was questioned by the House Committee on Un-American Activities about black radical Claudia Jones, a member of CPUSA's National Committee charged with violating the Smith Act, which made it illegal to advocate the violent overthrow of the U.S. government. Herndon knew Jones as an internationalist and feminist from the Young Communist League, but he refused to answer any questions about her. Ultimately she was deported to England.

Herndon remained in Chicago during the McCarthy era, and for the last forty years of his life he wrote nothing, nor did he espouse any causes or advocate for any political positions. On December 9, 1997, at the age of eighty-four he died in Sweet Home, Arkansas.

12 ▎ BIG SANDY   A Murder and Two Lynchings

> Poverty is the worst form of violence.
> —attributed to Mahatma Gandhi

The day after Judge James Horton ordered Haywood Patterson's new trial, three young black men from Tuscaloosa County were charged with the rape and murder of Vaudine Maddox, a twenty-year-old white sharecropper's daughter.

The girl's desperately poor family had recently moved to Big Sandy Creek, a black community twelve miles south of Tuscaloosa, and were illegally subletting a two-room shack. Vaudine's father used it to distill and sell moonshine.[1] She had been caring for her brothers and sisters since their mother's death nine years earlier. Her twenty-five-year-old cousin, Leland Fowler, also lived with the family.[2]

Vaudine Maddox left home on Monday morning June 12, 1933, to go to her job, caring for an elderly couple. Forty-eight hours later her sisters found her body in a ravine half a mile away. Their father had assumed she'd been staying with a friend. W. T. Maddox explained that he and his daughter had "some dispute" over a young male visitor who'd "called for her at their home."[3] Maddox believed that his daughter was staying away because she was still angry with him.

The crime scene was gruesome. The girl's skull was crushed, and it looked as if her body had been dragged from the road into the ravine. A bloodied stick and two bloody rocks were found near her body. Decomposition made it difficult for Coroner S. T. Hardin to determine if she'd been raped.[4]

The police theorized that Vaudine knew her murderer because she'd set down, rather than thrown down, the bucket she was carrying. That indicated that her attacker had not surprised her. The *Tuscaloosa News* explained that "some of the evidence would indicate a typical attack case involving a negro but for the fact that it appears the Maddox girl either stood or sat on a log and talked with someone at a point near the trail leading down to the ravine." The implication was, of course, that a white woman would never sit on a log with a black man.[5]

Rumors circulated that Maddox had been raped—and there were several theories about who'd done it. It was well known, for example, that white women in and around Big Sandy Creek were charging black men for sex. Speculation grew about Vaudine's possible involvement. Several of Big Sandy's black residents told Walter Chivers (who'd come with Arthur Raper to investigate) that she'd been seeing an older white man by the name of Powell. Some conjectured that Powell may have discovered Vaudine entertaining black clients and killed her. Evidently this scenario did not impress the police, since they arrested a black teenager on June 16.

Eighteen-year-old Dan Pippen lived in Big Sandy with his parents, worked with his father, and sang in his church choir. A white man, who the *Baltimore Afro-American* reported owed Pippen money for work he'd done, told the police that he'd seen the young man near the Maddox home on Monday morning "carrying a rock and looking angry."[6]

Pippen admitted to knowing Maddox but said that he'd been draining a swamp with his father on the day she was murdered. The police, however, pressured to quickly solve what was looking more and more like a case the Reds might get interested in, chose to concentrate on what they had—a solid lead. They apparently never tried to find "Powell," the older man who Vaudine was allegedly seeing, or to identify the young man who'd provoked the quarrel between her and her father. There's no record of their interviewing Leland Fowler the twenty-six-year-old cousin who lived with the Maddoxes either.

The Suspects

On June 18, fifteen-year-old A. T. Hardin, a friend of Dan Pippen, was also arrested. Hardin, who'd never been in trouble before, was so frightened that he told the police he'd seen Pippen murder the white woman. The following day he recanted and swore that he'd only heard her scream. A few hours later he said he hadn't seen or heard anything at all.

In fact, it was not unusual for police to rely on fear to get young black men to produce statements they thought the authorities wanted to hear in order to ensure their own release; fear of police was particularly high among blacks, for obvious reasons. It happened when the Scottsboro teens were grilled by police officers who were also under pressure to quickly solve a sensational crime. At their first trials, Clarence Norris and Haywood Patterson testified that they'd witnessed all the other boys rape the two white women in the freight car, but that they had not taken part. Later Norris explained:

"we was scared and I don't know what I said. The prison guards told us if we didn't confess they'd kill us—give us to the mob outside."[7] At just fifteen years old, A. T. Hardin was likely terrified of what might happen to him in custody.

Two days after Hardin's arrest, a white mob surrounded the Tuscaloosa jail to demand that Pippen and Hardin be released to them. Circuit Judge Henry Foster, Tuscaloosa's former mayor, ordered Sheriff Shamblin to take the two to the Birmingham Jail for their safety. Willie Peterson was there awaiting trial for a rape, two murders, and a shooting he swore he had not committed.

Then, on June 23, Tuscaloosa County police arrested twenty-eight-year-old Elmore "Honey" Clark, who had a reputation in the white community as a "mean nigger." He'd been cast as the ringleader of the attack on Maddox despite the fact that he had one shriveled, virtually useless arm. Several witnesses swore that he was with them on a fishing trip the day that she was murdered.[8]

The following day, Harden and Pippen returned from Birmingham to join Clark for a grand jury hearing. Judge Henry Foster presided. Hardin, nearly hysterical, swore that the police had pressured him to confess. Revising his story several times, he finally testified that Pippen and Clark had murdered Vaudine Maddox.

Clark's shriveled arm made it unlikely that he'd attacked Maddox, and Pippen's father and his boss, Will Jemison testified that Dan had worked with them all day. Amazingly, Judge Foster ordered Dan Pippen Sr. and Jemison, both black, arrested for interfering with the investigation, and they were removed from the courtroom.

The prosecution alleged that Clark had planned the crime and that he and Pippen killed Maddox while Hardin served as lookout. Arthur Raper reported, "The mutual charges and alleged confessions on the part of the suspects themselves constituted the case against them. On these their guilt was assumed and the three were indicted."[9]

Three trials were scheduled beginning with Dan Pippen's on August 1, 1933. The Pippen and Clark families hired white attorneys Charles La France and Jack McGuire to defend their sons. The Hardins chose J. Monroe Ward. There were also rumors that Pippen's mother, Lucinda, was talking with the Reds.

As Judge Foster was unfamiliar with La France, McGuire, and Ward, and since a bunch of Red lawyers had recently gotten a Scottsboro guilty verdict overturned because of "inadequate counsel," on July 29 he assigned to the case three attorneys who he did know. They were John D. McQueen, past president of the Alabama Bar Association; Fleetwood Rice, a former circuit court judge; and Reuben H. Wright, a prominent Tuscaloosa attorney. He charged them with assisting (and essentially keeping an eye on) the other three. McQueen tried to refuse, but the judge was firm.[10] In the end, there were six attorneys for the defense (not counting any potential help from the ILD).[11]

Unwelcome Assistance

The summer of 1933 was reportedly Tuscaloosa's hottest on record. On August 1, as Dan Pippen's jury was being sworn in, attorney Frank Irwin of Birmingham (a member of the Scottsboro defense team) and his colleagues Allan Taub and Irving Schwab (who'd represented the Kentucky coal miners and the Camp Hill sharecroppers) entered the courtroom. They were apparently anticipated, since nearly four hundred people, including reporters and a cadre of national guardsmen, were waiting inside. In the August 1933 issue of the *New Masses*, Taub gives an account of what followed.[12]

Frank Irwin, the most militant of the three, produced a retainer agreement signed by Lucinda Pippen, and stated that he and the other ILD attorneys had been refused admission to the jail to consult with their client. Irwin demanded, therefore, that Judge Foster end the proceedings and grant a continuance.

Without missing a beat, Allan Taub observed that "this procedure bears a remarkable resemblance to another hearing on April 6, 1931 in Scottsboro in the case of nine Negro boys accused of rape."[13] He cited the U.S. Supreme Court's recent ruling that denial of counsel amounted to denial of due process. Because they hadn't been able to speak with their client, Taub explained, they were not prepared to proceed with a defense. He seconded Irwin's request for a continuance. Tuscaloosa's worse nightmare was beginning.

Finally, Irving Schwab asked that the record reflect the unusually crowded courtroom and the presence of armed national guardsmen. At that point, Judge Foster asked Pippin which attorney he wanted to represent him. The frightened young man, whose face was badly bruised, said he wanted LaFrance and McGrath. His terrified mother insisted that she had not requested help from the Red attorneys and that she did not want them defending her son.[14]

Irwin commented that Pippen had obviously been beaten and likely forced to renounce the ILD. At that point defense attorneys La Frank and Maguire produced their own retainer agreements allegedly signed by Lucinda Pippen.

Judge Foster, wiping the sweat from the back of his neck, examined all the documents and ruled that the ILD attorneys had no jurisdiction in the case. He denied them permission to interview Pippen, dismissed the jury, and rescheduled Pippen's trial for August 22.

As he was about to leave the bench, a court officer handed him a telegram. The judge read it, threw it down, clenched his fists, and shouted, "God damn the son of a bitch that sent this! I'll make him answer for it. I'll go to Birmingham—I'll go to New York—I'll kill the son of a bitch!"[15] There was a long silence before the courtroom began to buzz.

The wire, sent by ILD national secretary William Patterson, informed the judge that "two hundred thousand members and affiliates of the International Labor Defense demand you withdraw troops in the trial of Pippen, Clark and Harden, withdraw the local lynch lawyers and permit defense by ILD attorneys retained by the families of the defendants. Will expose your illegal maneuvers nationally as counterpoint to Scottsboro."[16]

"Son of a bitch! I'll kill the son of a bitch," the judge howled. One of the court officers allegedly responded, "you don't have to do it, Judge. We'll do it for you."[17]

Word of the ILD's attempted hijacking spread quickly, and a crowd began to gather outside the courthouse. University of Alabama professor Clarence Elmore Cason described it as the kind that "had often gathered in front of those very same steps on other hot August days to hear Senator Tom Heflin elucidate his theories of white control. They were of the opinion that something ought to be done about those three little Jewish lawyers being paid to spread ideas of social equality among the Alabama Negroes."[18]

Attorney John McQueen encouraged Judge Foster to provide protection for the Reds. If harm came to them, he reasoned, Tuscaloosa would pay. Foster, who'd finally regained his composure, asked the attorneys if they wanted an escort. Irwin responded, "Judge, you know this county better that we do." Foster arranged for national guardsmen to take them (in disguise) to the railroad station and put them on the 4:30 to Birmingham.

Patterson's telegram was subsequently printed in the *Tuscaloosa News*, and rumors that the Birmingham Reds were returning to take over the Maddox case circulated throughout the city. Irwin, Taub, and Schwab had raised to a situation of national consequence a local murder trial that might have been newsworthy for a few days at most. To the horror of white Tuscaloosa, all the wire services had picked it up.

The Citizens' Protective League

Tuscaloosa's unemployment rate was high and still rising. By 1930 many of the farms outside the city were on the auction block for back taxes. As in Birmingham, Chattanooga, and Atlanta, unemployed miners, mill and foundry workers, and displaced croppers flocked to the city looking for work. There wasn't any. By the time construction of Tuscaloosa's veterans' hospital was completed, so many municipal workers had been laid off that no one was left to attach the pipes to the waterworks. Municipal foremen had to hire day laborers to dig the trenches. Workers who still had homes received water bill credits as payment, and the homeless got a small daily stipend.[19]

Red organizers from Birmingham were recruiting unemployed workers in Tuscaloosa and encouraging blacks and whites to march to city hall to demand financial relief. White Tuscaloosa grew increasingly angry and fearful. All Negro gatherings—whether in churches, lodge halls, or social clubs—became suspect, and the city council passed an ordinance making it illegal for blacks to congregate after sunset.

The police doubled down on Jim Crow statute enforcements, and white residents organized a Citizens' Protective League to ferret out communists. The league rewarded spies and encouraged them to infiltrate Red cells whenever possible.[20] League members conducted night raids, wore masks and hoods reminiscent of the Klan, and illegally searched black homes for communist literature. The league's popularity soared after the ILD attorneys attempted to grab the Maddox case.

The only bona fide communist the organization uncovered was Louis Harper, the black Tuscaloosa schoolteacher who'd encouraged the Pippen, Harden, and Clark families to hire ILD attorneys. He boarded a train to Birmingham just fifteen minutes before a posse came looking for him.[21]

League officials held the Reds responsible for every trouble the South was suffering—including what they contended was a new rash of blacks raping white women. This was the kind of thing communists were "known to encourage." They'd been found agitating down in Big Sandy Creek—encouraging croppers to demand a share of the federal land furlough money.²² Harden, Pippen, and Clark were all croppers, and the ILD was trying to link their arrests to what they called "the planters' reign of terror." Tuscaloosa was fearful of becoming the next Scottsboro. The Citizens' Protective League vowed that would never happen.

On August 10, Tuscaloosa County sheriff R. L. Shamblin allegedly received an anonymous tip that a mob was planning to storm his jail and take his prisoners. He informed Judge Foster, who deliberated for two days about whether or not to move Harden, Pippen, and Clark to Birmingham. Finally, he ordered the transfer. Foster would later deny giving that order.²³ Sheriff Shamblin, who Arthur Raper described as "elderly and inefficient," apparently took his time making the arrangements and openly discussed them at the police station as residents walked in and out all day.²⁴ The prisoners finally left Tuscaloosa at 9:30 p.m.

Ten officers were assigned the escort duty. Hardin, Pippen, and Clark, handcuffed together, rode in a van with Sheriff Shamblin and three deputies: Murray Pate, Harley Holeman, and W. I. Huff. Four officers followed in a second vehicle. When they completed twenty miles without incident, the sheriff ordered the second car back to Tuscaloosa.

The prisoners' van reached Woodstock, Alabama (thirty-five miles south of Birmingham) at midnight. There, they were either ambushed by a dozen armed masked men, as reported, or they turned their prisoners over to a mob, as suspected. Any need for trials ended right there. Harden and Pippen were shot to death, but Elmore Clark, who lay trapped beneath them, played dead and survived.

After the killers left, Clark freed himself and walked for nearly twenty-four hours before he risked stopping at a farmhouse near Vance, Alabama. A black woman took him in and sent a neighbor to Tuscaloosa to get Dr. B. B. Mitchell, a black physician. After Mitchell treated Clark, he called the police. Clark was taken to the Montgomery County Jail, where he repeatedly swore that he could not identify his attackers.²⁵

A terrified Clark confirmed Deputy Pate's account—that the mob had overtaken them, disarmed the officers, taken the prisoners, and shot them. The police inexplicably offered no resistance to the kidnappers, nor had they pursued them. No shots were fired. Clark swore that pursuit had not been possible.

But other theories began to circulate about how the prisoners had died and who might be responsible. Some said that the lynchers were Citizens' Protection League vigilantes. Judge Foster lent credibility to that when he remarked that "Tuscaloosa County was willing to see the Negroes tried and was willing to give them a fair trial, but some were not willing to have us go through another Scottsboro case."[26]

The ILD maintained that there was no mob, that the police had shot the prisoners themselves on orders from Sheriff Shamblin. Deputy Sheriff Murray Pate had been selected for escort duty despite his recent boast of killing "eleven niggers in the line of duty." The day after Harden and Pippen were murdered, the *Tuscaloosa News* reported that Pate and Deputy Holeman killed Jack Pruitt, a black Tuscaloosa resident, after he resisted arrest for disturbing the peace.[27]

An editorial in that same edition held the ILD attorneys responsible for the prisoners' deaths because they'd "spread their poisoned Communistic propaganda among our contented Negro population."[28]

The Inquest

Governor Benjamin Meek Miller ordered an inquest, and a grand jury was impaneled on August 14, with Judge Foster presiding. Attorney General Thomas Knight Jr. (who would be elected lieutenant governor three months later) conducted the investigation.

In an open letter addressed to the grand jury, Frank Irwin, who'd disrupted the Pippen grand jury proceedings, demanded that indictments for first-degree murder be brought against Sheriff Shamblin, the deputies who'd escorted the prisoners, and Judge Foster himself. Irwin wrote: "The International Labor Defense accuses Deputy Sheriffs Murray Pate, Harley Holeman and W. I. Huff, all of Tuscaloosa, of shooting with their own hands, murdering and lynching Dan Pippen Jr. and A. T. Harden, Negro boys on the night of August 12, 1933 while these boys were in their custody." Irwin further charged that Foster and Shamblin "directed the lynching plot and should be treated as accomplices."[29]

He challenged the officers' sworn statements that they'd left Tuscaloosa at 9:30 p.m. and were ambushed around midnight twenty-three miles south of

Birmingham. The entire forty-mile trip, he argued, should not have exceeded ninety minutes. He contended that "they made a circuitous route in order to find a quiet spot out of the way in order to murder the prisoners."[30]

Irwin pointed out that no autopsy had been ordered, crime scene evidence was reportedly destroyed, and that Pippen and Harden had been hurriedly buried the following day.[31]

The grand jury met four times between August 15 and October 2, 1933. Elmore Clark was called as the first witness. As he was brought into the court room a shot ran out and he dove to floor. He was unharmed. The bullet grazed Attorney General Knight's ankle, and the incident was explained as a court officer's gun unexpectedly discharging—an accident. Still Clark could not stop shaking. As the only eyewitness, he fully expected to be shot.[32]

Still under indictment for the murder of Vaudine Maddox, Clark swore that he could not identify any of the men who'd shot him. He repeated that the lynchers "had their guns on Mr. Pate" and while "Mr. Pate" did not want to turn the prisoners over, "Mr. Pate" had no choice.[33] Of the three officers who'd escorted him, Pate was by far the most vicious, and Clark was terrified of him. On the stand and under oath, Elmore Clark couldn't say enough good things about him. Perhaps most astoundingly, the testimony of a black witness was received by this all-white, all-male grand jury as entirely credible.

The jurors were informed that all the crime scene evidence had been taken by "souvenir hunters," and after hearing testimony from the coroner and the Bibb County sheriff who'd discovered the bodies, they recessed for two weeks to await a ballistics report.[34]

The September 5 session opened with testimony from Sheriff Shamblin, the police officers, and the volunteers who'd searched for Clark. The ballistics report indicated that Harden and Pippen were killed with .38 caliber bullets. Knight noted that the police carried only .44 caliber weapons. Apparently, no attempt was made to determine if any of the police owned a .38 caliber gun. Deputies Pate, Holeman, and Huff did not testify.

On October 2, the grand jury returned a "no true bill"—no indictments. The foreman explained that the evidence was insufficient. They did, however, express full faith and confidence in Sheriff Shamblin. On October 3 the *Tuscaloosa News* concluded that Pippen and Harden were "not victims of the mob, but rather victims of the ILD's invasiveness."

No one was ever charged with the murders of Harden and Pippen or the attempted murder of Elmore Clark, and no one was ever convicted of the murder of Vaudine Maddox. Clark was released from jail on May 23, 1934, and the Commission on Interracial Cooperation assisted him in relocating from Alabama.

Life in Alabama went on. The 1933 cotton harvest was more successful than the previous year's, which was very bad news indeed. Intensive cultivation of the acreage that had not been furloughed, combined with the planters' use of new and more powerful equipment (which many could afford because of their federal subsidy payments) had increased cotton production. Land furlough had not solved the surplus problem. Still, the Agricultural Adjustment Administration chose to reduce acreage by another 40 percent in 1934—a total of fifteen million additional acres.[35] Inevitably, more croppers and tenants would be displaced.

At the same time, croppers were continuing to demand their fair share of the federal land furlough payments and refusing to sign the government checks that were jointly issued to them and the planters. Because both signatures were required, the planters could not cash them either. Angry and frustrated, they blamed "the nigger union, the uppity niggers and the nigger-loving Reds" for all this defiance. Raids on cropper cabins increased. In Chambers County, a group of planters bribed Paul Powell, a black cropper, to join the union and make a list of all the members. Sheriff Frank Wood swore that he would kill anyone whose name was on it. When the croppers discovered what Powell was up to, they beat him so badly that he nearly died.[36]

13 ■ THE LYNCHING OF DENNIS CROSS

> Cruelty requires no motive outside of itself; it only requires opportunity.
> —George Eliot, *Scenes of Clerical Life*

On Thursday afternoon, September 7, 1933, six weeks after the murders of A. T. Hardin and Dan Pippen and the attempted murder of Elmore Clark, Alice Johnson walked into Tuscaloosa's Emergency Relief Office and reported that a Negro man had attacked her. Johnson, eighteen years old and white, was a familiar face at the center and famous for her vivid imagination. A staffer took her report and referred her to the police, who took another report.

Four days later, Alice's husband asked the police if they had any suspects in his wife's attack. He was told that no arrests had been made. On September 12, Alice returned to the relief office and passed Dennis Cross in the hall. He was a forty-nine-year-old semi-paralyzed black man who she may have recognized from one of her earlier visits. Johnson told the staffer who'd taken her report that Cross was her attacker. She maintained that he'd approached her on the street and lunged at her. When she resisted, he ripped her dress and ran. Cross was arrested.[1]

One look at Dennis Cross would convince anyone that he could never have run anywhere for any reason. He needed his brother's help to get dressed every morning. Nonetheless, on Alice Johnson's word he was arrested, jailed, and later released on $300 bond. That was unusual. A black man accused of attacking a white woman was never eligible for bail. Cross's boss, A. J. Hinton, a white man who owned Hinton's Hardware, had provided the bond.

At 2 a.m. Sunday, September 24, six white men came to the Cross home and identified themselves as officers of the court. They told Dennis's brother that additional bail was required, and they had to take Dennis into custody. They assured him that he could settle the matter in the morning.

It took three men to lift Cross out of his bed and carry him to the car. They brought him to the scene of the alleged assault and shot him dead. Early Sunday morning a local black undertaker was called and informed that "there's a dead nigger down the road, you'd better come pick him up."[2]

The Accuser

Alice Johnson, who had grown up as poor as Vaudine Maddox had, was as resourceful as Victoria Price. Her mother had died when she was a child, and a county social worker described the home of her father, J. L. Pannal, as "filthy and demoralized." When Alice was fourteen, she ran away to Jacksonville, Florida, with a forty-year-old man. When he deserted her in Gadsden, Alabama, she had to find her own way back home. The following year she ran to Florida with another man. At sixteen, she fled to Tallahassee alone and returned with a husband.

Between the Florida trips, Alice frequented Tuscaloosa's hobo camps and neighbors often complained to her father about her erratic behavior. She wanted more out of life and was not shy about demanding it from the staff at the Emergency Relief Office.[3] On the morning of September 7, however, she'd tried a new approach.

Alice went to visit a "society lady" who'd once been kind to her. Between racking sobs, she told the woman that she'd been accosted by a black man who'd torn her dress when she tried to get away. Alice's worn, thin, and dirty dress was indeed ripped. The lady, as Alice anticipated, offered to buy her another one and asked if she'd reported the attack. When Alice said she hadn't, the woman encouraged her to do so.

In Arthur Raper's report of the Cross murder for the Southern Commission on the Study of Lynching, he'd asked incredulously, "Had [Alice Johnson] trumped up the charge to get a dress?" and, "Did she accuse Cross because she had to identify someone?" After two years of investigating mob murders and lynchings, including the Emelle, Scottsboro, and Big Sandy cases, the heartlessness of Cross's death left Raper deeply shaken.

In the Scottsboro case, two destitute white women, Ruby Bates and Victoria Price, lied nine innocent black men into death sentences that morphed into long prison terms. All to avoid arrest themselves. Although Bates eventually recanted, Price never dropped the rape charges.

In the Shades Mountain murders, Nell Williams, a white debutante, lied an innocent, sick black man into a life sentence for a crime she knew he did not commit in order to protect three sullied reputations. Dennis Cross had the bad luck to cross the path of a desperately poor white woman who lied him into the hands of vigilantes—for a new dress.

An obsession with interracial sex—specifically, white fear of black men seducing or raping white women—was the common denominator in all these cases. Despite their class differences, all these women were confident that they would be believed. White women who accused black men were always believed. When they identified Willie Peterson, Dennis Cross, Charlie Weems, Ozie Powell, Clarence Norris, Olen Montgomery, Willie Roberson, Haywood Patterson, Eugene Williams, and Andy and Roy Wright as their attackers, knowing full well that all were innocent—and in the cases of Willie Peterson, Willie Robeson, Olin Montgomery, and Dennis Cross that they were physically incapable of committing the crimes—Victoria Price, Ruby Bates, Nell Williams, and Alice Johnson's accusations were acknowledged and acted on by white law enforcement and the white judicial system.

As Sheriff Shamblin, who'd botched the Maddox investigation, began his inquiries into the Cross murder, the white *Birmingham Age Herald*'s columnist John Temple Graves II called it "one of the most shameful affairs with which Alabama has ever had to deal."[4]

The subsequent grand jury session was unproductive. On October 14, foreman Ben Eddins announced a no true bill—no indictments. "We have used every means at our command to ascertain the parties guilty of the Cross lynching but we have been unable to secure enough evidence on which to base an indictment at this time." The panel recommended, however, that the case be continued.[5]

The National Committee for the Defense of Political Prisoners

Two weeks after the Cross grand jury disbanded, the National Committee for the Defense of Political Prisoners (NCDPP; journalists who had organized the hearings in Harlan County, Kentucky, in 1931) dispatched a delegation to Tuscaloosa to investigate the deaths of Dan Pippen, A. T. Harden, Dennis Cross, and Jack Pruitt, the twenty-four-year-old black man killed by Officer Murray Pate one day after Harden and Pippen's executions.[6]

On November 2, 1933, the NCDPP delegation arrived in Tuscaloosa. They included four southerners: Virginians Bruce Crawford, publisher of *Crawford's Review*, and Howard Kester; Georgians Grace Lumpkin, the novelist;

and Professor C. Vann Woodward, of Georgia Tech. The Yanks were Hollis Ransdell of the ACLU, Jessica Henderson of NCDPP's Boston chapter, and NCDPP national director Alfred Hirsch. All were white. On November 10, Hirsh wrote a brief describing their reception. "The Ku Klux Klan, masked and in full regalia and a full hundred strong" had greeted them. When they requested access to transcripts of all the grand jury hearings, Attorney General Knight, who'd prosecuted both Haywood Patterson and Dan Pippin, told them "I refuse that request. Moreover, if any person permits you to see those records or gives you any information concerning the records it will be my duty to prosecute him." Hirsch had alerted the national press earlier that day, "It is our aim to surround our findings on these lynchings with the broadest and most searching of publicity. We want to bring these crimes before the Court of World Opinion so clearly and sharply that extra-legal lynchings—which are becoming a recognized short cut to terrorization as the fight for Negro legal rights grows—may become impossible."[7] Tuscaloosa's nightmare had returned.

The committee subsequently learned that Dan Pippen Sr. and his boss, Willie Jamison, had disappeared. Arrested during the Pippen trial for interfering with the prosecution after Pippen Sr. attempted to substantiate his son's whereabouts at the time of the murder, rumors had spread through the black community that they'd been "done away with." Judge Henry Foster, scoffing at that, insisted that they'd left town "for their own safety."[8]

The delegation also learned of a possible motive for Dennis Cross's murder, one involving his boss, A. J. Hinton, the white man who'd posted bail. The minimal $300 bail had puzzled many people at the time. Why was it so low? Why had a black man accused of molesting a white woman been granted bond in the first place?

The investigators determined that Cross was one of three Hinton Hardware employees—all black—who'd witnessed the boss kill another black employee who he suspected of having an affair with his wife. Hinton had charged the other two with stealing from his inventory, and both were serving long prison terms. Cross was the last man who could connect him to the murder.

Some committee members conjectured that Hinton had used Alice Johnson's accusations to motivate the Citizens' Protective League to take care of Cross. Whether Johnson had randomly picked Cross as her attacker or if Hinton had influenced her in any way was not known, but complicity between

Hinton, law enforcement, and the judicial system likely explained the low bail and Cross's release. The men who went to his home in the middle of the night posing as court officers told his brother that there'd been a problem with the bail bond.

In his final report, the NCDPP's Arthur Hirsch attested that "lynching is now being used, deliberately, to 'teach' negroes that outsider organizations must not be permitted to defend them in court, though they are on trial for their lives. It is no longer a question of individual defendants. Nor is it a question of the crime of which the individual happens to be accused. It is, for the lynchers, a question of covering institutions, just as they are, against implicit challenge even in the courts of law."[9]

The NCDPP's visit did not result in any arrests, indictments, or convictions, but it did produce a substantial increase in the membership roles of the Citizens' Protective League.

The Plight of Tuscaloosa

In December 1933, Arthur Raper submitted his report on the Tuscaloosa murders to the Southern Commission on the Study of Lynching. The commission published it as "The Plight of Tuscaloosa: Mob Murders, Community Hysteria, Official Incompetence—A Case Study of Conditions in Tuscaloosa County Alabama"; it addressed both the Maddox and Cross cases. The black *Pittsburgh (PA) Courier* hailed it as an "unofficial grand jury" report.[10]

Raper had documented the rise of the Citizens' Protective League, called out specific county officials for dereliction of duty, and criticized law enforcement and the judicial system for failure to locate and punish the lynchers. Although critical of the district 17 Reds for "adding to the hysteria," Raper considered them scapegoats.

"There is a good deal of agitation among the whites over rumors of communist propaganda which is unjustified by the facts," he wrote. "The emphasis on alleged activities of the communists persists largely because it affords the community a means of diverting attention from its own neglect and failure."[11]

Raper concluded that in the Maddox case "the residents of Tuscaloosa [had] lynched two black men, not because of any particular crime, but to send a message that New York lawyers were not to interfere with Southern issues of race."[12]

"If the community were really afraid of Communism," he explained, "its best defense would lie in extending the Negroes full protection under the law. . . . Tuscaloosa could hardly have placed itself in a worse light than it did by insisting that the Negroes' defense be left in local hands and then permitting them to be lynched and the lynchers to go unpunished."[13]

Raper strongly recommended that Sheriff Shamblin be prosecuted, and he appealed to Governor Miller and to the Alabama Supreme Court to "impeach the offenders who failed in their duties."[14] Nothing happened.

After Alabama authorities refused to prosecute either the sheriff or his deputies, Charles Hamilton Houston and two of his associates submitted a brief on behalf of the NAACP to Attorney General Homer Cummings at the U.S. Justice Department. They demonstrated that the federal government had the power under existing law to intervene and to prosecute the Tuscaloosa law enforcement officers who had allowed the lynchings. They cited section 53, chapter 3, title 18 of the U.S. Code. The sheriff and his deputies had willfully subjected Pippen and Harden to deprivation of rights protected by the Constitution. Houston never received a response.[15]

14 ❙ MEMPHIS   Mayhem and Mistaken Identity

> I wonder why they gave it such a name of old renown;
> This dreary, dismal, muddy, melancholy town.
> —William Howard Russell, *London Times* correspondent, 1863

Early in 1933, Al Murphy traveled to New York City to deliver his annual report to the CPUSA Central Committee. Murphy could boast that by the beginning of its third year five new Alabama Share Croppers' Union chapters were up and running with nearly three thousand members in total. Harry Haywood, a Central Committee official and president of the League of Struggle for Negro Rights who was in the audience that day, decided it was time for him to visit Tallapoosa County.[1] Instead, he spent his time that spring in Atlanta with Ben Davis getting up to speed on the Angelo Herndon defense.

Now, in the spring of 1934, Haywood was on his way to Birmingham to meet with Nat Ross to discuss plans for building a revolutionary movement in Memphis. He wanted to make sure that Ross understood just how important that city was. The nation's largest inland cotton market, it was also a bastion of segregation and labor violence. Tom Johnson had never been able to get any traction at all there.

District 17's only ally in the Bluff City was the party-affiliated IWO, which provided affordable health and life insurance and medical and dental clinics on a nonsegregated basis. The motto of this working-class organization was "Serving Labor and Promoting Security." Members were committed racial justice advocates. As in Chattanooga, the Memphis membership was largely Jewish.

The IWO was desperate to bring an ILD chapter to Memphis because of increasing police brutality in the black community and because the city's chief political power broker, "Boss" Edward Crump, was blatantly anti-Semitic. When the IWO offered to subsidize two organizers, Haywood wanted to make sure that Ross followed up. Three years earlier, Tom Johnson had worked with Horace Davis a professor at the city's Southwest College, his wife Marian, the IWO, and a few local clergymen to raise funds for the defense of the Atlanta Six—four black male and two white female unemployed worker council organizers charged with inciting insurrection. During the fund-raising campaign, a *Memphis Appeal* reporter asked Marian Davis if she really believed that blacks and whites ought to be treated equally. When she said she did, the next day's headline screamed, "Negro for Governor Is Planned Social Equality Meeting to Be Held." Tom Johnson and Horace Davis were arrested. Johnson was put on a train back to Birmingham, and Davis was released on a promise that he and his wife would leave the city.[2]

In the summer of 1932, Johnson sent Mack Coad in. Coad operated underground for nearly a year before he trusted two black undertakers who ultimately betrayed him to "Boss" Crump. The Boss could be very generous to black businessmen who played ball with him. His agents in the Memphis Police Department nearly beat Coad to death before dumping him on a freight car back to Birmingham.[3] That was the whole of district 17's experience with Memphis. The city desperately needed help.

Ross told Haywood that he planned to send Harold Forsha, a white ILD organizer currently working in Chattanooga, and a yet-to-be-named black comrade. Blaine Owen (Boris Israel), who was preparing an article about southern organizing for the *New Masses*, would join them to cover the story. Haywood volunteered to go along. "I was anxious to undertake this assignment," he recalled, "my first organizing job in the South. I figured I could stay there a little while to help get things started and make contacts in the black community."[4] Like Owen and Forsha, who were both from New York City, Haywood was not a southerner. Born in Omaha and raised in Minneapolis, he made his home in Chicago.

On March 20, 1934, Haywood, Forsha, and Owen arrived in Memphis and were welcomed by an IWO contingent. As they toured the city, Haywood picked up a copy of the *Memphis Appeal*. An article on page three caught his attention. Six police officers had been cleared in the beating death of seventeen-year-old Levon Carlock, a black man suspected of raping a white woman. An inquest had determined that their actions—including breaking his neck and shooting him four times, amounted to justifiable homicide since he'd resisted arrest. Haywood handed the paper to Forsha and told him, "here's our issue."

After getting some background from their hosts, Owen went downtown to investigate. This wasn't difficult, since the *Appeal* had published the names and addresses of both Carlock and his alleged victim. Owen learned from sixteen-year-old Mrs. Eula May Carlock that she and Levon had recently arrived from Mississippi, where they'd been sharecroppers. They lived in a rooming house on South Second Street, and Eula May worked as a maid in one of the "evening establishments" in the red-light district. Levon was still unemployed. Because South Second Street was dangerous, he picked her up every night after her shift.

On Saturday February 25, as Carlock waited for his wife, police officers O. D. Sanders and J. P. Freeman approached him and demanded to know what he was doing out so late. As he started to explain, one of them shouted, "you're the nigger that raped that white woman."[5] He'd apparently been mistaken for a black man who'd escaped after raping a prostitute at the Cordova Hotel. As Carlock protested his innocence, they handcuffed him and sent two officers to the Cordova to get Ruby Morris, the woman who'd made the complaint. When Owen interviewed Morris, she admitted that, while she had never seen her attacker's face, she'd recognized Carlock's voice.

Eula May Carlock introduced Owen to eyewitness Fannie Henderson, a fifty-nine-year-old black woman who was helping to care for the terrified young woman. Henderson told Owen that on the night of the murder she'd been staying with a friend in the apartment house next to the hotel on Vance Avenue. She'd seen everything from a window overlooking the alley between the buildings. Carlock's screams woke her at three o'clock in the morning, and she watched the police drag him into the alley.

Levon Carlock pleaded for his life, she said, but they kept beating him with clubs until they broke his neck. She knew that because at one point he could no longer lift his head. Then "they shot him down in cold blood, right there." Fannie Henderson had not known Eula May Carlock previously. She'd reached out to the young woman because Eula May had no family in Memphis. Henderson was scared, but she was angry too, and she agreed to provide the NAACP with a sworn affidavit.[6]

Forsha, Owen, and Haywood helped the IWO organize rallies to protest the police brutality. Their banners read "Levon Carlock Must Be the Last." The ILD, the National Committee for the Defense of Political Prisoners, and the League of Struggle for Negro Rights all contributed funds, as did Lewis O. Swingler, black editor of the *Memphis World*. Forsha led black and white ministers, educators, and fraternal lodge members in the effort to organize block councils. They scheduled several rallies to allow Eula May Carlock to tell her husband's story. The local NAACP seemed eager to help, but their officers in Washington, still smarting from the public battles with the ILD over Scottsboro, discouraged them.

When Forsha, now spokesman for the new Memphis ILD chapter, demanded that the police officers involved in Carlock's death be fired, retaliation was swift. "Boss" Crump called their campaign "a red invasion." Blaine Owen was arrested for sedition and the Commercial Appeal reported that the communists' support for "political prisoners and the Scottsboro Boys" proved beyond a doubt their "unvarying support for violence and criminal activities." A page-one banner headline charged "Reds Plot Destruction of All Churches in Memphis."[7] It was classic dirty fighting. While Owen sat in jail, Fannie Henderson disappeared. Without an eyewitness, there was no case.

The Carlock campaign lasted just six weeks. Haywood returned to Chicago, and when Owen was released from jail he went back to Chattanooga. Forsha remained in Memphis to build the fledgling chapter.

Memphis would continue to play a bloody role in U.S. labor history. CIO organizers would battle with the bosses, the police, and the Crump machine over issues of workers' rights and social justice. The 1937 southern campaign to organize food processing, lumber, and dock workers failed miserably. In 1939 Crump's men beat and nearly killed Thomas Watkins, a black longshoreman who'd led a Mississippi River dock hands strike, and black activist Robert Cotton disappeared from the docks one day, never to be seen again.

Ford Motor's corporate security guards, aided by white workers fearful of losing their jobs, mercilessly beat chief organizer Norman Smith. As in Birmingham and Chattanooga, labor organizing threatened Memphis's chief asset—its cheap labor supply. The Crump machine knew how to protect the interests of those it served. [8]

BOOK TWO
THE LATE GREAT DISTRICT 17

> There have been periods of détente with the Soviet Union, but never really with the American Left.
> —Carl Bernstein, *Loyalties*

15 ▎ REAPING THE WHIRLWIND

> For they have sown the wind, and they shall reap the whirlwind; it hath no stalk: the bud shall yield no meal: if so be it yield, the strangers shall swallow it up.
> —Hosea 8:7

In December 1934, Al Murphy sailed for Moscow as a delegate to the Seventh World Congress. He and Nat Ross had reached the point of no return over the issue of integrating the Alabama Share Croppers' Union. Ross had pushed to integrate, Murphy had resisted, Murphy left. He remained in the Soviet Union for three years, married a Russian woman, and returned to the States in 1937.

Early in 1935 Ross had replaced Murphy with Clyde Johnson, the white organizer who'd assumed leadership of Atlanta's unemployed worker movement after Angelo Herndon's arrest. Ross tasked him with fashioning a mainstream biracial union from Murphy's black underground resistance movement. Collaboration with socialists and progressives was becoming a priority for CPUSA general secretary Earl Browder. Ross and Sid Benson were planning an All Southern Conference for Civil and Trade Union Rights for May 1935 in partnership with Tennessee socialists Myles Horton and James Dombrowski, who ran the Highlander Folk School.

Horton and Dombrowski also hoped that this conference would increase enthusiasm for a unified progressive southern labor movement. Since 1932 their adult school had trained hundreds of workers of both races for union leadership positions. Highlander supported organizing drives, demonstrations, and strikes. Ross believed that he and Horton shared enough similarity of purpose to make such a joint venture possible.

Their conference announcement called for building "a common front of urban workers, rural sharecroppers and the unemployed." It encouraged liberals and progressives to unite against the ruling class in the South. "This conference," it proclaimed, "is the first great step in that action."[1]

On May 26, 1935, two hundred delegates from labor, religious, social service, and political organizations arrived in Chattanooga for the three-day event. As they made their way to the Negro Pythian Temple, the police barred their entry. Apparently, the commander of the local American Legion Post had alerted the authorities that an integrated "Communist convention" was being held.[2] After several unsuccessful attempts to find a venue to accommodate them, they decided to use the Highlander School in Monteagle. Only seventy-five of the two hundred delegates drove the nearly fifty miles to get there. Hardly an auspicious beginning.

Over the two remaining days, the delegates focused on three issues: repeal of sedition and antilabor laws, support for labor's right to organize unions, and joining the national campaign to secure a federal death penalty for lynchers. They discussed whether or not they could rely on the AFL for support since William Mitch, president of the Alabama Federation of Labor, had been interested enough to come to Chattanooga, but he had not followed them to Monteagle.[3]

In the end, the conference generated more hope than results. It was not a question of bad faith—everyone wanted similar outcomes. Rather, the problem was a classic clash of political philosophies. Economic freedom was a higher priority for socialists than black social equality. Socialists considered blacks just another sector of the working class. As trade unionists, socialists often aligned with segregated unions. The Reds, however, agreed with W. E. B. Du Bois (who was not yet a party member), that black workers considered their greatest enemies not necessarily the bosses, but their white fellow workers. Eliminating racism in the ranks was a priority for communists. The conference, therefore, experienced some difficulty getting off the ground.

A Walk-Off

Shortly before Al Murphy left Alabama in December 1934, the ASCU's cotton pickers and choppers had submitted a list of demands to planters in Tallapoosa, Lowndes, Lee, Chambers, Dallas, and Montgomery Counties. They wanted to be paid a minimum rate of $1 per hundred pounds of picked cotton. The going rate was 40 cents, and a young picker in a ripe field could handpick about two hundred pounds a day. That would yield him exactly 80 cents for twelve hours of work.

In Tallapoosa and Montgomery, the union negotiated an increase to 65 cents per hundred pounds, a raise in croppers' monthly credit allowances from $10 to $15, and on a few plantations the right to independently gin their cotton. But in Lowndes and Dallas Counties, the planters refused to bargain. By the spring of 1935, the pickers and choppers there were talking about striking.

On August 19, 1935, during the height of picking season, fifteen hundred men and women dropped their sacks and walked off Lowndes's massive Bell and Bates plantations. Clyde Johnson, the new union president with just six months on the job, requested solidarity from the Southern Tenant Farmers' Union, whose members were also threatening to strike. He hoped to spark a general action, but the STFU refused to join them.[4]

The planters were beside themselves. A delay of just a few days could mean loss of the entire crop. Dallas County sheriff R. E. Woodruff drove out to the Bell Plantation to "talk some sense" into the strikers. He cornered one of the organizers, Willie Witcher, who told him "I don't care to listen to strike-breaking talk" and walked away. Woodruff ordered him to stop. When Witcher stopped and turned around, the sheriff shot him. His deputy also fired. They put Witcher in the back seat of their police car and drove him to the Haynesville jail. Willie Witcher died there.[5]

Woodruff subsequently deputized landlords and overseers to raid six of the strikers' cabins. They beat some of the croppers and drove others miles into the country and left them there so they had to walk back. J. W. Davis, a white tenant farmer believed to have assisted the black croppers, was flogged.[6]

Jim Press Merriweather, another Bell Plantation strike leader, was murdered two days later. His widow, Annie Mae, a captain in Capitola Tasker's ASCU Sewing Club network, described what Vaughn Ryles and Ralph McQuire, two posse members, did to her while her husband was being killed.

> They started tearing up the place looking for leaflets and found some under a mattress.... I said I didn't know about the meeting because I had been working. Ryles started doubling a rope and told me to pull off all my clothes. He said, "Lay down across the chair, I want naked meat this morning." I lay down across the chair and Ralph McQuire held my head for Ryles to beat me.... He was beating me from my hips on down, and [then] he hit me across the head. They said, "Now see if you can tell us what you know." They were all cussing.... Ryles put a loop in the rope....

> He threw the rope over the rafters... drew me up about two feet from the floor.... I heard a gun firing.... They told me about my husband being shot... They were lynching him then.[7]

The last thing she remembered was losing consciousness.

Blaine Owen went to Dallas County to cover the story for the *Federated Press*. After his foray in Memphis, he'd been organizing steelworkers in Birmingham and made the mistake of meeting with a few of them in one of the company housing units. Afterward, he was followed, kidnapped, thrown into the back seat of a black sedan, and beaten unmercifully. Two men demanded the names of his comrades, and when he refused, they pulled out fistfuls of his hair and drove him into the countryside, where they flogged him and left him.[8]

Owen's luck wasn't much better in Dallas County. An angry deputy sheriff arrested him as soon as he arrived, bellowing, "we got eight niggers to every white man here... we got a hard-enough time keeping down trouble without you coming around and stirring things up." The following day, the sheriff released him to two men who took him outside Selma, stripped him, beat him, and left him on a deserted road. They swore he would be lynched if he ever returned.[9]

On September 2, 1935, Fort Deposit deputy sheriff Ed Arrant's posse killed Ed Bracy, the Hope Hull ASCU chapter president. That week sixteen strikers, including organizer Robert Washington, were arrested in Selma. Washington was released to a white mob who beat him nearly to death.[10] Joe Spinner Johnson, a leader of Hale County's Greensboro chapter, was arrested and taken to the Dallas County jail. His landlord, B. J. Young, bailed him out and turned him over to a mob who killed him. Johnson's battered body was later found in a Greensboro field. Al Murphy's friend Charles Tasker was also arrested for leading striking WPA workers who'd refused to provide scab labor for the fields.[11]

When the *Montgomery Advertiser* called the strike a "communist rebellion," a desperate Governor Miller called on Tallapoosa sheriff J. Kyle Young who had some experience with cropper uprisings. Young came to Lowndes, bringing the Wetumpka State Prison bloodhounds with him to ferret out strikers hiding in the swamps. His intervention apparently made a difference. The strike ended that fall.[12]

Although strikers in Tallapoosa and Lee Counties won some minor financial concessions, the 1935 pickers and choppers strike was crushed in Dallas and Lowndes. In December the newly widowed Annie Mae Merriweather told Clyde Johnson, "this terror we suffered lately didn't give strength to the landlords. It only showed us that they'd rather see us die at the point of lynchers guns than give us a living wage."[13]

Mechanization

By the time the ASCU's pickers and choppers struck, most of the members of union locals in Georgia, Mississippi, North Carolina, and Louisiana were displaced croppers who'd become hourly workers or day laborers. This was the result of Texas farmer John Rust's invention of a mechanical cotton harvester that could do the work of fifty to a hundred hand pickers 75 percent cheaper. Rust boasted that "the sharecropper system of the Old South will soon be abandoned," and he wasn't wrong.[14]

Thanks to their land furlough stipends, planters could afford to experiment with new technologies. Intensive cropper labor was required for only about ten weeks a year, yet croppers needed year-round shelter. Sharecropping was a wasteful system, created and maintained basically to protect white privilege. Now that it was unraveling what did the future hold for the displaced?

Nat Ross's failure to achieve collaboration with socialists on his antilabor violence campaign, Johnson's failure (after several attempts) to achieve solidarity with the Southern Tenant Farmers' Union, and the crushing defeat of the ASCU strike precipitated a second district 17 reorganization. Ross and Benson left. Johnson stayed.

Early in 1936 Rob Hall, a white native Alabamian, replaced Ross. A 1932 graduate of Columbia University he had a degree in agricultural economics and his first Party assignment was organizing farmers in Nebraska and editing the Farmers' National Weekly. He was the first white Southerner to head the District. Born in Pascagoula, Mississippi, and raised in Mobile, Alabama, Hall was a tall, stocky extrovert—a great storyteller and an obsessive pipe smoker. More approachable than Ross, he seemed truly interested in getting to know his comrades.[15]

Attorney Robert Wood subsequently replaced Donald Burke as ILD secretary, and Sid Benson went to Chattanooga to edit and publish the *Southern Worker*.[16]

The ILD's national leadership also changed. In the summer of 1934, William Patterson had passed out in his New York City home and was diagnosed with a collapsed lung. On July 21 he sailed to the Soviet Union for treatment and rehabilitation at a sanitarium on the Black Sea. In the interim, Anna Damon was appointed acting ILD national director. Patterson did not return in 1935. He would not come back to the States until 1937, and Damon would ultimately succeed him.[17]

In Alabama, Rob Hall got to work reconfiguring district 17. He chose to keep Clyde Johnson. They'd studied together at Columbia University and had worked with the National Students League there. In May 1936, Hall approved Johnson's request to relocate ASCU headquarters from Montgomery to New Orleans, where the Louisiana Farmers' Union (originally an ASCU chapter) had an interracial membership of almost a thousand. Johnson wrote an article for the *Southern Farm Leader* that summer encouraging a merger of the black Alabama Share Croppers' Union with the integrated Southern Tenant Farmers' Union and the white National Farmers' Union—which would create an organization with sixty thousand members. The NFU expressed interest, but STFU once again declined. Its Socialist president, J. R. Butler, had recently been denied a seat at the Arkansas Federation of Labor convention because of his radical politics. Merging with the Reds could only bring more rejection. By 1936 unionism, integration, atheism, and communism were virtually interchangeable terms in the South.

Hall was pleased when Johnson completed the merger of the Alabama Share Croppers' Union and the National Farmers' Unions, which was celebrated at ASCU's October 1936 convention. Leaders of the new alliance pledged to fight for the right of croppers to sell their own cotton; to inspect and review their accounts; to apply for federal relief without the landlords' authorization; and to abolish the southern wage differential, the commissary system, and the poll tax.[18]

By 1937, all the former SCU chapters in Alabama, Georgia, and Louisiana were operating as National Farmers' Union locals. The membership participated in a massive march on Washington, D.C., to demand an emergency relief bill for farmers and to repeal the Bankhead Cotton Control Act. This 1935 legislation had further restricted cotton production by taxing planters who refused to participate in the land furlough program. It triggered evictions of thousands more croppers and made them hourly workers overnight. Unemployment, poverty, and hunger increased.

In 1936 Franklin Roosevelt created the President's Commission on Farm Tenancy to study the situation. In April 1937, Clyde Johnson and Annie Mae Merriweather testified before that commission, requesting that the members consider creating a land purchasing program and settling former tenant farmer on small plots of land. They also proposed graduated land taxes to keep large landholders, banks, and insurance companies from co-opting the program.

The final report of the Commission on Farm Tenancy to President Roosevelt advised him that no existing federal agency had adequate power to cope with the massive rural poverty in the South in a comprehensive, unified and integrated way.[19] The president's acceptance of their conclusions directly led to creation of the Farm Security Administration and passage of the Bankhead-Jones Farm Tenancy Act, which authorized the federal government to buy up vacant land, rehabilitate it, and relocate farm tenants. A welcomed improvement, but still not a long-term solution.

Scottsboro, the Home Stretch

The 1935 wave of change that washed over the nation, the South, the party, and district 17 did not spare the Scottsboro defense team.

In October 1934, the ILD's Ben Davis, who'd defended Angelo Herndon, met with the Scottsboro teens in Kilby Prison to inform them that the Leibowitz-Brodsky partnership was over. While all nine initially chose to remain with Brodsky, some would eventually return to Leibowitz.

After Haywood Patterson and Clarence Norris signed affidavits naming Leibowitz as their counsel, Leibowitz ramped up his public criticism of Brodsky, accusing him of making a deal with Lieutenant Governor Thomas Knight Jr. to accept life sentences for the teens in return for their repudiating the ILD. Brodsky vehemently denied this and countercharged that Leibowitz and the NAACP had joined forces to bargain over jail time instead of fighting for the young men's freedom.

On January 7, 1935, the U.S. Supreme Court agreed to hear Norris and Patterson's appeals. Knowing that this was the teens' last chance and that continuing their feud would seriously damage it, they called a truce. Leibowitz agreed to represent Norris, and Brodsky to represent Patterson.

On April 1, 1935, the U.S. Supreme Court overturned both Norris and Patterson's convictions in *Norris v. Alabama*. The justices confirmed that they had been denied trials by juries of their peers, since blacks were systematically excluded from serving on juries in Alabama. That ruling made U.S. constitutional history.

Leibowitz and Brodsky completed the last rounds of Scottsboro trials under the watchful eye of a Scottsboro Defense Committee, organized (in good Popular Front fashion) in December 1935 by the NAACP, the ILD, the ACLU, the League for Industrial Democracy (LID), and the Methodist Federation for Social Services. Both attorneys agreed not to make any decisions or to devise any strategies without consulting the committee.

By the end of 1936, Alabama officials were sick and tired of the cycles of trials and retrials and all the wretched publicity that Scottsboro brought them. Although Leibowitz had never gotten his acquittal, he'd finally broken the prosecution's will and Alabama was ready to negotiate. After relying on Victoria Price's testimony sixteen times, prosecutors approached her with an offer of immunity from perjury if she would drop the charges. She wasn't interested. In the end, Alabama would parole four of the nine despite their rape convictions. What kind of future could these men, raised to adulthood in prison, expect? By the time the last one was released in 1950, they each had lost between six and nineteen years of their lives.

Haywood Patterson, who'd been tried and convicted four times, broke out of Kilby Prison in 1948 and fled to Detroit, where within a year he was arrested for killing a man in a bar fight. He was convicted of manslaughter and sent to an Illinois prison, where he died of cancer in 1952. Clarence Norris, paroled in 1944, also fled Alabama, was captured, returned to prison, and paroled again in 1946. He assumed his brother's identity and began to rebuild his life. Norris was pardoned by Governor George Wallace in 1976; he died of complications from Alzheimer's disease in 1989. Andy Wright, paroled in 1943, also left Alabama, was arrested for breaking parole, and finally released in 1950. He moved to New York City. His younger brother, Roy, acquitted in 1937, joined the army and later the merchant marines. Roy married and appeared to have made a new life, until he came home on leave in 1959 to find his wife with another man. He killed her and then himself. Ozie Powell, paroled in 1946, went home to his sharecropping family in Georgia. Charlie Weems, paroled in 1943, married, moved to Atlanta. and found steady employment in an industrial laundry. Eugene Williams, paroled in 1937, moved to St. Louis, where his surviving relatives welcomed him. Olin Montgomery, also paroled in 1937, attempted to make a career in vaudeville but was not successful. He began drinking heavily, lived for a time in New York City, and finally returned to Atlanta, where he'd been raised. Willie Roberson, who had an IQ of 64 and no known living relatives, was also paroled in 1937. There is apparently no record of what happened to him after that.

In 2013 Powell, Patterson, Weems, and Andy Wright—the four who were all either paroled or released in 1936 with rape convictions hanging over them—were issued posthumous pardons by the State of Alabama.

Historian Douglas Linder maintains that Scottsboro "launched and ended careers, wasted lives, divided America's left, created sectional strife, and fueled a fledging civil rights movement. Nine lives were saved, thanks in large measure to the Reds, but nine young men still languished in prison, living with fear, suffering and bitterness. The Reds made plenty of mistakes in their defense, but they did not make martyrs of the Boys to further their own cause. The judicial system martyred them, the communists were right on that issue, and the judicial system gave them what legacy they have."[20]

16 ▌ A POPULAR FRONT

> The revolution, it seemed, was farther off—perhaps a lifetime or two away—and the practical work of bringing it about would be more prosaic than I had previously believed.
> —Junius Scales, *Cause at Heart*

Hosea Hudson returned to Birmingham in 1936 and found a job as an iron molder. He'd worked hard in Atlanta, but had gotten tired of living hand to mouth. The Magic City had changed during the two years he was gone, and Hudson wasn't impressed with district 17's new leader, Rob Hall, or with the party's new direction, for that matter. "The Party wasn't what it was when I left," he recalled. "Now we got this open Party office and you go up there, walk in, and have classes on a Sunday."[1]

Most of his section leader comrades—Frank Williams, Al Murphy, Ted Burton—were gone. The TUUL had been dismantled, and some of the old organizers were working for the CIO now. After a few weeks in town, Hudson himself was recruited by the Steel Workers Organizing Committee.

Jane Speed, the young white Montgomery girl with the long red hair who kept getting herself arrested was back managing a communist bookstore downtown. It was a gathering place, a hangout, for the new comrades. Rob Hall didn't hold with Nat Ross's rigid management style, and Hudson wasn't sure how he felt about that.

All this change began with Hitler. The spread of fascism in Europe caused the Comintern to put the goal of world revolution on hold. Survival became the first priority. On July 25, 1935, at the Seventh World Congress, Secretary General Georgi Dimitrov introduced the People's Front against Fascism and War policy. He told the European parties to collaborate with antifascist leftists in order to fight the scourge.[2] He told communist parties in the capitalist democracies to adopt "realistic perspectives on their own national realities."[3]

Unlike Nat Ross, Rob Hall admired national party secretary Earl Browder, and both championed the Popular Front strategy. Hall believed that Browder was absolutely the right man to navigate the party through this crisis. Raised in Kansas, Browder had grown up among populists and pacifists, and he said communism was just another American revolutionary tradition.

"We are not un-American," he liked to say. "When did it become un-American to struggle to overthrow a tyrannical and destructive system?"[4] Many comrades and fellow travelers agreed. They recognized an affinity with the American Revolution and the Abolitionist and Populist movements.

Chairman Browder stopped insisting that capitalism be overthrown. He replaced the party's "For a Soviet America" slogan with "Communism is Twentieth Century Americanism." The party dissolved the League of Struggle for Negro Rights and replaced it with the National Negro Congress, a more broadly progressive organization whose consensus issues included supporting organized labor, resisting fascism, and challenging discrimination. The NAACP's Charles Hamilton Houston supported the NNC, but Walter White did not. Both John L. Lewis and A. Philip Randolph, president of the Brotherhood of Sleeping Car Porters, endorsed it.

Earl Browder would ultimately champion Roosevelt's New Deal and partner with Lewis to strengthen the CIO.

In June 1936, CPUSA's Ninth Congress met in New York City to discuss a U.S. Popular Front strategy. While some comrades resented cooperating with the enemy (wasn't collaboration a betrayal of the revolution?) and others feared that Popular Front ideology blurred the distinctions between reformism and radicalism, most younger Reds welcomed the new direction. Journalist James Wechsler, then a twenty-one-year-old college student, recalled: "When the Popular Front program was proclaimed in Moscow I felt better about being a Communist. I deeply believed that it was not a momentary tactic but a great turning point in political history."[5]

Browder explained that "the American bourgeoisie was never able to fully unite our country into one nation. It compromised with all sorts of localisms and particularisms which divide the people. . . . We Communists must become known as the most energetic champions of the full national unification of our country."[6] And so, the task was to build coalitions of liberals, radicals, trade unionists, and socialists—black and white—and to push back against the fascist threat.

At the same time, Birmingham whites were dealing with ongoing antilabor violence. Section 7A of the 1933 National Industrial Recovery Act granted workers the right to form unions and to bargain collectively, but the Magic City's corporate leaders were ignoring, if not openly flouting that section. Their security forces, assisted by the police and the Klan, continued to employ violence. Birmingham rose to third on the ACLU's list of the most violent cities in the United States.⁷ Commercial and even local businesses were being hurt by all the adverse publicity.

The Reds were no longer charged with creating every problem in the city. This was a very subtle shift that Hall took full advantage of by operating the district more openly. He was, after all, a white Alabamian and he understood white Alabamians. He made it clear that he was ready to cooperate with anyone willing to cooperate with him. Hall subsequently found an ally and a comrade when he met Joe Gelders—a white Birmingham native, University of Alabama professor, a Jew, and someone whose help Nat Ross had rejected.

Professor Gelders

Joe Gelders's family was well respected in Birmingham. His parents, Louis and Blanche, ran a high-class restaurant over in Red Mountain and were civic-minded citizens. Their only son, Joe was a physics professor at the University of Alabama in Tuscaloosa. As the Great Depression descended, Joe campaigned for FDR. But as the New Deal solutions began to roll out, his enthusiasm waned—especially after the Agricultural Adjustment Act resulted in destroying perfectly good wheat and corn and massacring farm animals to jumpstart the economy.

Gelders came to the Communist Party in his own idiosyncratic way. Most southern Reds, black or white, were recruited by friends or fellow workers, but Joe read his way to communism and tried to argue his way into a chapter that wasn't interested in having him. It all started in 1934, as waves of strikes and antilabor violence shook Birmingham. The professor asked himself: If New Deal liberalism wasn't the answer, what were the other options? He systematically read the works of the utopian socialists, then Marx and Engels, and he listened to Norman Thomas's speeches. But it wasn't until he found a copy of Stalin's *Foundations of Leninism*, however, that the pieces started coming together. Gelders admired Lenin's attempt to apply the principles of science to government.

Joe Gelders was a tall wiry man with a long rather sad face and a nervous temperament. During his 1934 semester break, he'd traveled to New Orleans for much-needed ulcer surgery. When his nurse saw the books he'd piled on his nightstand, she asked (furtively) if he would like to meet the local party leader. Their subsequent encounter put Gelders on the path to party membership.

He returned to Tuscaloosa in May to find Birmingham's Mine, Mill and Smelter Workers union striking Republic Steel over union recognition. Republic's security forces were brutalizing organizers, and its management team threatened to fire anyone who associated with them. It was an act of courage, therefore, when in July 1933 the East Thomas Blast Furnace's predominantly black workforce overwhelmingly voted to be represented by Mine, Mill. Management refused to recognize the election, however, and ordered company guards to break up all interracial meetings. Twenty-five men were fired. In late May 1934, Mine, Mill, whose president was white and vice president was black, called a strike.

Pickets marching outside the East Thomas plant were physically attacked and during one scuffle a Jefferson County sheriff's deputy fired a machine gun into the crowd, killing two black strikers. After that, there was no going back for Gelders. He drove to Birmingham to find Nat Ross and apply for party membership. Unfortunately, Ross suspected that he was just another bored intellectual looking for excitement and brushed him off. District 17 needed workers, not more thinkers.

The setback proved to be only temporary for Gelders. When he returned to Tuscaloosa, he organized a campus study group and encouraged his students to draft a petition opposing the proposed Downs literature ordinance, which would make possession of subversive literature a felony punishable by six months on a chain gang. This legislation was specifically designed to harass labor organizers, since being a radical was not a crime, nor was membership in the Communist Party. As his students collected signatures, Gelders's colleagues complained to university president George Denny that involving students in political protest was inappropriate. Although Denny took no action, Gelders sensed that his days on campus were numbered.

The Gelderses' home was opened to like-minded colleagues, neighbors, and friends for discussion and debate, and his living room became a gathering place for free thinkers in the tradition of Montgomery's Norman Thomas Study Club. Gelders actually had a connection with the Montgomery group. Sadie Franks, his wife's sister, and Dorothy Lobman, her cousin, were both charter members.

John Catchings, Mine, Mill's white president, was subsequently arrested for assault, and his wife and eight children were evicted from company housing. After a grand jury refused to indict him, Catchings was rearrested and charged with dynamiting the home of a strikebreaker. This time he was convicted and sentenced to 526 days at hard labor. During the course of this long strike, 160 miners—black and white—lost their jobs.

Gelders returned to Birmingham to find Nat Ross, who sent him to Sid Benson this time. Benson was genuinely impressed, and he introduced the professor to Robert Wood, Donald Burke's replacement at the ILD. Wood was still recuperating from a beating he'd been given on May 1 when a police car stopped him on a Birmingham street and four men came out of nowhere, grabbed him, pushed him into another car, drove into the countryside, stripped, and flogged him.[8] Wood suggested that if Gelders really wanted to get involved, he should contact the National Committee for the Defense of Political Prisoners, an ILD adjunct. Gelders did.

In June, the determined professor drove to New York City, ostensibly to take graduate courses at Columbia University but actually to attend the party's National Training School. Despite his wife's reservations, Gelders wanted to work for the party. While in New York he learned that Wood had been kidnapped and beaten twice more and that he'd finally left Alabama.[9]

For Gelders, the only good news that summer was Congress passing the National Labor Relations (Wagner) Act and creating a permanent National Labor Relations Board with authority to supervise union elections and to represent members who brought charges of unfair labor practices. When he returned to Tuscaloosa, he learned that his teaching contract wasn't going to be renewed. His in-laws (with the exception of Sadie Franks) encouraged his wife to divorce him.[10] She didn't, but Tuscaloosa wasn't home for either of them anymore. In October, just as the Downs literature ordinance became law, Joe and Esther Gelders and their two daughters left for New York City, where he was appointed Harlem delegate to the National Committee for the Defense of Political Prisoners.

After completing a year at this assignment, Gelders returned to Birmingham to serve as the NCDPP's first southern representative. In August 1936, he opened an office and hired an attorney. Nat Ross was gone by then and Rob Hall was in charge. Hall and Gelders, men of different generations and very different temperaments, raised and radicalized in the South, would forge a strong working partnership. All their lives they'd been assured that the South could solve its own problems if left alone to do so. They'd come to accept about half of that, and with a caveat. In their desperation to confront the region's seemingly intractable problems, they were willing to collaborate with outsiders, to accept help—even (God forbid) federal assistance—if it would advance the South economically, politically, or socially in building a foundation for equal justice under the law. Gelders, through the NCDPP, would serve as the link between the Reds and the liberal-progressive community, both in the South and beyond. For that reason, Hall asked him to keep his party affiliation a secret—something that was only possible outside Birmingham.

The Cost

One month before Gelders returned to Alabama, the office of district 17's Bessemer organizer Bart Logan had been raided. When the police found copies of the *Southern Worker*, he was arrested for violating the city's seditious literature ordinance (Bessemer's version of the Downs law). He was found guilty and, despite suffering from tuberculosis, was sentenced to 180 days at hard labor and denied bail. His wife, Belle, was referred to Gelders, who provided legal representation and demanded medical attention. When this was denied, Gelders and Belle Logan led a delegation to Mayor Jap Bryant's office in Bessemer on September 21, 1936. Although the mayor refused to speak with them, he arranged for a medical examination, and Logan was subsequently sent to a sanatorium.[11]

Two days later, Gelders was clubbed from behind on a Birmingham street and dragged into a car, just as Wood had been. Four men drove him fifty miles to Clanton, stripped and beat him with blackjacks, and left him there. He was lucky that a farmer discovered him and helped. After his release from the hospital, Gelders recuperated at his sister-in-law's home in Montgomery. One of his broken ribs had punctured his heart muscle.[12]

With Joe's parents, relatives, and their influential friends demanding an investigation, Governor Graves ordered an inquest. He assigned the case to Alabama State Police special investigator James McClung.

McClung discovered that on the day after Gelders's beating, a man had been seen dumping a large package into an empty lot in Birmingham. He appeared very nervous, and a passerby who sensed "something wasn't right" wrote down his license plate number and gave it to the police. The package contained Gelders's wallet and a baseball bat. The license plate number led McClung to a captain and subsequently to a lieutenant in the Alabama National Guard. They were Walter J. ("Crack") Hanna, TCI's security chief, and Dent Williams, a Birmingham attorney (the same Dent Williams who'd shot

Willie Peterson in 1931).[13] Gelders positively identified both men as his attackers, yet neither was indicted.

Apparently, shortly after Gelders's flogging, U.S. Steel (the parent company of TCI) announced a $31 million expansion of its Birmingham facilities. That raised hopes for new jobs in the Magic City, and apparently saved the two national guardsmen on TCI's payroll from indictment.[14] Nobody wanted to make the TCI officials angry enough to change their corporate plans.

Disappointed, but not finished, in the fall of 1937, a full year later, Gelders took his case to the new LaFollette Committee in Washington, D.C. This senate committee had been created under the auspices of the National Labor Relations Board with a mandate to investigate industrial espionage, private police agencies, strike-breaking services, and other management attempts to disrupt legal union activity. Wisconsin senator Robert M. LaFollette chaired. Gelders, now thirty-nine years old, angry, and considerably worse for wear, was described by one comrade as "a white-haired avenging angel."[15]

Gelders told the committee that TCI employed terrorists. Investigator McClung confirmed that and testified that fifteen of the seventeen officers of the Alabama State National Guard were on U.S. Steel's payroll.[16] Crack Hanna and Dent Williams were just two of them.

McClung attested that "any opposition against Captain Hanna—even a $10 fine—anything that might bring a civil suit would antagonize TCI, and they [Jefferson County's residents] were looking forward to an expenditure of 31 million dollars."[17]

"That is why," McClung, concluded, "the Jefferson County Solicitors Office failed to press vigorously for indictments against Hanna and Williams."[18]

Despite powerful rebuttals by TCI attorneys and the testimonies of respected Birmingham businessmen, TCI's corporate practices proved to be indefensible. Crack Hanna had flogged the wrong radical this time. TCI was ordered to make restitution, and on March 7, 1937, U.S. Steel signed an agreement with the CIO to schedule a union election. The bad news was that no one went to prison and that TCI never expanded its Birmingham operation.

Gelders's long ordeal reinforced his conviction that local jurisdictions could not be counted on to handle civil liberties violations impartially. He'd been lucky to have McClung's support, but even that had not resulted in justice. Only the federal government had the muscle to accomplish that.

Comrade Browder

While CPUSA did not formally endorse Franklin Roosevelt in 1936, Earl Browder denounced the Republican challenger, Alf Landon. He insisted that the campaign issues of 1936 were not socialism versus capitalism, but rather between democracy and fascism, and he argued that Governor Landon was moving in the wrong direction. That year, Browder and James Ford, a black Birmingham steel worker whose grandfather had been lynched, headed the party's presidential ticket. This made Ford the first black American to be nominated for a national office. CPUSA's platform included universal social security, health insurance, government employment at union wages, public housing, and racial equality. Jane Speed managed their campaign.

Browder's speeches were inspired by some of the "American exceptionalism" philosophy of his predecessor, Jay Lovestone, who'd argued that real revolution could never get traction in the United States because Americans were so thoroughly corrupted by capitalism. Lovestone believed that the United States required a more nuanced and longer-term strategy, and Browder heartedly agreed. Popular Front policy freed the U.S. party leaders to act somewhat more independently of Moscow, and Browder would eventually support New Deal reforms and reformers. He'd learned a lot by watching Roosevelt, who was also trying to pull together a broad coalition of left-leaning supporters.

Browder had a keen sense of timing. He'd paid attention in 1931 when African Americans failed to embrace the Black Belt self-determination policy. In 1933, he'd watched the souring of the party's attempts to organize a midwestern farm-labor coalition. Reds who'd organized heartland wheat and dairy farmers and who'd led demonstrations to stop evictions and prevent foreclosures and land auctions had wrongly concluded that the farmers' animus toward bankers, middlemen, and the government would radicalize them. Few considered that the New Deal programs might (and eventually did) generate optimism as their effects began to be felt in 1934.[19]

According to Nebraska attorney Anan Raymond, the midwestern farmers who rebelled against evictions and market manipulation in 1933 were defending, not repudiating, the principle of private property. "Real revolution," he said, "would have followed any attempt to herd such farmers, the most individualist of all [Americans], into collective or state-owned farms."[20]

Finally, the CIO's success with industrial organizing offered Browder yet another example of the U.S. desire for inclusion—as opposed to revolution. Factory, mill, and mine workers, like the midwestern farmers and the Black Belt sharecroppers, wanted their slice of the American pie and were willing to fight for it.[21]

Raymond concluded that "for communism to succeed in America it would have to cooperate in some ways with capitalism."[22] Browder understood that. And so did Rob Hall.

Hall knew that Popular Front cooperation would require that CPUSA's racial justice goals be muted in order to attract white southern progressives. It meant reaching out to the black middle class, to the NAACP, and making peace with the clergy. Collaboration with the CIO was also essential, and John L. Lewis was willing to hire Red organizers for his industrial and agricultural labor campaigns. Lewis appreciated how hard the Reds worked, how skilled they were at negotiating, how well they ran meetings, and how they stood up to authority. He also appreciated their ability to recruit across racial lines. But the Reds who worked for him had to deny their party affiliation.

Alabama sharecroppers resented all the Popular Front emphasis on industrial workers, and the requirement that cropper demands be balanced against the needs and concerns of the party's new partners. One year after ACSU's merger with the National Farmers Union, it had been absorbed by the CIO's United Cannery, Agricultural, Packing and Allied Workers of America. An angry Harry Haywood charged that "those responsible for liquidating the Sharecroppers Union were motivated by . . . a feeling that the existence of an independent and mainly Black union with the explosive potential of the Share Croppers Union would frighten off our new democratic front allies: the Roosevelt New Dealers, the Southern moderates and the C.I.O. leadership."[23]

The party's need to modify its revolutionary stance meant ending strategic tactics like mass protest. Former ILD national director William Patterson had sensed this coming in 1934, and it made him furious since his biggest successes were based on those methods.

Change was unremitting. In 1937, district 17's territory shrank to inside the borders of Alabama. The party restructured along more traditional political party lines, complete with a national headquarters and state chapters. Rob Hall became Alabama state secretary, and Sid Benson was appointed state secretary for Tennessee. Benson would concentrate on organizing Chattanooga TVA workers and building a united front with the Tennessee Socialist Workers' Party.

In the meantime, Joe Gelders was determined to resurrect the dream of a united southern progressive labor movement, the one that was deferred a few years earlier in Monteagle, Tennessee.

The Southern Conference for Human Welfare

On August 10, 1938, the National Emergency Council released its *Report on the Economic Conditions of the South*, a study commissioned by President Roosevelt, who'd become concerned about his eroding Democratic support in the region. The council maintained that the South's resources had been squandered over many generations and in fifteen sections the authors addressed what the region required in the areas of health care, housing, public services, infrastructure, and land use. The South's railroads, utilities, and much of its industry was controlled by outsiders, and the best and brightest left for opportunities elsewhere. The researchers concluded that the federal government had a responsibility to intercede since widespread poverty was such a major factor.

While many white southerners considered the report inaccurate, distorted, and/or politically motivated, Joe Gelders welcomed it. It wasn't perfect, since it omitted two of the most contentious issues of 1938—race and organized labor—but it was a start, something to work with, and he'd been making allies who he believed might become partners in facing this challenge. One was the CIO's Lucy Randolph Mason, whom he'd met during a cotton mill strike in Tupelo, Mississippi, in April. They'd talked about sponsoring a joint CIO/NCDPP regional conference to address the antilabor violence.[24] After the report's release, Mason mentioned their discussion to her friend, First Lady Eleanor Roosevelt, and assured her that both the majority of southern blacks and the white working class supported the president, but most couldn't vote for him because of poll tax restrictions. Mason proposed including the poll tax as an issue in any potential regional conference.[25]

Mason asked Gelders to join her when Mrs. Roosevelt arranged a meeting with the president. Franklin Roosevelt warmed to their proposal but requested that the conference be structured as a response to the *Report on the Economic Conditions of the South*. That meant broadening the scope from antilabor violence, civil liberties, and the poll tax to include economic issues. All agreed that the additions would make it appeal to a wider audience of progressives. Gelders and Mason did not spearhead the conference—too many politicians, and social theorists scrambled for that position, but Gelders led the charge in Alabama.

He spent July 1938 scheduling meetings, recruiting staff, financial support, and political, economic, and social science experts, drafting statements of purpose and preparing advance publicity. The Alabama Policy Committee officially sponsored what would become the Southern Conference for Human Welfare (SCHW), and the CIO underwrote most of the cost. Birmingham was chosen as the site, not only because it was the epicenter of antilabor violence, but it was also convenient to most transportation. Judge Louise O. Charlton, recently appointed to Birmingham's Federal District Court, chaired the steering committee. Joe Gelders served as conference secretary, and Rob Hall and the CIO's William Mitch made all the local arrangements.

In the meantime, Hosea Hudson, who'd just started a new job with the federal Workers Project Administration was asked to represent the unemployed. Finally, the University of North Carolina president Frank Porter Graham, who'd helped draft the original NEC report, was appointed honorary chair.

They sent out a call at the end of summer: "There are many liberal thinkers and leaders in the South. Their number is rapidly increasing. Progressive ideas and the desire for progressive action are spreading. Their leaders have heretofore been isolated and scattered, the effectiveness of their work limited by their lack of coordination. [This] Conference, by providing a meeting ground for all Southern progressives will promote mutual trust and cooperation between them for greater service to the South."[26]

On Thanksgiving weekend 1938, a thousand white and two hundred black delegates arrived at the city's municipal auditorium for the SCHW. Only southerners by birth or residence qualified as delegates, but registration was open to anyone. The fee was one dollar to allow sharecroppers and unemployed workers to attend, but if they didn't have that dollar, they paid what they could. Labor, government, education, social service and volunteer organizations, the clergy, and the southern press were all well represented. Delegates met national figures, like newly appointed U.S. Supreme Court justice Hugo Black; Aubrey Williams, director of the National Youth Administration; and Mary McLeod Bethune, director of its Office of Minority Affairs. The First

Lady also attended. The stated goal was to develop a regional agenda, and expectations ran the gamut from supporting industrial democracy to ending segregation. The only consensus was that change was overdue.

In his keynote address, Graham challenged the South to catch up with the rest of the nation. "We desperately need the aid of the federal government," he said,

> to equalize educational opportunities, to improve wages, housing and healthcare, to allow full political participation to close the economic, social and cultural gaps between the South and the rest of the nation.
>
> In this day when democracy and freedom are in retreat everywhere in the face of totalitarian powers and their regimentation of youth and persecution of minorities, let us raise the flag of freedom and democracy where it counts most here in our own land. The black man is the primary test of American democracy and Christianity. The Southern Conference for Human Welfare takes its stand here tonight.[27]

While Graham raised the race issue, he did not call for ending segregation. But it hardly mattered, since the following day race became the overriding issue anyway. As panelists brought propositions forward and the resolutions committee drafted proposals, blacks and whites worked side by side until Public Safety Commissioner Bull Connor burst into the auditorium and ordered everyone to "separate or face arrest." After the First Lady protested the eviction by moving her chair to the middle of the center aisle, the press focused on little else.

Despite this, over the long weekend resolutions were proposed to petition state legislatures to shorten work hours for women, improve workers' compensation benefits, enforce the child-labor provisions of the Fair Labor Standards Act, and enact civil service employment reforms. Farm tenancy reform, abolishing the poll tax, and endorsing a federal antilynching statute were high on the agenda. Finally, a resolution calling for the release of the Scottsboro teens still incarcerated was passed by acclamation.

More radical proposals at the SCHW included equal pay for equal work regardless of race and permitting qualified black physicians to admit patients to state-funded hospitals.[28] On the last day, the delegates voted to become a permanent organization with state committees meeting annually in nonsegregated facilities. They also passed a resolution—later regarded as suicidal—to follow the Popular Front strategy of cooperating with all democratic and progressive organizations. Communists were eligible for full membership.[29]

The SCHW, by its endorsement of federal antilynching legislation and condemnation of Jim Crow laws, caused *Montgomery Advertiser* editor Grover Hall to moan, "surely there was enough work for this conference to do to soften these rigors of life in the Deep South without challenging the folkways of our people and raising extraneous issues."[30]

By "folkways" he was alluding to segregation that, it was widely believed, would disappear once more basic problems (like poverty) were solved. One had to have patience. Hall, who'd initially supported the conference, ended up calling it "a gratuitous insult which spit in the face of the Southern people and their way of life."[31]

Many white southerners, even some who were progressive, believed that the SCHW was attempting to link black economic and political equality to social equality—a full frontal attack on white supremacy.

While Rob Hall was unhappy with the overwhelming focus on labor (giving rural poverty the short shrift), and disturbed by the paternalism he'd witnessed, as well as the unwillingness of many white delegates to challenge Birmingham's segregation laws, he publicly declared himself pleased with the outcome.[32] In January 1939 he wrote that "here was a gathering of intensely patriotic Southerners wrapped up in southern problems and jealous of their obligations to solve these problems. But that did not mean the narrow, fanatical sectionalism of the past.... The Southern Conference indicated that the Southern people, harassed by deep-seated problems ... are determined to secure for themselves and their families more of the fruits of the New Deal."[33]

Hall had written this in response to a December 9, 1938, *Tuscaloosa News* editorial describing the SCHW as "a slap at the Party as it has been constituted for years in the South—and an open revelation that the New Dealers are more concerned with the Negro than with anything else."[34] It would not end there, of course.

In May 1938, the U.S. House of Representatives established the Committee on Un-American Activities (HUAC), chaired by Texas congressman Martin Dies, to investigate disloyal and/or subversive activities of individuals and/or organizations to determine if any had ties to the Communist Party. In the summer of 1940, the Dies Committee began a series of hearings to investigate Communist influence in Birmingham's steel industry and in the offices of Chattanooga's Tennessee Valley Authority. In their final report they mentioned the Southern Conference for Human Welfare as a radical communist front. Although Senators John Bankhead and Lister Hill, Governor Bibb Graves, and Representative Luther Patrick subsequently withdrew their initial promotion of the idea of the SCHW, the conference was subsequently defended by an unlikely candidate, editor Grover Hall:

> The Dies Committee on Un-Americanism, whatever un-Americanism may be, sticks its long nose into the affairs of the Southern Conference for Human Welfare which the *Advertiser* has denounced for certain offenses it committed in its resolutions ... [but] no citizen said anything at Birmingham that he did not have a right, under the United States Constitution to say.... It is not the business of the federal Congress to know who suggested and organized the Conference. It is not the business of the federal Congress to know whether attendants were Republicans, Democrats, Socialists, Communists or Populists.... So, the *Advertiser* ... wishes to express its contempt and scorn for the impudent Dies Committee that now dares to question the free-born citizens that originated and participated in this ill-fated Conference.[35]

Nearly eighteen years later, in 1955 Kenneth Douty, chair of the Illinois ACLU, took issue with Mississippi senator James O. Eastland's 1954 report to the Internal Security Subcommittee (the senate's counterpart to HUAC) concerning the origins of the SCHW. Eastland maintained that the SCHW was a front invented by the CPUSA to destroy democracy in the South by spreading communism.

Douty offered another explanation. "An organizational vacuum existed in the South in 1938," he wrote. "There was no general counterweight to Southern conservative opinion, there was no general shelter for the New Deal Southern political figures, there was no South-wide organization for liberals and others aroused by the Report on Economic Conditions, there was no citizens group that could interpret for the labor movement and none where white and Negro could talk to each other. To fill this vacuum the Southern Conference for Human Welfare was born."[36]

17 ▎ A CULTURE OF OPPOSITION

> Struggle is a never-ending process. Freedom is never really won.
> You earn it and win it in every generation.
> —Coretta Scott King, *My Life with Martin Luther King, Jr.*

On August 23, 1939, Josef Stalin, who'd championed the Popular Front Against War and Fascism, entered into a nonaggression pact with Adolf Hitler, effectively destroying the European antifascist coalition and threatening united front collaboration in the United States. Progressive white southerners lost one of the best excuses they had for cooperating with the Reds.

Citizens on both sides of the Atlantic who'd witnessed fascism crawl across Europe feared another world war was inevitable. When Hitler invaded Poland two weeks later and Britain and France declared war on Germany, Stalin accused them of "perpetrating an imperialist war." Earl Browder struggled mightily to translate that into something positive. Suddenly England and France were no longer allied with the Soviet Union in the fight against fascism but were rather imperialists promoting a war that Stalin wanted no part of.

Many U.S. communists experienced this mind-bending reversal as a bitter betrayal. One wrote sadly that "during the height of the Popular Front, despite the show trials, Russians stood for all that was good, rational and progressive and Germany stood for all that was evil, barbaric, and reactionary." But the pact with Hitler caused many to wonder if there was any moral distinction between communism and fascism.[1]

Browder undercut his own leadership when he chose to toe the party line and defend the pact as a "master stroke for peace." He tried to frame it as an attempt to delay and possibly prevent another European war. William Patterson also argued that signing the pact did not mean "that the Soviets endorsed fascism any more than the signing of such a pact with the United States indicated that the Soviets endorsed lynching and Jim Crowism."[2] That didn't fly. And what did Germany get out of it? Nothing less than a guarantee that it would not have to fight on two fronts again.

Stalin's treachery was insufficient to destroy CPUSA or its united-front policy. Despite the fact that many faithful comrades and fellow travelers abandoned their posts, enough hard-liners remained, as did those who were determined to continue their work on the local fronts. The greatest losses were counted among the alliances that had been so carefully constructed and the good-faith coalitions that were destroyed.

The district 17 Reds had muted their radicalism as the old Popular Front strategy mandated, but they had not buried it. As their alliances began to unwind in 1939, the district pivoted left to build new coalitions of what historian Robin Kelley calls "independent radicals, rebellious youth, Christian socialists, black nationalists and budding feminists." A "culture of opposition" was fostered in Birmingham that year.[3]

Back in 1937, Hosea Hudson had established the Right to Vote Club in an effort to reach out to the black middle class. At the time, he and Rob Hall believed that the NAACP, black clergy, and black businessmen could be persuaded to join with the district in assisting poor and working-class blacks to navigate the voter registration process. Right to Vote Club volunteers coached first-time voters through the obstacles that registrars were likely to throw before them.

Hudson was convinced that he could replicate the success that he, Henry Mayfield, and Mack Coad had within the black labor–civil rights coalition led by Hartford Knight, black district representative of the United Mine Workers, and Emory Jackson, editor of the *Birmingham World*. But the Magic City's black middle class remained elusive. Collaboration with Reds would endanger their standing with the city's white elite.

Undaunted, Hudson continued to conduct his voting clinics, teach his citizenship classes, and to file charges every time a club member was denied registration. As a result, between 1938 and 1940, the percentage of Jefferson County black voters nearly quadrupled. In 1939 he began working with the Southern Negro Youth Congress (SNYC), an organization founded in 1937 in Richmond, Virginia, as the youth component of the National Negro Congress. James Jackson, its twenty-two-year-old chair (and a party member), described the SNYC as "dedicated to challenging white supremacy, ending segregation and lynching."[4] Angelo Herndon, who'd been appointed chair of the Young Communist League that year, attended SNYC's inaugural meeting and was recruited as an advisor.

In 1938 SNYC declared itself an independent southern black-led interracial organization of teachers, young professionals, intellectuals, sharecroppers, domestic and industrial workers, and the unemployed—its focus was regional reform. Membership was open to those of all races, classes, and political leanings. But it was essentially a militant movement—one that did not seek confrontation but refused to avoid it.[5]

Southern Negro Youth Congress volunteers joined forces with Hudson in Birmingham, with the CIO, and with a growing number of local black fraternities and churches. Several SNYC members joined black churches in order to establish trust with the preachers and solidarity with the congregations. Whatever their religious beliefs, or lack of them may have been, SNYC's social justice mission came first. SNYC also collaborated with Birmingham's white League of Young Southerners (LYS), founded in 1938 as the youth division of the SCHW. SNYC and LYS members jointly offered literacy and leadership classes in the city's black Prince Hall Masonic Temple and organized voter registration drives and campaigns to end the poll tax. SNYC members assisted the NAACP with antilynching campaigns and promoted the National Urban League's vocational education programs as well as the CIO's labor organization drives. This cooperation reflected a high-water mark in a budding Southern Freedom movement in the Magic City.

In April 1938, Hosea Hudson attended SNYC's second annual conference in Chattanooga, and in November SNYC sent several delegates to the Southern Conference for Human Welfare. In 1939, SNYC held its annual conference in Birmingham and the following year moved its headquarters from Richmond to the Magic City. Rob Hall was thrilled by the infusion of energy. Here was a new crop of young radicals stepping up—dedicated, smart, tough, and right on time—district 17 needed all the help it could get.

Theophilus "Bull" Connor, a popular radio sportscaster was Birmingham's new commissioner of public safety. Just as Chief Fred McDuff once made life miserable for Tom Johnson and Harry Jackson, so Connor continued the tradition. Early on he had demonstrated his anti-Red zeal by attempting to close down Birmingham's SCHW in 1938.

That year the CIO launched a massive organizing campaign focused on southern tobacco, rubber, lumber, and textile workers. Unfortunately, John L. Lewis's Red organizers, who'd demonstrated great skill in utilizing sit-down strikes in 1936, were unable to replicate those successes. Sit-down strikes had eliminated strikebreaking in 1936, but two years later HUAC had struck them down as "conspiracies in restraint of interstate commerce."

Philip Murray, who succeeded Lewis in 1940, considered himself a labor-management advocate, and under his watch CIO organizers were instructed to quash all sit-down strikes.⁶ This caused the remaining Red organizers to bitterly regret scrapping the old TUUL unions, which were "revolutionary" rather than "reform" operations. Vladimir Lenin himself had counseled that "workers who put their trust in reformists are always fooled."⁷

On January 25, 1940, Joe Gelders, chair of the SCHW Standing Committee on Civil Rights, launched a weekly tabloid, the *Southern News Almanac*. It served the functions that the defunct *Southern Worker* once had—keeping its constituents informed, motivated, and connected. His white coeditor Sam Hall (no relation to Rob Hall), a chubby, affable former North Carolina district organizer, was another Alabama native and former editor of the *Anniston Star*. He'd helped Gelders launch the SCHW.⁸

The *Southern News Almanac* published essays, editorials, and general news about labor issues, police brutality, the coming war in Europe, antiwar activity in the United States, racism, and capitalism. Contributors ran the gamut from organizers, politicians, students, radical clergy, and musicians, to social philosophers, hourly workers, and anarchists. Gelders tried to reach as broad a constituency as possible.

Fred Maxey, a white former negotiator with the U.S. Department of Labor and pastor of the Mount Hebron Baptist Church near Leeds, Alabama, wrote a weekly column "Pulpit in Print." Maxey had worked among Kentucky coal miners for years. A fiery social gospel preacher, he accused the church of turning its back on the New Testament mandate of caring for the poor. The Jesus he proclaimed preached radical social justice and would have opposed the poll tax and supported black voting rights.⁹

Don West, a white ordained Presbyterian minister who'd left the church to preach the social gospel and organize workers, strikers, and the unemployed, also contributed a column titled "The Awakening Church."

In October 1940, folksinger Pete Seeger visited a struggling coal miner's family in rural Kentucky and wrote a piece about his experience for the *Southern News Almanac*. In a second article, "No More Labor Wanted Until Further Notice: Camp Blanding, Florida," he documented the story of hundreds of unemployed men who'd been lured to Florida by the prospect of building a new army camp. When they arrived and found there was no work, many were rendered homeless as well as jobless.¹⁰

In 1941, Gelders, in partnership with Montgomery activist Virginia Durr, founded an independent National Committee to Abolish the Poll Tax and petitioned Congress to eliminate the tax in federal elections. That was the year Germany invaded the Soviet Union and Japan attacked Pearl Harbor, changing Josef Stalin's worldview radically. He subsequently pursued an alliance with the United States and Great Britain. Incredibly, a capitalist, a colonialist, and a communist formed a successful alliance of convenience to overcome fascism. The coming of war had changed everything.

During the war the CIO's Philip Murray declared a moratorium on strikes and demanded that all his organizers sign no-strike pledges. Harry Haywood deeply resented that mandate, as he did Murray's subsequent refusal to support a march on Washington to demand opportunities for black workers in defense plants. In 1942, despite the large number of blacks in the CIO ranks, Murray refused to recognize the *Pittsburgh (PA) Courier*'s popular "Double V" campaign for Victory over fascism abroad and Victory over racism at home. Murray argued that both the march and the Double V campaign would distract from the war effort.[11]

By early 1942, James Jackson and Ed Strong of SNYC, Rob Hall, Sam Hall, Joe Gelders, and many of Birmingham's steel and smelter workers, coal miners, and district organizers had either enlisted in the armed forces or had been drafted. The *Southern News Almanac* stopped publishing at the end of 1941.

While the Allies were ultimately victorious, the alliance with the Soviet Union did not survive the peace and Earl Browder's leadership barely survived the war. In his 1944 decision to dissolve CPUSA and replace it with a "political association," he'd clearly overplayed his hand. The Comintern expelled him a year later.

After the war, Rob Hall accepted a journalistic assignment in Washington, D.C., Nat Ross subsequently returned to Birmingham as southern district director. He worked with Sam Hall, recently discharged from the navy. The International Labor Defense, the National Negro Congress, and the National Federation of Constitutional Liberties ultimately merged to create the Civil Rights Congress, led by William Patterson.

The LYS never reassembled after the war, and the SCHW disbanded in 1948. On April 23, 1948, SNYC held its eighth and final conference in the Magic City. In 1949 the organization was placed on the U.S. Attorney General's list of subversives. Nearly fifteen years later Bull Connor would still be grousing, "the trouble with this country is communism, socialism and journalism."[12]

Phil Murray fired the last of John L. Lewis's Red organizers in 1949. They were a bad fit in the new postwar anticommunist environment.[13] In 1950 the Birmingham City Council drafted legislation to outlaw the Communist Party within city limits. Bull Connor vowed to make an example of Sam Hall. Since Nat Ross was gone by then, Hall was the city's "top commie." In June, members of Connor's Red Squad arrested him for vagrancy, the charge that Sheriff McDuff had so successfully utilized. Despite the fact that Hall could verify his employment with the Communist Party, he was indicted anyway since his employer was considered "disreputable." Sylvia Hall contacted a local attorney to get her husband released on bond and they drove to New York City. While they were there, the Birmingham City Council passed the anticommunist ordinance. Reds had forty-eight hours to leave town; if they refused, they would be subject to both a $100 fine and 180 days in jail.

While in New York, Sam Hall consulted with William Patterson at the Civil Rights Congress who engaged attorney John Coe of Pensacola, Florida. Coe brought suit in federal court to invalidate the ordinance because it violated the Fourteenth Amendment's "due process" clause. In October 1950, he argued before U.S. District Judge Seybourn Lynne of the Fifth Circuit of Appeals that "by passing such ordinances we rush headlong into fascism because we are afraid of communism." Coe allowed that a member of the Communist Party might be excluded from a sensitive government position, but as a general rule Americans should not be imprisoned for their beliefs, even if those beliefs extend to the overthrow of the government.[14]

Judge Lynne concurred, not only invalidating the ordinance but overturning the vagrancy charge against Hall. Bull Connor complained that "if the Fourteenth Amendment protects communists in this country then it is time for Congress and the people to start amending the Fourteenth Amendment."[15] The Halls returned to Birmingham staying just long enough to pack and leave Alabama permanently.

In 1951 the Birmingham City Council passed a Communist Control Law requiring members of the party to register with the Department of Public Safety. Clifford Durr, a white Montgomery attorney who'd chaired the Federal Communications Commission during the New Deal years, recalled that "life in the South in the early 1950's could be pleasant only if one took a firm stand in opposition to the boll-weevil and in favor of white face cattle and crimson clover and avoided the petty issues of domestic and international politics."[16]

The struggle to build a strong interracial southern social justice coalition eventually passed to a new generation. While district 17, the ILD, the SCHW, SNYC, LYS, and the NNC were all gone, they'd provided working models for the generation that would shape the movement culture in Birmingham. New organizations emerged: SNCC (the Student Non-Violent Coordinating Committee) and CORE (Congress of Racial Equality), whose shock troops helped to sustain Martin Luther King Jr.'s Southern Christian Leadership Conference and Fred Shuttlesworth's Alabama Christian Movement for Human Rights. Projects like the Freedom Rides, the Mississippi Summer, the Freedom Schools, and the Mississippi Free Democratic Party have district 17's influence woven all through them.

History may be cyclical, but there is still that arc of the moral universe to consider. While it reveals itself to be long and bending toward justice, it still requires human beings to do the heavy lifting.

18 ▍ ALL THINGS CONSIDERED . . .

> The story of the Communist Party is in some measure the story of the rise and fall of a dream of human betterment. To scrutinize the dream while respecting the dreamers is the historian's special challenge.
> —Michael Kazin, *American Dreamers*

In January 1950, Gerald W. Johnson, a popular white southern journalist who was not a communist, wrote an article for *Harper's* magazine titled "Why Communists Are Valuable."

"If the American Communist Party had done nothing more than force the issue of racial justice onto the national agenda and energize American industrial workers, it would have accomplished a great deal," he said. "The Party has had a very definite educational and moral value for the ordinary American. . . . Americans think more about oppressed minorities than we could have without the Communists, and labor leaders work harder and think faster than they would without them." Johnson considered Reds "antidotes to apathy in a democracy," since they demonstrated that "ideas cannot be put down by law."[1]

Just a month later, Wisconsin senator Joseph McCarthy called a press conference to announce that he'd identified more than two hundred "card carrying members of the Communist Party" in the U.S. State Department. It marked the beginning of a six-year effort to flush out Reds and fellow travelers in government, in Hollywood, in schools and universities, and in the armed forces. Defenders of radical ideas became targets. U.S. communists were suspected of subversion, spying, and of operating as foreign agents. Many lost their jobs. Careers were destroyed, and families divided in the frenzied, anti-Red panic of the 1950s.

Ironically, just two decades earlier, communists were engaged in expanding the Fourteenth Amendment's equal protection clause. In *Powell v. Alabama* in 1932, ILD attorneys appealed the Scottsboro convictions on the basis that the black teens did not receive fair, impartial, and deliberate trials and that they were denied the right to competent legal counsel guaranteed by the Sixth and Fourteenth Amendments.[2]

After the State of Alabama countered that the Sixth Amendment right to legal counsel applied only to the federal courts, the U.S. Supreme Court ruled on appeal that legal counsel is guaranteed by the U.S. Constitution to everyone facing a potential death sentence. This had major implications for how justice would subsequently be pursued in the state courts.

In *Norris v. Alabama*, three years later, the ILD charged that the Scottsboro teens were tried by all white juries and therefore not juries of their peers. The high court agreed, holding that exclusion of African Americans from jury service did in fact violate the equal protection clause of the Fourteenth Amendment.

Both appeals, fought entirely on constitutional issues, saved the Scottsboro teens' lives. This strategy prevented state courts from convicting the young men and Alabama from executing them. If the lower courts had not been so careless, the teens might have died.[3]

In February 1937, in *Herndon v. Lowry*, the ILD exposed Georgia's use of the criminal justice system to make Angelo Herndon a political prisoner by threatening him with death for attempting to incite insurrection. In April 1937, the U.S. Supreme Court determined that a state must show a direct connection between revolutionary speech and an actual attempt to overthrow the government in order to prosecute an "inciting insurrection" charge. Possession of radical literature was not sufficient to convict. This decision broadened the protections of the First Amendment entitlement of free speech.

Despite substantial legal, political, and even social contributions, however, the party's failures tend to be more vividly remembered. While the Reds fought oppression of the poor, of minorities, and of the working class, while they dragged oppressors into the national spotlight and generated public outrage, they made a lot of mistakes.

Their mass protest tactics subjected them to accusations of sacrificing the Scottsboro teens for political ends, and their fight for Black equality (and nearly everything else) was often attributed to promoting Moscow's agenda. With respect to labor, historian Theodore Draper maintains that Red organizers were "allergic to compromise, and employers were usually determined not to compromise with them.... A Communist strike was an all or nothing gamble."[4]

It is true at the same time, however, that without the Reds' tenacity much injustice in the United States would have gone unreported. Communists were skilled in putting oppressors on the defensive. NAACP legal counsel

Charles Hamilton Houston admired the ILD's fiery national secretary, William Patterson, for just that reason.

"Through their bold and uncompromising intervention, the communists have been the first to fire the masses with a sense of their raw potential power and the first to preach openly the doctrine of mass resistance and mass struggle." he told the YWCA national convention in Philadelphia on May 5, 1934. "They make it impossible for any aspirant to Negro leadership to advocate less than full economic, political and social equality and expect to retain the respect and confidence of the group."[5]

Fifteen years later, the NAACP's staunchly anticommunist Henry Lee Moon wrote that "offering no quarter the Communists put the South on the defensive in the eyes of the whole world. They stirred the imagination of Negroes and inspired the hope of ultimate justice."[6]

Finally, historian Michael Kazin's more contemporary assessment maintains that the Reds' greatest legacy may have been "putting pressure on Franklin D. Roosevelt and other New Deal liberals to dismantle barriers between people who were deemed worthy of government help and those who were not."[7]

Any legacy at all, however, was threatened on February 25, 1956, when Russia's premier Nikita Khrushchev delivered his "Secret Speech" before a closed session of the Twentieth Congress of the Soviet Communist Party. The text was subsequently acquired by the CIA and published in the *New York Times* several months later. Khrushchev told his comrades:

> When we analyze the practice of Stalin in regard to the direction of the party and of the country, when we pause to consider everything which Stalin perpetrated, we must be convinced that Lenin's fears were justified. The negative characteristics of Stalin, which in Lenin's time, were only incipient, transformed themselves during the last years into a grave abuse of power by Stalin, which caused untold harm to our party.
>
> We have to consider seriously and analyze correctly this matter in order that we may preclude any possibility of a repetition in any form whatever of what took place during the life of Stalin, who absolutely did not tolerate collegiality in leadership and in work, and who practiced brutal violence, not only toward everything which opposed him, but also toward that which seemed to his capricious and despotic character, contrary to his concepts.[8]

Twenty-five years later, Steve Nelson, a member of the CPUSA Central Committee who'd organized countless workers and the unemployed and served with the Abraham Lincoln Brigade in Spain, recalled the effect of this revelation:

> The words... were like bullets, and each found its place in the hearts of the veteran communists. Tears streamed down the faces of men and women who had spent forty or more years, their whole adult lives, in the movement. I looked into the faces of people who had been beaten up or jailed with me and thought of the hundreds that I had encouraged to join the Party. My head was swimming. I thought, "All the questions that were raised along the way now require new answers, and there's no longer one seat of wisdom where we can find them. We're on our own now."[9]

The Communist Party of the United States was decimated as many thousands of members resigned and fellow travelers simply walked away.

Nat Ross, Rob Hall, Ralph Ellis, Lowell Wakefield, and Jesse Wakefield left the party. Angelo Herndon was expelled in 1944, Earl Browder in 1946, and Harry Haywood in 1959. William Patterson, Joe Gelders, Ben Davis, Sid Benson, Jim and Isabelle Allen, Jane and Darlie Speed, Rabbi Benjamin Goldstein, Don and Alice Burke, Hosea Hudson, Joseph Brodsky, Amy Schechter, and Al Murphy all stayed.

A higher percentage of black than white comrades remained. The Soviet Union, after all, had no history of enslaving black people. The party fought to end segregation and to achieve economic equality, and Moscow welcomed black American émigrés during the Great Depression. William Patterson and Ben Davis maintained that Moscow would never let up on the United States for its Jim Crow hypocrisy and would guarantee that segregation remained at the forefront of American political discourse. Patterson felt personal solidarity with Moscow because of the Soviet Union's aid to national liberation movements in Africa, a cause that Washington opposed.[10]

Others, including fellow travelers, could not forget the decisive role that the Red Army had played in the recent Allied victory. The Russians suffered more than fifteen million casualties—the highest, by far, of any of the combatants.

U.S. party members, some naively, had accepted the Soviet model as one that could best serve the interests of the United States. During the Great Depression, those who'd visited Moscow reported that there was no unemployment there and that race discrimination was not practiced. Capitalism, they believed, could never reform itself. Communism worked in the Soviet Union because the party was organized like the military. Decisions came from the top, and orders were carried out on the ground. They had faith in this efficient interim structure as the path to full democracy.

In the 1930s, Americans benefitted from CPUSA's involvement wherever life was hard. Home evictions were reversed; utilities were turned back on; people were fed, sheltered, and defended; labor and the unemployed were organized; and ordinary men and women found the courage to stand up to their oppressors. Many who abandoned the party in the late 1950s, regardless of their feelings about Stalin, continued to have faith in the viability of communism with a "small c." CPUSA, after all, had addressed some of the most critical issues of the Depression era. It had shaped domestic history by helping to advance a national progressive agenda. After Khrushchev's "Secret Speech," however, comrades who'd spent their entire adult lives working to build the party felt unmoored. The revelations were mind-bending, frightening, heartbreaking, and humiliating.

19 ▌ THE REST OF LIFE

> We have an interval, and then our place knows us no more.
> —Walter Pater, *Studies in the History of the Renaissance*

For most district 17 Reds, black and white, the years spent in the South proved to be pivotal. Like returning combat veterans many would have difficulty integrating what they'd experienced into the years to come. What, after all, could compete with larger than life confrontations with security guards, police officers, and southern judges? What could ever feel as good as even temporary victories gained over those who wanted you dead? Staying alive, especially in Alabama, came with an adrenaline rush.

While working for the party they'd admittedly often felt terrified, enraged, exhausted, or disgusted, but their mission infused their lives with the sort of meaning that conventional lifestyles could never deliver. Some would spend years reflecting on the choices they'd made, many continued to work for social justice in other venues, and still others strove to re-create themselves and win social acceptance.

In 1937, *Mack Coad*, first liaison to the Tallapoosa County sharecroppers, enlisted in the Abraham Lincoln Brigade. He served with the Mackenzie-Papineau Battalion to defend the Spanish Republic, under attack by General Francisco Franco's fascists. *Blaine Owen* (Boris Israel) and *Harold Forsha*, comrades from the Memphis organizing campaign, also volunteered for America's first (unofficial) integrated fighting unit. *Harry Haywood* (Haywood Hall), who'd served in France during the first World War, enlisted in the International Brigade's 15th Brigada Mixta unit at about the same time.

By the time Spain fell in 1939, the Abraham Lincoln Brigade had suffered a casualty rate greater than 50 percent, but Corporal Mack Coad, Private Harold Forsha, and Regimental Commissar Harry Haywood all made it home. Twenty-seven-year-old Blaine Owen, however, who'd been beaten and jailed in Birmingham, Selma, and Memphis and shot in Harlan County, Kentucky, was reported missing in action. He was believed to have been sent to a hospital near Barcelona, but there is no record of what happened to him after that.[1]

Mack Coad eventually returned to South Carolina and worked as a crane operator, a train fireman, and a coalminer. He was killed in a mining accident in 1967, still working at the age of seventy-three. Harold Forsha returned to Pennsylvania in 1939, served in World War II, raised a family, and died in Pittsburgh in 1977 at the age of seventy-one.

Harry Haywood served in the merchant marine during World War II; in 1956 he married historian Gwen Midlo and they had two children. Haywood had always been critical of Earl Browder's Popular Front policy and in 1957 began speaking out against both the CPUSA's decision to formally disavow the policy of self-determination in the Black Belt and Khrushchev's destalinization revolution. The party expelled him in 1959 and he later aligned with the new Chinese Communist Party. In 1978 he published his autobiography, *Black Bolshevik*. Haywood died on January 4, 1985, and was buried in Arlington National Cemetery.

In 1932, *Lowell* and *Jesse Wakefield* left Chattanooga to establish a regional ILD office in Seattle, Washington. Wakefield, who was not an attorney, made a bad judgment call that year in the case of Iver Moe, leader of a hunger march in Anacortes, Washington, which was coincidentally Lowell's hometown. During the march, Moe was arrested for raiding a grocery store. Wakefield believed that media pressure would be sufficient to get the charge dismissed and he did not get Moe a lawyer. Ultimately, Iver Moe went to prison.

Wakefield was replaced by Morris Rappaport.[2] He subsequently wrote for the *Daily Worker* and edited the *Voice of Action* until 1936, when he apparently left the party. In 1939 he enlisted in the navy; after the war he returned to Anacortes to manage the family salmon cannery business. He began experimenting with canning king crab, eventually making a fortune. After retiring in the early 1970s, Wakefield helped to develop quality-control legislation for the Pacific Northwest fishing industry. He and Jesse raised three children and Lowell died in 1977 at the age of sixty-eight.[3]

Jim and *Isabelle Allen* (Solomon Auerbach and Ida Kleiman/Helen Marcy) published the *Southern Worker* from July 1930 until autumn 1931. Allen replaced Harry Haywood as chair of the party's Negro Commission in 1938 and in 1941 was appointed foreign editor of the *Daily Worker*. Drafted in March

1944 at the age of thirty-eight, Allen was honorably discharged seven months later, as he was too old to be sent overseas and, as he often joked, too risky to be assigned to the Office of Strategic Services.

In 1946, he chaired the CPUSA Veterans' Commission, and from 1958 to 1966 served as general secretary of national programs. For fourteen years, Allen was executive editor of International Publishers, a Marxist press, where Isabelle served as educational director. They had one son, Jesse. After Isabelle died in 1972, Jim retired. Having written more than twenty books on black history, philosophy, and political science, he died in 1986 at the age of eighty.[4]

In 1939 *Sid Benson* (Solomon Bernstein/Ted Wellman) returned to his native New York City to work with the Group Theater Collective. His colleagues there included Lee Strasberg, Clifford Odetts, and Elia Kazan. Kazin recalled that Benson (who he knew as Ted Wellman) looked "like a boxer whose sole purpose in the ring was to be the punching bag for one opponent or another."[5]

Benson married Elizabeth Savage in the 1940s; they made their home in Greenwich Village, where he taught at the Communist Workers School on East Fourteenth Street.

Nat Ross (Rosenberg) left district 17 in 1935 to become secretary of district 9 (Minnesota, North and South Dakota), where he organized for the Farm Labor Party while his wife Janet worked with the Minneapolis Theater Union. In 1939 they moved to Moscow, where he worked for the Comintern and she wrote for the *Daily Worker* under the name Janet Weaver. In 1946, they returned to the States and Ross went back to Birmingham as the party's southern director. He resigned from the party in 1954 and subsequently became a successful businessman.[6]

Rabbi Benjamin Goldstein (George B. Stern/Ben Lowell) left Montgomery in 1932. Three years later, still unable to find a congregation in New York City, he took his family to Los Angeles, where he got work as a film distributor for Artkino Pictures.

In 1945 the Goldsteins divorced. Two years later he married Juliet Lowell and took her surname. They moved back to New York, where in 1948 Ben Lowell was appointed administrative assistant for the B'Nai Brith Hillel Foundation. That year he spoke at a Joint Anti-Fascist Refugee Committee testimonial dinner honoring Dr. Edwin Barsky, who'd been director of International Medical Services during the Spanish Civil War. Barsky was subpoenaed by HUAC and ordered to turn over not only the names of Americans who'd donated to the Lincoln Brigade, but also of those still working underground in Spain. He chose to go to prison in 1950 rather than release the files. Goldstein's tribute to Barsky cost him his job.

After a failed second marriage, the rabbi found a congregation in Elmhurst, Queens, but his contract was not renewed. He briefly led another congregation in Cuba before moving to San Francisco in 1953 to live with his sister. He died there of leukemia at the age of fifty-two.[7]

In 1936, *Jane Speed* attended the Communist National Training School in upstate New York, where she met and fell in love with Cesar Andrew Iglesias, president of the Puerto Rican Communist Party. In 1937, they married and in 1939 Jane, Cesar, and her mother moved Puerto Rico.

Using the surname Speed de Andreu, Jane worked in the rural districts with Partido Comunista Puertorriqueno, an underground women's organization. Fluent in Spanish, she would identify herself as a Tampax sales representative in order to scatter the men and give her time alone with the women.

In 1954, Jane and Iglesias were briefly imprisoned after four members of the Puerto Rican National Party demanding independence for Puerto Rico opened fire in the U.S. House of Representatives and wounded five members of Congress. The Puerto Rican territorial government subsequently ordered mass arrests of local nationalists and Communists; Jane and her husband were among them. They had one son, Nicholas. Jane died of a cerebral hemorrhage in 1958 at the age of forty-eight. Her mother, Darlie, died four years later. Caesar Iglesias worked in Puerto Rico as a journalist, novelist, and playwright and lived there until 1970.[8]

In 1937 the ILD dispatched *William Patterson* to Chicago to establish the Workers' School. A decade later he returned to New York City to serve as national secretary for the Civil Rights Congress (CRC), successor to the merged ILD and National Negro Congress.

Patterson led his staff in defending controversial clients like Willie McGee, a black man accused of raping a white housewife in Laurel, Mississippi; the Martinsville Seven, seven young black men accused of raping a white woman in Martinsville, Virginia; and the Trenton Six, six black men alleged to have beaten William Horner, a white small-business owner, to death in Trenton, New Jersey.

The outcomes were universally tragic. By 1951, Willie McGee and the Martinsville Seven had been executed. On August 6, 1949, Patterson appealed to the New Jersey Supreme Court in the Trenton Six case after four of them were declared guilty. He managed to get the lower court decision reversed and deferred to his nemesis, Walter White. They agreed that the NAACP would handle the new trial. HUAC had cited the CRC as a disloyal and subversive organization and Patterson feared that would negatively impact the appeal. Three years later, on June 14, 1951, all four were exonerated.

Patterson subsequently took the CRC into the international arena when he indicted the United States for genocide. Arguing that the postwar Nuremburg Trials had established the principle of collective guilt, he applied it to the U.S. government.[9] He delivered his petition, "We Charge Genocide" to United Nations delegates at the Palais de Chaillot in Paris on December 17, 1951. His friend and colleague Paul Robeson simultaneously delivered a copy to the United Nations in New York City.

"The federal government claimed it had nothing to do with lynchings," one CPUSA official commented, "but the petition said, you knew about it and you did nothing." Patterson had documented nearly every lynching since the Civil War and he'd cited ongoing conspiracies to deny blacks the right to vote by using poll taxes, literacy tests, and terrorism. He maintained that by the United Nations' own definition, "any intent to destroy, in whole or part, a national, racial or religious group is genocide." Patterson's passport was subsequently revoked, he was charged with disloyalty and subpoenaed to appear before the House Committee on Un-American Activities. In 1956 the CRC was dissolved. When Patterson was again summoned before HUAC in 1959, he calmly responded, "Let me assure you that your hatred for what I represent can never equal my contempt for that for which your committee stands."[10]

Defiant to the end, he died on March 5, 1980, at Union Hospital in the Bronx at the age of eighty-nine.

Al Murphy (Albert Jackson), former president of the Alabama Share Croppers' Union, returned from an assignment in the Soviet Union in 1937 to work with Harlem's Scottsboro Defense Committee. A year later he was sent to St. Louis, Missouri, as a National Training School instructor. In January 1939, he and

Owen Whitfield, black former vice president of the Southern Tenant Farmers' Union, organized the Committee for the Rehabilitation of Sharecroppers to assist 1,700 displaced croppers who were living in makeshift tents, improvised shelters, church basements, and abandoned barns along Highways 60 and 61 around Swamp East, near Sikeston, Missouri. Securing funding from the CIO, the Urban League, and the Federated Council of Churches, by June Murphy and Whitfield had purchased ninety acres near New Madrid, Missouri, where they relocated many of the families.[11]

In 1940, Murphy ran (unsuccessfully) for lieutenant governor of Missouri on the CPUSA ticket. Two years later he protested the lynching of Cleo Wright, a young black Sikeston, Missouri, man arrested for attempting to rape a white woman. Although the police repeatedly shot him, Wright survived, only to be kidnapped from his jail cell, tied to the bumper of a pickup truck, and dragged to the center of town, where a mob literally burned him alive. His gruesome murder was one of the many cases that fueled the "Double V" campaign during the Second World War—the demand that victory over European fascism abroad include victory over racism at home. Murphy later worked in St. Louis as a porter, a sheet metal worker, a meat-packer, and a night watchman before returning to Sikeston in 1951. He died there in 1978.[12]

Hosea Hudson began working for the CIO Steel Workers' Organizing Committee in 1936. From 1942 to 1945 he served as president of the Steel Workers Local in Ensley, Alabama, and as a delegate to the Birmingham Industrial Union Council. After his appointment to the National Committee of the Communist Party in 1945, he lost his job at the Alabama Foundry Company and his position on the union council. His wife, Sophie, divorced him the following year, and he moved to New York City in 1954, where he found work as a mason and a janitor. Hudson remarried in 1965; he and his wife made their home in Atlantic City, New Jersey, until 1984, when they retired to Florida. He died there in 1988.[13]

Rob Hall, discharged from the army in 1946, was appointed managing editor of the *Daily Worker* that year. He later became its Washington correspondent. Hall resigned from the party in 1954 after reports of Stalin's atrocities were confirmed. He subsequently moved to the Adirondack region of New York state with his wife Euphemia (Mickey) and their five children, joined the Republican Party, and in 1962 began publishing *Adirondack Life* magazine. Eight years later, Hall was named editor of the *Conservationist*, a journal of the New York State Department of Environmental Conservation. He also served as publicity director for the Essex County Republican Committee.[14]

In 1987 he completed an oral history with professor Robin Kelley. Hall, who virtually never expressed regret, shared with Kelley some of the guilt he felt about the Tallapoosa County sharecroppers. He said that before being appointed to district 17, he'd worked in Kansas and Nebraska and had written extensively about how the wheat and dairy farmers there suffered from the unintended consequences of the Agricultural Adjustment Act. They'd impressed him with their battles against foreclosures and with their willingness to disrupt law enforcement and bypass the judicial process by setting up "penny auctions." They would show up at a farm auction holding pitchforks and shotguns to discourage outsiders from bidding on the property, then buy it back themselves for one cent.

Almost fifty years later, Hall still wondered if enthusiastic party comrades like his younger self, overly encouraged by the success of the farm holiday movement, hadn't set up the Camp Hill and Reeltown croppers to openly defy southern planters. The midwestern farmers could count on local support, something that was never available to the Alabama sharecroppers. They were on their own in the Black Belt, and the failed 1935 strike had proved devastating. Hall was still haunted by the possibility that Al Murphy had been right all along when he argued that the ASCU should remain an underground movement.[15]

Hall died on August 27, 1993.

Joe Gelders was discharged from the army after World War II and moved his family to California, where he became an instructor at the UC Davis while he completed his PhD in physics on the GI Bill. In 1949 the university implemented a loyalty oath, and Gelders was fired the following year for refusing to sign it. He died a year later at age fifty-two after suffering a series of heart attacks. An autopsy revealed that the 1935 flogging he'd suffered in Birmingham not only damaged his heart muscle but had also crushed his chest. Long-term complications from those injuries had shortened his life.[16]

Joseph Brodsky, chief counsel for the International Labor Defense during the Scottsboro trials, became a founding member of the National Lawyers' Guild in 1937. An alternative to the American Bar Association, the guild was the first racially integrated attorneys' organization in the nation.

In April 1946, Brodsky was appointed to the National Board of the Civil Rights Congress, where he worked with his old friend William Patterson. When Brodsky died on July 28, 1947, Vito Marcantonio, member of Congress from East Harlem, eulogized him as "my friend whose name is a synonym to many of devotion to the common people. We will carry on the fight he left us to finish."[17]

Brodsky's sometimes-partner *Samuel Leibowitz*, lead counsel for the Scottsboro teens' appeals, was elected justice of Kings County (Brooklyn) Court in December 1940. Reelected in 1954, he was appointed to the New York State Supreme Court in 1962. Justice Leibowitz developed a reputation as one of the toughest judges in the city. He would often berate prosecutors, defense attorneys, police officers, and sometimes other judges and was an outspoken advocate for the death penalty. Leibowitz ran unsuccessfully for mayor of New York City twice, retired in 1969, and died on January 11, 1978, at the age of eighty-four. He lived to see Alabama governor George Wallace pardon Clarence Norris, the last living Scottsboro defendant, in 1976.

Finally, and ironically, on election night 2008, the African American Macedonian Church of God in Christ in Springfield, Massachusetts, burned to the ground. Two months later, three white men were charged with arson. They said they'd been enraged by the election of Barak Obama.

The church's seventy-four-year-old pastor, Bishop Bryant Robinson Jr., was the grandson of Preacher Tom Robinson, who'd been murdered by a white posse in Emelle, Alabama, in 1931. He was also the grandnephew of Esau Robinson, who'd been lynched there. Bishop Robinson's parents had moved the family to Massachusetts over seventy years earlier to ensure their safety.[18]

NOTES

Prologue

1. Allen, *Organizing*, 128–29.
2. Draper, *Roots*, 1.
3. Ibid.
4. Howe and Coser, *American Communist Party*:; Klehr, *Heyday*; Klehr and Haynes, *American Communist Movement*.
5. Isserman, *If I Had a Hammer*; Isserman, *Which Side On?*; Kelley, *Hammer and Hoe*; Solomon, *Cry Was Unity*.
6. Maurice Isserman quoted in Storch, "Moscow's Archives." Kazin, *American Dreamers*.
7. O'Connor, *Mysteries and Manners*, 81.

Backstory

1. Postgate, *Bolshevik Theory*, 184.
2. Haywood, *Black Bolshevik*, 234.

Chapter 1. District 17 Headquarters

1. Painter, *Narrative*, 373.
2. Herndon, *Let Me Live*.
3. Ibid., 85. See also Herndon, *You Cannot Kill the Working Class*, 13.
4. T. Johnson, "We Are Illegal Here," 475. See also Pennybacker, *From Scottsboro to Munich*, 21.
5. *Southern Worker*, October 4, 1930.
6. "Report of Comrade Tom Johnson to Politboro [sic], May 1931," quoted in T. Johnson, "We Are Illegal Here," 464.
7. Davidson, "Sociologist in Eden," 110.
8. For background about the sharecropping system, see Rogers, *One-Gallused Rebellion*, 11–14, and H. Mitchell, *Mean Things*, 47–50.
9. Robinson, *Bridge*, 57.
10. *Southern Worker*, January 17, 1931, 2.
11. Ibid.
12. C. Martin, *Angelo Herndon Case*, 7–8.
13. Newton, *White Robes*, 75.

14. Herndon, "You Cannot Kill the Working Class," 17–18.
15. Ibid., 19.
16. Harris, "Running," 21–25. See also *Daily Worker*, June 3, 1935.
17. *Daily Worker*, July 17, 1931.
18. Allen, *Negro Question*, 177.

Chapter 2. The *Southern Worker* and the Dynamo of Dixie

1. Allen, *Organizing*, 33–38.
2. Hamilton, "Chattanooga's Radical History."
3. Schechter, "How Solomon Schechter's Daughter."
4. Carter, *Scottsboro*, 54–55.
5. Allen, *Organizing*, 39–40; *Southern Worker*, November 22, 1930.
6. Shay, *Judge Lynch*, 121–25.
7. *Macon (MO) Chronicle Herald*, July 5, 1930; *Big Spring (TX) Daily Herald*, July 6, 1930, 1, 6.
8. Stefani Evans, "Family's Encounter with Racism Recalled," *Las Vegas Sun*, December 8, 2008.
9. *Lawrence (KS) Daily Journal*, July 5, 1930, 1.
10. *St. Petersburg (FL) Independent*, July 5, 1930.
11. Raper, *Tragedy*, 66.
12. *Southern Worker*, July 14, 1931, 2.
13. Segrave, *Lynchings*, 158–62.
14. Raper, *Tragedy*, 68.
15. *Southern Worker*, August 30, 1930.
16. Ibid., 1, 2.
17. Willie, "Walter R. Chivers," 245.
18. Raper, *Tragedy*, 60–61.
19. *Southern Worker*, October 18, 1930.
20. Raper, *Tragedy*, 70–71.
21. Ibid., 74.
22. Willie, "Walter R. Chivers," 246. Long, *Against Us*, 29–32.
23. *Southern Worker*, November 15, 1930.
24. Ibid.
25. *Southern Worker*, December 5, 1930.
26. Ibid.
27. Raper, *Tragedy*, 82.

Chapter 3. Scottsboro

1. Acker, *Scottsboro*, 19.
2. *Huntsville Times*, March 25, 1931.

3. Patterson, *Man*, 129.
4. Carter, *Scottsboro*, 24.
5. Acker, *Scottsboro*, 25.
6. Janken, *White*, 150.
7. Allen, *Smash the Scottsboro Lynch Verdict*.
8. Wilson, "Freight Car Case."
9. Acker, *Scottsboro*, 40. See also *Amsterdam News*, July 16, 1930, 2.
10. *Birmingham Age Herald*, June 18, 1931. *Montgomery Advertiser*, April 14, 1931, 4.
11. Arthur Raper quoted in Goodman, *Stories*, 297. Mazzari, *Southern Modernist*, 169–70.
12. Allen, *Organizing in The Depression South*, 82–85.
13. Solomon, *Cry Was Unity*, 198.
14. Hollace Ransdell, "Report on the Scottsboro, Alabama Case," ACLU, New York City, May 21, 1931, p. 3, frame 175, reel 3, part 6, "Scottsboro Case 1931–1950," Papers of the NAACP.
15. Ibid., May 27, 1931, p. 19.
16. Ibid., 20–21.
17. Broeg, "Belle versus Beast," 208–10.
18. Ransdell, "Report," 11.
19. Ibid., 21.
20. Braden, "Free Thomas Wansley."

Chapter 4. An All-Purpose Jesus

1. Marx, "Contribution," 175.
2. Davies, *Infected Christianity*, 106. Matt. 19:30 (AV).
3. Grubbs, *Cry*, 65–68.
4. R. Martin, "Prophet's Pilgrimage," 521.
5. Haselden, *Mandate*, 40.
6. Ibid., 40–41.
7. Evans, "Klan Spiritual," 3.
8. Baker, *Gospel*, 28–30.
9. Wright, "Klansman's Criterion."
10. Feldman, "Beginning," 135.
11. Oppenheimer, *Exit Right*, 51.

Chapter 5. The Massacre at Camp Hill

1. *Crisis*, March 1936, 75.
2. Mjangkij, *Organizing Black America*, 25–27.
3. TAM 218, box 3, folder 2, Solomon and Kaufman files.
4. Rosengarten, *All God's Dangers*, 57–59.

5. Wilson, "Freight Car Case."
6. Carter, *Scottsboro*, 121–23. See also Allen, *Organizing*, 89–90.
7. Allen, *Organizing*, 71.
8. Beecher, "Share Cropper Union," 125.
9. *Crisis*, March 1936, 75, 92.
10. Feldman, *Irony*, 262.
11. Watkins, *Hungry Years*, 145–46.
12. *New York Times*, July 18, 1931. *Time*, July 27, 1931.
13. *New York Times*, May 29 and July 24, 1931.
14. Stone, "Agrarian Conflict," 523. Allen, *Organizing*, 73.
15. Chiassen, *Press*, 18.
16. Stone, "Agrarian Conflict," 525.
17. Carter, *Scottsboro*, 127.
18. *New York Times*, July 19, 1931.
19. Ibid.
20. Ibid., July 25, 1931.
21. Solomon, *Cry*, 123.
22. Allen, *Organizing*, 74
23. Howard Kester to Walter White, August 15, 1931, letter accompanying Kester's final report, part 6, reel 23, file 1, NAACP Legal Files.
24. John Henry Calhoun, *Indianapolis Record*, August 1, 1931.

Chapter 6. The National Miners' Union, Southeastern Kentucky

1. Herndon, *Let Me Live*, 131.
2. Ibid., 129–31. See also Herndon, *You Cannot Kill the Working Class*, 17. See also *Southern Worker*, March 7, 1931.
3. *Selma Times Journal* headline quoted in Herndon, *Let Me Live*, 139.
4. Allen, *Organizing*, 33.
5. Portelli, *They Say in Harlan County*, 189–92.
6. "Pittsburgh Convention."
7. Finley Donaldson quoted in the *Scranton-Republican* (Scranton, PA), November 9, 1931, 2.
8. Portelli, *They Say in Harlan County*, 195–96.
9. Soodalter, "Price of Coal."
10. *Kentucky Miners' Struggle*, 10.
11. Portelli, *They Say in Harlan County*, 187.
12. Dreiser, *Harlan Miners*, 81. Gannes, *Kentucky Miners*, 9–10.
13. West, "Romantic Appalachia," 213–14.
14. Portelli, *They Say in Harlan County*, 75.

15. Dreiser, *Harlan Miners*, ix.
16. Gannes, *Kentucky Miners*, 28. See also *Kentucky Miners' Struggle*.
17. Gannes, *Kentucky Miners*, 2.
18. Testimony of James C. Garland, "Hearings before Subcommittee of the Committee on Manufacturers," U.S. Senate 32nd Cong., May 11, 12, 13, and 19, 1932 (LaFollette Committee), May 11, 1932.
19. Cowley, "Kentucky Coal Town."
20. Bethell, foreword, 5–6.
21. Sullivan, *Days of Hope*, 78–79.
22. Hevener, *Which Side?*, 80–81.
23. Weller, *Yesterday's People*, 130.
24. Ibid., 131.
25. Callahan, *Work and Faith*, 187. Portelli, *They Say in Harlan County*, 205.
26. *Advocate Messenger* (Danville, KY), February 29, 1932.

Chapter 7. The Shades Mountain Rape and Murders

1. For background on the Shades Mountain Murders, see Kelley, *Hammer and Hoe*, 83–90, and Morrison, *Murder*.
2. *Birmingham News*, August 6, 1931.
3. *Labor Defender*, April 1, 1934, 5.
4. Ibid.
5. *Labor Defender*, April 1, 1934, 5, 19. See also Herndon, *Let Me Live*, 148–57.
6. *Southern Worker*, August 15, 1931.
7. Herndon, *Let Me Live*, 163.
8. Charles Hamilton Houston, "Confidential Memo, the State v Peterson, Birmingham Alabama, September 2, 1933," August Meir Papers.
9. Ibid.
10. *Southern Worker*, December 9, 1931, 2.
11. "Was Victim Shot to Seal His Lips?," *Pittsburgh (PA) Courier*, October 17, 1931, 1.
12. Ibid.
13. Ibid.
14. Ibid.
15. Herndon, "You Cannot Kill the Working Class," 19–20.
16. "Willie Peterson Trials," folder 0021524-024-0542, Papers of the NAACP.
17. Part 6, group I, series D, reels 23 and 24, legal files, "Willie Peterson Trials," Papers of the NAACP.
18. Charles McPherson to Walter White, December 9, 1931, series D, box D65, part 06, legal files, Cases Supported: Willie Peterson 1931–1937, Papers of the NAACP.

19. *Southern Worker*, January 16, 1932.

20. Roderick Beddow to Walter White, March 1, 1932, Correspondence, part 06, folder 001469-015-002, "Willie Peterson Trials," Papers of the NAACP.

21. Ibid.

22. Kelley, *Hammer and Hoe*, 84.

23. *Tuscaloosa News*, May 18, 1933, 4.

24. Oscar W. Adams Sr., *Birmingham Reporter*, April 1, 1933.

25. Houston, "Confidential Memo."

26. Box 144, file 8, August Meir Papers.

27. *Evening Independent* (St. Petersburg, FL), March 9, 1933. See also *Southern Worker*, October 17, 1931.

28. July 1933, "Scottsboro Case," Papers of the NAACP.

29. Charles Hamilton Houston to Robert Moton, July 29, 1933, box 144, file 8, August Meir Papers. *Southern Worker*, February 10, 1934, 2.

30. Horne, *Black Revolutionary*, 48.

31. Ibid., 48.

32. *Pittsburgh (PA) Courier*, January 20, 1934, 6.

33. *Southern Worker*, February 10, 1934.

34. *Labor Defender*, January 1934, 2.

35. John W. Altman to Charles McPherson, box 144, folder 8, August Meir Papers.

36. *Southern Worker*, March 25, 1934.

37. *San Antonio Register*, March 16, 1934.

38. *Southern Worker*, March 25, 1934.

39. Walter White to Robert Moton, February 5, 1934, box 144, August Meir Papers.

40. *Tuscaloosa News*, March 6, 1934.

Chapter 8. Staying the Course

1. Pennybacker, *From Scottsboro to Munich*, 25. See also Allen, *Organizing*, 127.

2. Pennybacker, *From Scottsboro to Munich*, 22.

3. Alice Burke (Jarvis), oral history.

4. Kelley, *Hammer and Hoe*, 25.

5. Solomon, *Cry Was Unity*, 118.

6. Painter, *Narrative of Hosea Hudson*, 110–13.

7. Lawson, "In Dixie Land."

8. Kelley, "Comrades Praise Gawd," 62–63.

9. *Militant* 5, no. 51 (December 31, 1932): 2. And Burke (Jarvis), oral history.

10. Rosen and Rosengarten, "Shootout at Reeltown."

11. Allen, *Organizing*, 76.

12. Kelley, *Tell Me More*.

13. Brooks, *Boycotts, Buses, and Passes*, 124.

14. Ibid., 125.
15. Theoharis, *Rebellious Life*, 15. See also McGuire, *At the Dark End*, 11–13.
16. Jankin, *White*, 152. See Also Dray, *At the Hands*, 310.
17. Folder 27, Olive M. Stone Papers.
18. Olive M. Stone, 3B oral history interview.
19. Ibid., 4B.
20. N. Read and D. Read, *Deep Family*, 240–42.
21. Ibid., 213–21.
22. Stanton, *Hand of Esau*, 69–70.
23. Ibid., 71. L. Kaufman, "Beatrice Holzman Schneiderman."
24. Hollis, *Alabama Newspaper Tradition*, 78.
25. Stone, *Agrarian Conflict*, 522.
26. Harris, "Running," 31.

Chapter 9. Reeltown Radicals

1. "What Happened in Tallapoosa County?"
2. Solomon, *Cry Was Unity*, 225.
3. Gray, *Tuskegee Syphilis Study*, 74–76.
4. "What Happened in Tallapoosa County?"
5. Lelyveld, *Omaha Blues*, 103.
6. Ibid., 103.
7. Shapiro, *White Violence*, 234. See also Carter, *Scottsboro*, 176–78, and Kelley, *Hammer and Hoe*, 49–51.
8. Shapiro, *White Violence*, 234.
9. For background material on the AAA, see Biles, *South and the New Deal*, 39–47.
10. Biles, *South*, 40.
11. John P. Davis, "Black Inventory."

Chapter 10. Reversals and Bombshells

1. Chambers, *Witness*, 221–24, 232–34. See also Tanenhaus, *Whittaker Chambers*, 58.
2. Goodman, *Stories*, 101.
3. Acker, *Scottsboro*, 54.
4. Acker, *Scottsboro*, 55.
5. Ibid., 54–56.
6. Ibid.
7. Rossi, "First Scottsboro Trials."
8. Allen, *Organizing*, 302–5.
9. Goodman, *Stories*, 120.
10. Ibid., 124.
11. Carter, "Reasonable Doubt."

12. Jonathan Daniels, *Raleigh News and Observer*, April 8, 1933. Quoted in Goodman, *Stories*, 172.
13. Ibid.
14. John Spivak, *Daily Worker*, April 10, 1933.
15. *Montgomery Examiner*, April 6, 1933. Carter, *Scottsboro*, 259.
16. Stanton, *Hand of Esau*, 69–70.
17. Stanton, *Journey toward Justice*, 112.
18. Olive M. Stone, 4B oral history interview.
19. Fosl, "Life and Times." N. Read and D. Read, *Deep Family*, 17–20.
20. Stone, 4B oral history interview.
21. *New York World Telegram*, August 5, 1933.
22. Linder, "Without Fear or Favor," 567.
23. Reynolds, *Courtroom*, 280.
24. Isadore Schneider, *Labor Defender* 11, no 8 (August 1933): 30.
25. Ibid.
26. Linder, "Without Fear of Favor."
27. Bellamy, "Scottsboro Boys," 32.
28. Solomon, *Cry Was Unity*, 245–47.
29. Leibowitz quoted in Acker, *Scottsboro*, 142–23. Carter, *Scottsboro*, 312.
30. Damon, "Scottsboro."
31. Carter, *Scottsboro*, 244.

Chapter 11. Justice for Angelo Herndon

1. This chapter relies primarily on Herndon's autobiography, *Let Me Live*, published by Random House, New York City, 1937.
2. Herndon, *Let Me Live*, 203,345.
3. Ibid., 205.
4. T. Johnson, "We Are Illegal Here," 462.
5. Herndon, *Let Me Live*, 228.
6. *Southern Exposure* review.
7. Angelo Herndon quoted in C. Martin, *Angelo Herndon Case*, 52.
8. Herndon, *Let Me Live*, 346.
9. Ibid., 238.
10. Ibid., 250.
11. Ibid., 352.
12. *Labor Defender*, August 1935, 8,10.
13. Mack, *Representing the Race*, 170.
14. C. Martin, *Angelo Herndon Case*, 140–41.
15. C. Martin, *Angelo Herndon Case*, 168.
16. Ford, "Let My People Live."

17. George H. Dession, "The Making of a Radical," *Saturday Review*, April 3, 1937, 11. Rose C. Field, *New York Herald Tribune*, March 14, 1937. Correspondence, box 1, folder 6, *Let Me Live*, Angelo Herndon Papers.

18. L. Jackson, *Ralph Ellison*, 345–46.

Chapter 12. Big Sandy: A Murder and Two Lynchings

1. Dray, *At the Hands*, 318.
2. *Tuscaloosa News*, June 15, 1933.
3. Ibid.
4. *Tuscaloosa News*, June 18, 1933.
5. *Tuscaloosa News*, June 15, 1933.
6. Ibid.
7. Bellamy, "Scottsboro Boys."
8. Hollars, *Thirteen Loops*, 19.
9. Raper, *Plight of Tuscaloosa*, 13.
10. *Harlem Liberator*, August 19, 1933.
11. Sharpe, "Tuscaloosa," 20.
12. Taub, "Prelude."
13. Ibid., 6.
14. Cunard, *Essays*, 212.
15. Taub, "Prelude," 6.
16. Ibid.
17. *Southern Worker*, September 20, 1933.
18. Cason, *Ninety Degrees*, 31.
19. McDonough, "Men and Women," 92–93.
20. Terry and Simms, *They Live on the Land*, xxxiii–xxxv.
21. Kelley, *Hammer and Hoe*, 88.
22. Shapiro, *White Violence*, 226.
23. *Chicago Tribune*, August 14, 1933, 7.
24. Raper, *Plight of Tuscaloosa*, 22.
25. Ibid., 32.
26. Dray, *At the Hands*, 320.
27. *Tuscaloosa News*, August 14, 1933, 1.
28. Ibid.
29. *Southern Worker*, September 20, 1933, 1–2.
30. Sharpe, "Tuscaloosa," 25.
31. *Southern Worker*, November 15, 1933.
32. *Labor Defender* 9, no. 9 (October 1933): 3.
33. Hollars, *Thirteen Loops*, 32.
34. *Time*, August 21, 1933, 10.

35. N. Ross, "NRA in the South."

36. *Southern Worker*, November 15, 1933.

Chapter 13. The Lynching of Dennis Cross

1. For background on Alice Johnson, see Raper, *Plight of Tuscaloosa*, 26–39.

2. NCDPP Briefing 2, November 17, 1933, p. 2, part 06, "Lynchings in Tuscaloosa," file 001-524-002-0101, NAACP Legal Files.

3. Raper, *Plight of Tuscaloosa*, 28.

4. Ibid., 30.

5. *Tuscaloosa News*, October 16, 1933.

6. Hollars, *Thirteen Loops*, 22.

7. Briefs dated November 10 and 17, 1933, both in part 6, "Lynchings in Tuscaloosa," November 1, 1933, to December 31, 1933, folder 001-524-002-0101, NAACP Legal Files. *San Antonio Register*, November 3, 1933, 1.

8. NCDPP Brief 2, November 19, 1933, 3, part 06, "Lynchings in Tuscaloosa," file 001-524-002-0101, NAACP Legal Files.

9. "Lynchings in Tuscaloosa, National Committee for the Defense of Political Prisoners, Alfred Hirsch Report," November 19, 1933, NAACP Papers.

10. *Pittsburgh (PA) Courier*, December 23, 1933.

11. Raper, *Plight of Tuscaloosa*, 37.

12. Ibid., 38.

13. Ibid., 37.

14. Ibid., 39.

15. Ibid., 39.

Chapter 14. Memphis: Mayhem and Mistaken Identity

1. Murphy, "Achievement and Tasks," 142–43.

2. Honey, *Southern Labor* 54. Charges against the Atlanta Six were not officially dropped until August 30, 1939.

3. Honey, *Going Down Jericho Road*, 12–14.

4. Haywood, *Black Communist*, 205.

5. Ibid., 207.

6. Fannie Henderson's affidavit quoted in Honey, *Black Workers* 22.

7. Honey, *Southern Labor*, 56.

8. Biles, *Memphis* 120.

Chapter 15. Reaping the Whirlwind

1. Lorence, *Unemployed People's Movement*, 139–40.

2. Adams, *James A. Dombrowski*, 89–93.

3. Ingalls, "Anti-Radical Violence."

4. Jamison, *Labor Unionism*, 298.
5. A. Jackson, "You Can Kill Me."
6. Kelley, *Hammer and Hoe*, 165–66.
7. Annie Mae Merriweather quoted in W. Kaufman, *Woody Guthrie*, 41.
8. Wood, *To Live and Die in Dixie*, 28–31.
9. Ibid., 31.
10. Shapiro, *White Violence*, 236.
11. Wood, *To Live and Die in Dixie*, 29.
12. *Montgomery Advertiser* quoted in A. Jackson, "You Can Kill Me." Olive Stone, "A Survey of Civil Rights in the South: A Summary for 1934–5, Chapel Hill: Southern Committee for People's Rights, April 1936, p. 12, Olive M. Stone Papers.
13. *Southern Farm Leader*, December 7, 1935.
14. Straus, "Enter the Cotton Picker," 390.
15. Scales and Nickson, *Cause at Heart*, 78.
16. Purcell, *White Collar Radicals*, 50–51.
17. Horne, *Black Revolutionary*, 65–68.
18. Kelley, *Hammer and Hoe*, 171–72.
19. Biles, *South and the New Deal*, 49–50.
20. Linder, "Without Fear or Favor."

Chapter 16. A Popular Front

1. Painter, *Narrative of Hosea Hudson*, 243, 245.
2. Ottanelli, *Communist Party*, 83–84.
3. Post, "Popular Front."
4. Ryan, *Earl Browder*, 103–4.
5. Wechsler, *Age of Suspicion*, 85–86.
6. Hall, "Earl Browder."
7. McWhorter, *Carry Me Home*, 43.
8. Ingalls, "Anti-Radical Violence," 538–41.
9. Feldman, *Politics, Society*, 242–43.
10. Gelders, "Teachings of Marx," 49.
11. Ingalls, "Anti-Radical Violence," 529.
12. Rittenberg, "We're C.I.O.s."
13. Gelders, "Teachings of Marx," 51.
14. Ingalls, "Anti-Radical Violence," 532–33.
15. Scales and Nickson, *Cause at Heart*, 120.
16. Ingalls, "Anti-Radical Violence," 536.
17. Pat Barr, "Disarm Industry," *Southern Worker*, March 1937, 6.
18. Ibid.
19. Ottanelli, *Communist Party*, 116.

20. Raymond, "Prairie Fire," 975.
21. Ibid.
22. Ibid.
23. Haywood, *Black Communist*, 199–200.
24. Virginia Durr, oral history interview.
25. Sullivan, *Days of Hope*, 61.
26. Sosna, *In Search*, 88–104, quotation on 90.
27. Egerton, *Speak Now against the Day*, 188.
28. Kenneth Douty, "The Southern Conference for Human Welfare," SCHW Collection.
29. Reed, *Simple Decency*, 50.
30. Krueger, *And Promises*, 33.
31. Grover Hall quoted in ibid., 33. See also Feldman, *Irony*, 142.
32. Kelley, *Hammer and Hoe*, 189.
33. Hall, "Southern Conference," 64–65.
34. *Montgomery Advertiser*, December 15, 1938, 2.
35. Governor Grover Hall quoted in Hall, "Southern Conference," 64–65.
36. Douty, "Southern Conference."

Chapter 17. A Culture of Opposition

1. Ryan, *Browder*, 125, 186.
2. Ibid., 127. Horne, *Black Revolutionary*, 86.
3. Kelley, *Hammer and Hoe*, 195.
4. Kelley, "Jacksons," 178.
5. Ibid.
6. Salmond, *Miss Lucy*, 78. See also Smith, "Sit-Down Strikes."
7. Lenin, "Marxism and Reformism."
8. Taylor, *History*, 147.
9. Flynt, *Alabama Baptists*, 375.
10. Cohen and Capaldi, *Pete Seeger Reader*, 57.
11. Fried, *Communism in America*, 49–50.
12. "How Alabama Newspapers Failed to Cover Segregation in 1963," *Guardian*, November 11, 2011.
13. Smith, "1930's."
14. Brown, *Standing against Dragons*, 94.
15. Connor, "Birmingham Wars."
16. Brown, *Standing against Dragons*, 93.

Chapter 18. All Things Considered . . .

1. G. Johnson, "Why Communists," 93.
2. "Scottsboro—What Now?"

3. Acker, *Scottsboro*, 154.

4. Draper, "Communists and Miners," 391.

5. Charles Hamilton Houston, "An Approach to Better Race Relations," speech to YWCA Convention, May 5, 1934, Philadelphia, Pennsylvania, www.law.cornell.edu/houston/ywcatxt.htm.

6. Moon, *Balance of Power*, 123.

7. Kazin, *American Dreamers*, 156.

8. Nikita Khrushchev quoted in Harrison Salisbury, "Khrushchev Talk on Stalin Bares Details of Rule Based on Terror," *New York Times*, June 5, 1956, 1.

9. Steve Nelson quoted in Fried, *Communism in America*, 394–95.

10. Horne, *Black Revolutionary*, 11, 216.

Chapter 19. The Rest of Life

1. Abraham Lincoln Brigade Archives (ALBA), www.alba-valb.org; also Abraham Lincoln Brigade Archives.

2. "Investigation of Communist Activities in the Seattle, Washington Area, Part 2," Hearings before the Committee on Un-American Activities, U.S. House of Representatives, 84th Cong., 1st Sess., March 18 and 19, 1955, p. 421.

3. Alvarez, "How Lowell Wakefield."

4. Guide to the James S. Allen Papers.

5. Elia Kazan quoted in Schwartz, *Marilyn Revealed*, 58.

6. Kelley, *Hammer and Hoe*, 125, 225. See also Klehr, Haynes, and Firsov, *Secret World*, 287–88.

7. Lelyveld, *Omaha Blues*, 154–60.

8. Fosl, "Life and Times." See also "Rosario Morales, 1930–2011," obituary, Puerto Rican Students Association, posted by Aurora Levins Morales, April 2011, www.PuertoAmericanStudies.org.

9. Horne, *Black Revolutionary*, 97.

10. Wheeler, "We Charge Genocide." Article 3, Genocide Convention, approved by UN General Assembly December 9, 1948. Horne, *Black Revolutionary*, 169.

11. Roll, *Spirit of Rebellion*, 148.

12. Capeci, *Lynching of Cleo Wright*.

13. Painter, *Narrative of Hosea Hudson*, 341–62.

14. Kelley, *Hammer and Hoe*, 125–26.

15. Rob Hall, oral history.

16. Ingalls, "Flogging."

17. Meyer, *Vito Marcantonio*, 14.

18. Don Barry, "Up from the Ashes: The Hate That Does Not Win," *New York Times*, September 25, 2011.

BIBLIOGRAPHY

Archival Collections and Oral Histories

Abraham Lincoln Brigade Archives. "Brigade Archives, Roll Call—American Volunteers in the Spanish Civil War" (alphabetical listing search), Tamiment Library and Robert F. Wagner Labor Archives, New York University.

Allen, James S. Papers. TAM 142, box 5, folder 20, Tamiment Library and Robert F. Wagner Labor Archives, New York University.

Burke (Jarvis), Alice. Oral History. Oral History Collection OH.040. Tamiment Library and Robert F. Wagner Labor Archives, New York University. Interviewed by Robin Kelley.

Durr, Virginia. Oral History Interview G-0023-2, Southern Oral History Program Collection 4007. University of North Carolina at Chapel Hill. Interviewed by Sue Thrasher, March 13–15, 1975.

Hall, Rob. Oral History. Oral History Collection. OH.040 Tamiment Library and Robert F. Wagner Labor Archives, New York University. Interviewed by Robin Kelley, September 18 and 19, 1987.

Haywood, Harry. Papers, 1948–81. MG398, Schomburg Center for Research in Black Culture, New York Public Library.

Herndon, Angelo. Papers, 1932–40. MG 124, Schomburg Center for Research in Black Culture, New York Public Library.

Jackson, James. Oral History Collection. OH.040, Tamiment Library and Robert F. Wagner Labor Archives, New York University. Interviewed by Robin Kelley.

Meir, August. Papers. Alabama 1931–37, "The Willie Peterson Case," box 144, folder 8, Schomburg Center for Research in Black Culture, New York Public Library.

NAACP. Legal Files. "The Scottsboro Case," microfilm, parts 6 and 7, reels 23 and 24, "Lynchings in Tuscaloosa," Schomburg Center for Research in Black Culture, New York Public Library. (Cited as NAACP Legal Files.)

NAACP. Papers. Part 6, "Scottsboro Case 1931–1950" and "Willie Peterson Trials," folder 0021524-024-0542, March 1, 1934–March 7, 1934; and folder 001524-024-0869, August 1, 1935–December 31, 1937, Schomburg Center for Research in Black Culture, New York Public Library. (Cited as NAACP Papers.)

Patterson, William. Papers. Paper 152, biography, 1–7. Moorland Spingarn Research Center, Howard University, Washington, DC (Digital Howard at Howard University).

Solomon, Mark, and Robert Kaufman files. Files on African Americans and Communism, Tamiment Library and Robert F. Wagner Labor Archives, New York University.

Southern Conference for Human Welfare (SCHW) Collection. Research manuscript SCHW, 1955 box 4, folder 3, Clark Foreman Files 1938–67, Robert W. Woodruff Library, Atlanta University Center.

Stone, Olive M. Papers, 1838–1977. Wilson Library Southern Historical Collection 04107, University of North Carolina at Chapel Hill.

Stone, Olive M. Oral History Interviews August 13, 1975, through October 14, 1975, G-0059-4, 4007, Southern Oral History Program, Southern Historical Collection, Wilson Library, University of North Carolina at Chapel Hill. Interviewed by Sherna Berger Gluck.

Other Sources

Acker, James R. *Scottsboro and Its Legacy: The Cases that Challenged American Legal and Social Justice.* Westport, CT: Praeger, 2008.

Adams, Frank T. *James A. Dombrowski: An American Heretic, 1897–1983.* Knoxville: University of Tennessee Press, 1992.

Allen, James S. *The Negro Question in the United States.* New York: International, 1936.

———. *Organizing in the Depression South: A Communist's Memoir.* Minneapolis: MEP, 2001.

———. *Smash the Scottsboro Lynch Verdict.* Pamphlet. New York: Workers Library (April 1933): 5.

Alvarez, Sharon. "How Lowell Wakefield Made Crab King." *Entrepreneurship and Innovation Exchange*, October 11, 2016. www.eix.org.

Baker, Kelly J. "The Gospel According to the Klan: The Ku Klux Klan's Vision of White Protestant America, 1915–1930." PhD diss., Florida State University, 2008.

Beck, E. M., and Stewart E. Tolnay. "The Killing Fields of the Deep South: The Market for Cotton and the Lynching of Blacks, 1882–1930." *American Sociological Review* 55: no. 4 (August 1990): 526–39.

Beecher, John. "Reflections of a Man Who Once Stood Up for Freedom." In *John Beecher, Hear the Wind Blow: Poems of Protest and Prophecy.* New York, International Publishers, 1950.

———. "The Share Cropper Union in Alabama." *Social Forces* 13 (October 1934): 124–32.

Bellamy, Jay. "The Scottsboro Boys: Injustice in Alabama." *Prologue*, spring 2014, 26–34.

Bernstein, Carl. *Loyalties: A Son's Memoir.* New York: Simon & Schuster, 1989.
Bethell, Thomas. Foreword to *Welcome the Traveler Home: Jim Garland's Story of the Kentucky Mountains*, by Jim Garland, with Julia S. Ardey, 6–29. Lexington: University Press of Kentucky, 1983.
Biles, Roger. *Memphis in the Great Depression.* Knoxville: University of Tennessee Press, 1986.
———. *The South and the New Deal.* Lexington: University Press of Kentucky, 1994.
Blackmon, Douglas A. *Slavery by Another Name: The Re-Enslavement of Black Americans from the Civil War to World War II.* New York: Anchor Books, 2008.
Braden, Anne. *Free Thomas Wansley: A Letter to White Southern Women.* Pamphlet. Louisville: SCEF Press, December 1972.
Broege, Henry Guston Kemp. "Belle versus Beast or Tramp Versus Child? Contested Representations of the Scottsboro Trials." Master's thesis, Sarah Lawrence College, May 2016.
Brooks, Pamela E. *Boycotts, Buses, and Passes: Black Women's Resistance in the U.S. South and South Africa.* Amherst: University of Massachusetts Press, 2008.
Brown, Sarah Hart. *Standing against Dragons: Three Southern Lawyers in an Era of Fear.* Baton Rouge: Louisiana State University Press, 1998.
Bush, Carletta A. "Faith, Power and Conflict: Miner Preachers and the United Mine Workers of America in the Harlan County Mine Wars, 1931–1939." PhD diss., West Virginia University, 2006.
Callahan, Richard J. *Work and Faith in the Kentucky Coal Fields: Subject to the Dust.* Bloomington: Indiana University Press, 2009.
Cane, Don, and Jacob Zorn. "Communist Organizing in the Jim Crow South." *Workers Vanguard* 925 (November 21, 2008): 1–10.
Capeci, Dominic J., Jr. *The Lynching of Cleo Wright.* Lexington: University Press of Kentucky, 1998.
Carlton, David, and Peter Colanis. *Confronting Southern Poverty in the Great Depression: The Report on Economic Conditions of the South with Related Documents.* Boston: Bedford/St. Martins Press, 1996.
Carter, Dan T. "A Reasonable Doubt." *American Heritage* 19, no. 6 (October 1968).
———. *Scottsboro: A Tragedy of the American South.* New York: Oxford University Press, 1969.
Cash, W. J. *The Mind of the South.* New York: Alfred Knopf, 1941.
Cason, Clarence. *Ninety Degrees in the Shade.* Chapel Hill: University of North Carolina Press, 1936.
Cather, Willa. *O Pioneers!* New York: Houghton Mifflin, 1913.
Chambers, Whittaker. *Witness.* New York: Random House, 1952.
Chiassen, Lloyd, Jr. *The Press on Trial: Crimes and Trials as Media Events.* Westport, CT: Greenwood, 1997.

Christian, Cornelius. "Lynching, Labor and Cotton in the U.S. South." *Voices across Borders* (blog), Oxford University, November 28, 2014. http://torch.ox.ac.uk/.

Cohen, Donald D., and James Capaldi, eds. *The Pete Seeger Reader*. New York: Oxford University Press, 2014.

"Conditions in Coal Fields in Harlan and Bell Counties, Kentucky." Hearings Before a Subcommittee of the Committee on Manufacturers. United States Senate, Seventy-Second Congress, First Session. S.Res.178, "A Resolution for an Investigation of Conditions. May 11, 12, 13 and 19, 1932." Washington, DC: US Government Printing Office, 1932. (Referred to as proceedings of the LaFollette Committee.)

Connor, Eugene (Bull). "Birmingham Wars on Communism." *Alabama Local Government Journal* 8, no. 2 (August 1950): 7, 36–38.

Conrad, Joseph. *Chance: A Tale in Two Parts*. New York: Oxford World Classics, 1914.

Cowley, Malcolm. "Kentucky Coal Town." *New Republic*, March 2, 1932, 67–70.

Cunard, Nancy. *Essays on Race and Empire*. Ontario: Broadview, 2002.

Damon, Anna. "Scottsboro: An Analysis." *Labor Defender*, December 1934, 22.

Daniel, Pete. *Breaking the Land: The Transformation of Cotton, Tobacco, and Rice Cultures since 1880*. Champaign: University of Illinois Press, 1986.

Davidson, Donald. "A Sociologist in Eden." In *The Southern Agrarians and the New Deal: Essays After "I'll Take My Stand*,*"* edited by Emily S. Bingham and Thomas A. Underwood, 104–23. Charlottesville: University Press of Virginia, 2001.

Davies, Alan. *Infected Christianity: A Study of Modern Racism*. Montreal: McGill/Queens University Press, 1988.

Davis, John P. "A Black Inventory of the New Deal." *Crisis* 42 (1935): 141–42.

Davis, Mike. *Prisoners of the American Dream: Politics and Economy in the History of the U.S. Working Class*. Brooklyn: Verso Press, 2000.

Diggins, John Patrick. *The Rise and Fall of the American Left*. New York: W. W. Norton 1992.

Dorr, Lisa Lindquist. *White Women, Rape, and the Power of Race in Virginia, 1900–1960*. Chapel Hill: University of North Carolina Press, 2004.

Draper, Theodore. "Communists and Miners 1938–1933," *Dissent* 19, no. 2 (spring 1972): 371–92.

———. *The Roots of American Communism*. Chicago: Ivan R. Dee, 1957.

Dray, Philip. *At the Hands of Persons Unknown: The Lynching of Black America*. New York: Modern Library, 2002.

Dreiser, Theodore, and the National Committee for the Defense of Political Prisoners. *Harlan Miners Speak: Report on Terrorism in the Kentucky Coal Fields*. Edited by Leonard W. Levy. New York: Da Capo Press, 1970 [1932].

Dykeman, Wilma, and James Stokley. *Seeds of Southern Change: The Life of Will Alexander*. New York: W. W. Norton, 1962.
Egerton, John. *Speak Now against the Day: The Generation before the Civil Rights Movement in the South*. New York: Alfred Knopf, 1994.
Eliot, George. *Scenes of Clerical Life*. London: William Blackwood & Sons, 1877.
Evans, H. W. "The Klan Spiritual." *Imperial Knight-Hawk*, October 22, 1924, 3–6.
Fannin, Mark. "Breaking the Circle: Klan Myth and Radical Rhetoric." Paper delivered at the Milan/Montpelier Group Symposium, University of Milan, June 22–24, 2005.
Feldman, Glenn. "Beginning of the End of the New Deal Coalition." In *History and Hope in the Heart of Dixie: Scholarship, Activism, and Wayne Flynt in the Modern South*, edited by Gordon E. Harvey, Richard D. Starnes, and Glenn Feldman, 124–57. Tuscaloosa: University of Alabama Press, 2006.
———. *The Irony of the Solid South: Democrats, Republicans, and Race, 1865–1944*. Tuscaloosa: University of Alabama Press, 2013.
———. *Politics, Society, and the Klan in Alabama, 1915–1949*. Tuscaloosa: University of Alabama Press, 1999.
Flynt, Wayne. *Alabama Baptists: Southern Baptists in the Heart of Dixie*. Tuscaloosa: University of Alabama Press, 1998.
———. *Poor but Proud: Alabama's Poor Whites*. Tuscaloosa: University of Alabama Press, 2001.
Ford, James. "Let My People Live." *Communist*, April 1937, 381.
Fosl, Catherine. "Life and Times of a Rebel Girl: Jane Speed and the Alabama Communist Party." *Southern Historian* 18 (July 13, 2010): 45–65.
Fried, Albert. *Communism in America: A History in Documents*. New York: Columbia University Press, 1997.
Gannes, Harry. *Kentucky Miners Fight*. Pamphlet. New York: Workers' International Relief, 1932.
Garland, Jim, with Julia S. Ardey. *Welcome the Traveler Home: Jim Garland's Story of the Kentucky Mountains*. Lexington: University Press of Kentucky, 1983.
Gelders, Marge. "Teachings of Marx for Girls and Boys Infiltrates Alabama." In *Red Diapers: Growing Up in the Communist Life*, edited by Judy Kaplan and Linn Shapiro, 41–60. Urbana: University of Illinois Press, 1998.
Gilmore, Glenda Elizabeth. *Defying Dixie: The Radical Roots of Civil Rights 1919–1950*. New York: W. W. Norton, 2008.
Goldfield, Michael. "Race and the C.I.O.: The Possibilities for Racial Egalitarianism During the 1930's and 1940's." *International Labor and Working-Class History* 44 (fall 1993): 1–32.
Goodman, James. *Stories of Scottsboro*. New York: Vintage/Random House, 1994.

Gray, Fred D. *The Tuskegee Syphilis Study: The Real Story and Beyond.* Montgomery: NewSouth Books, 1998.

Grubbs, Donald H. *Cry from the Cotton: The Southern Tenant Farmers' Union and the New Deal.* Chapel Hill: University of North Carolina Press, 1971.

Hall, Rob. "Earl Browder and the Southern People." *Communist*, June 1941, 559–60.

———. "The Southern Conference for Human Welfare." *Communist*, January 1939, 57–65.

Hamilton, Chuck. "Chattanooga's Radical History." Chattanoogan.com, March 25, 2013.

Harris, Lashawn. "Running with the Reds: African American Women and the Communist Party during the Great Depression." *Journal of African American History* 94, no. 1 (winter 2009): 21–43.

Haselden, Kyle. *Mandate for White Christians.* Richmond [VA]: John Knox Press, 1966.

Haywood, Harry. *Black Bolshevik: The Autobiography of an African American Communist.* Chicago: Liberator Press, 1978.

Haywood Harry, and Gwendolyn Midlo Haywood. *A Black Communist in the Freedom Struggle: The Life of Harry Haywood.* Minneapolis: University of Minnesota Press, 2012.

Herndon, Angelo. *Let Me Live.* New York: Random House, 1937.

———. *You Cannot Kill the Working Class.* Pamphlet. New York: International Labor Defense, 1937.

Hevener, John W. *Which Side Are You On? The Harlan County Kentucky Coal Miners, 1931–1939.* Champaign: University of Illinois Press, 2002.

Hollars, B. J. *Thirteen Loops: Race, Violence, and the Last Lynching in America.* Tuscaloosa: University of Alabama Press, 2011.

Hollis, Daniel. *An Alabama Newspaper Tradition: Grover C. Hall and the Hall Family.* Tuscaloosa: University of Alabama Press, 1983.

Honey, Michael. *Black Workers Remember: An Oral History of Segregation, Unionism, and the Freedom Struggle.* Berkeley: University of California Press, 1999.

———. *Going Down Jericho Road: The Memphis Strike, Martin Luther King's Last Campaign.* New York: Norton, 2007.

———. *Southern Labor and Black Civil Rights: Organizing Memphis Workers.* Urbana: University of Illinois Press, 1993.

Horne, Gerald. *Black Revolutionary: William Patterson and the Globalization of the African American Freedom Struggle.* Urbana: University of Illinois Press, 2013.

Howard, Walter T., ed. *Black Communists Speak on Scottsboro: A Documentary History.* Philadelphia: Temple University Press, 2008.

Howe, Irving, and Lewis Coser, with the assistance of Julius Jacobson. *The*

American Communist Party: A Critical History, 1919–1957. Boston: Beacon Press, 1951.

Ingalls, Robert. "Anti-Radical Violence in Birmingham during the 1930's." *Journal of Southern History* 47, no. 4 (November 1981): 521–44.

———. "The Flogging of Joe Gelders: A Policeman's View." *Labor History* 20, no. 4 (1979): 576–78.

Isserman, Maurice. *If I Had a Hammer: The Death of the Old Left and The Birth of the New Left.* New York: Basic Books, 1989.

———. *Which Side Were You On? The American Communist Party during the Second World War.* Urbana: University of Illinois Press, 1993.

Jackson, Al. "You Can Kill Me, But You Cannot Scare Me." *Labor Defender*, October 1935, 6.

Jackson, Lawrence Patrick. *Ralph Ellison: Emergence of Genius.* Athens: University of Georgia Press, 2007.

Jamison, Stuart. *Labor Unionism in American Agriculture.* Pamphlet. U.S. Department of Labor, Bureau of Labor Statistics, Bulletin 836. 1945. Reprint, New York: Arno Press, 1976.

Jankin, Kenneth Robert. *White: The Biography of Walter White, Mr. NAACP.* New York: New Press, 2003.

Jeffries, Hasan Kwame. *Bloody Lowndes: Civil Rights and Black Power in Alabama's Black Belt.* New York: New York University Press, 2009.

Johnson, Charles. "More Southerners Discover the South." *Crisis* 46 (January 1939): 14–15.

Johnson, Gerald W. "Why Communists Are Valuable." *Harpers*, January 1950, 93–95.

Johnson, Timothy V. "We Are Illegal Here: The Communist Party, Self Determination and the Alabama Sharecroppers Union," *Science and Society* 75, no. 4 (October 2011): 454–79.

Jones, Pam. "The Williams/Wood Murders." *Alabama Heritage*, winter 2006, 4–6.

deJong, Greta. "'With the Aid of God and the F.S.A.': The Louisiana Farmers' Union and the African American Freedom Struggle in the New Deal Era," *Journal of Social History* 34, no. 1 (fall 2000): 105–39.

Kaufman, Laura. "Beatrice Holzman Schneiderman: Civil Rights Activist and Committed Volunteer, 1906–1996." We Remember, Jewish Women's Archive. https://jwa.org/weremember/schneiderman-beatrice, accessed October 15, 2003.

Kaufman, Will. *Woody Guthrie, American Radical.* Urbana: University of Illinois Press, 2011.

Kazin, Michael. *American Dreamers: How the Left Changed a Nation.* New York: Alfred Knopf, 2011.

Kelley, Robin D. G. "The Black Belt Communists." *Jacobin* 22 (August 20, 2015): 6–15.

———. "Comrades Praise Gawd for Lenin and Them: Ideology and Culture among Black Communists in Alabama 1930–1935." *Science and Society* 52, no. 1 (spring 1985): 59–82.

———. *Hammer and Hoe: Alabama Communists during the Great Depression.* Chapel Hill: University of North Carolina Press, 1990.

———. "The Jacksons." *American Communist History* 7, no. 2 (2008): 175–80.

———. "Resistance, Survival and the Black Poor in Birmingham, Alabama 1929–1970." University of Wisconsin–Madison Institute for Research on Poverty, discussion paper 950–91, July 1991.

———. "Tell Me More." NPR Radio interview by Michael Morton, February 16, 2010.

The Kentucky Miners' Struggle. Pamphlet. New York American Civil Liberties Union, May 1932.

King, Coretta Scott. *My Life with Martin Luther King, Jr.* New York: Holt, Rinehart & Winston, 1969.

Klehr, Harvey. *The Heyday of American Communism: The Depression Decade.* New York: Basic Books, 1984.

Klehr, Harvey, and John Earl Haynes. *The American Communist Movement: Storming Heaven Itself.* New York: Twayne, 1992.

Klehr, Harvey, John Earl Haynes, and Fridrikh Igorevich Firsov. *The Secret World of American Communism.* Russian documents translated by Timothy D. Sergay. New Haven, CT: Yale University Press, 1995.

Krueger, Thomas A. *And Promises to Keep: The Southern Conference for Human Welfare, 1938–1948.* Nashville: Vanderbilt University Press, 1967.

Lawson, John Howard. "In Dixie Land We Take Our Stand: A Report on Alabama's Nazis." *New Masses*, May 29, 1934, 8–10.

Lelyveld, Joseph. *Omaha Blues: A Memory Loop.* New York: Farrar, Straus & Giroux, 2005.

Lenin, V. I. "Marxism and Reformism." In *Collected Works*, 19:372–75. Moscow: Progress Publishers, 1977. Accessed at Marxists International Archive, www.marxists.org.

"Leon Carlock, Lynched by Memphis Police." *Labor Defender* 9, no. 3 (March 1933): 31.

Linder, Douglas O. "Without Fear or Favor: Judge James Edwin Horton and the Trial of the 'Scottsboro Boys.'" *University of Missouri–Kansas City Law Review* 68 (January 2000): 549–83.

Long, Michael G. *Against Us, but for Us: Martin Luther King, Jr. and the State.* Macon, GA: Mercer University Press, 2002.

Lorence, James J. *The Unemployed People's Movement: Leftists, Liberals and Labor in Georgia, 1929–941.* Athens: University of Georgia Press, 2011.

Mack, Kenneth. *Representing the Race: The Creation of a Civil Rights Lawyer.* Cambridge: Harvard University Press, 2012.

Markovitz, Jonathan. *Legacies of Lynching: Racial Violence and Memory.* Minneapolis: University of Minnesota Press, 2004.

Martin, Charles H. *The Angelo Herndon Case and Southern Justice.* Baton Rouge: Louisiana State University Press, 1976.

Martin, Robert. "A Prophet's Pilgrimage: The Religious Radicalism of Howard Anderson Kester, 1921–1941." *Journal of Southern History* 48, no. 4 (1982): 511–30.

Marx, Karl. "Contribution to the Critique of Hegel's Philosophy of Law: Introduction": In *Collected Works*, by Karl Marx and Friedrich Engels, 3:175–87. Moscow: Progress Publishers, 1844 [1975].

Mazzari, Louis. *Southern Modernist: Arthur Raper, From the New Deal to the Cold War.* Baton Rouge: Louisiana State University Press, 2006.

McDonough, Julia Anne. "Men and Women of Good Will: A History of the Commission on Interracial Cooperation and the Southern Regional Council, 1919–1954." PhD diss., University of Virginia, 1993.

McGuire, Danielle L. *At the Dark End of the Street: Black Women, Race, and Resistance—A New History of the Civil Rights Movement from Rosa Parks to the Rise of Black Power.* New York: Alfred A. Knopf, 2010.

McWhorter, Diane. *Carry Me Home: The Climactic Battle of the Civil Rights Revolution.* New York: Simon & Schuster, 2001.

Meyer, Gerald. *Vito Marcantonio: Radical Politician, 1902–1956.* Albany: State University of New York Press, 1989.

Miller, James A. *Remembering Scottsboro: The Legacy of an Infamous Trial.* Princeton, NJ: Princeton University Press, 2009.

Miller, James A., Susan D. Pennybacker, and Eve Rosenhaft. "Mother Ada Wright and the International Campaign to Free the Scottsboro Boys." *American Historical Review*, April 2001, 387–430.

Mitchell, H. L. *Mean Things Happening in This Land: The Life and Times of H. L. Mitchell, Co-founder of the Southern Tenant Farmers Union.* Montclair, NJ: Allanheld, Osmun, 1979.

Mitchell, Patricia. "Recollections: Adventures of the Southern Worker." *Alabama Heritage*, spring 2008, 46–47.

Mjangkij, Nina. *Organizing Black America: An Encyclopedia of African American Associations.* New York: Garland, 2001.

Moon, Henry Lee. *Balance of Power: The Negro Vote.* Garden City, NY: Doubleday, 1948.

Morrison, Melanie S. *Murder on Shades Mountain: The Legal Lynching of Willie Peterson and the Struggle for Justice in Jim Crow Birmingham.* Durham, NC: Duke University Press, 2018.

Murphy, Al. "Achievement and Tasks of the Sharecropper's Union." In Fried, *Communism*, 142–43.
Newby, I. A. *Jim Crow's Defense: Anti-Negro Thought in America, 1900–1930*. Baton Rouge: Louisiana State University, 1965.
Newton, Michael. *White Robes and Burning Crosses: A History of the Ku Klux Klan from 1866*. Jefferson, NC: McFarland, 2014.
Norris, Clarence, and Sybil D. Washington. *The Last of the Scottsboro Boys: An Autobiography*. New York: Putnam, 1978.
O'Connor, Flannery. *Mysteries and Manners:: Occasional Prose*. New York: Farrar, Straus & Giroux, 1967.
Oppenheimer, Daniel. *Exit Right: The People Who Left the Left and Reshaped the American Right*. New York: Simon & Schuster, 2016.
Ottanelli, Fraser. *The Communist Party of the United States: From the Depression to World War II*. New Brunswick, NJ: Rutgers University Press, 1991.
Painter, Nell Irvin. *The Narrative of Hosea Hudson: His Life as a Negro Communist in the South*. Cambridge: Harvard University Press, 1979.
Pater, Walter. *Studies in the History of the Renaissance*. London: Macmillan, 1873.
Patterson, Haywood, Files Crenshaw Jr., and Kenneth A. Miller. *Scottsboro, The Firebrand of Communism*. Montgomery, AL: Press of the Brown Print Co., 1936.
Patterson, William L. *The Man Who Cried Genocide: An Autobiography*. New York: International, 1971.
Pennybacker, Susan D. *From Scottsboro to Munich: Race and Political Culture in 1930s Britain*. Princeton, NJ: Princeton University Press, 2009.
"Pittsburgh Convention Shows Need for Unity of Fighting Miners." *Militant* 4, no. 16 (July 25, 1931): 1, 6.
Portelli, Alessandro. *They Say in Harlan County: An Oral History*. New York: Oxford University Press, 2011.
Post, Charlie. "The Popular Front: Rethinking CPUSA History." *Solidarity: Against the Current* 63 (July–August 1996): 3–5. www.solidarity-us.org/node/2363.
Postgate, R. W. *The Bolshevik Theory*. New York: Dodd Mead, 1920.
Purcell, Aaron D. *White Collar Radicals: TVA's Knoxville Fifteen, the New Deal and the McCarthy Era*. Knoxville: University of Tennessee Press, 2009.
Raper, Arthur F. *The Plight of Tuscaloosa: Mob Murders, Community Hysteria and Official Incompetence: A Case Study of Conditions in Tuscaloosa County, Alabama, 1933*. Atlanta: Southern Commission on the Study of Lynching, 1933.
———. *The Tragedy of Lynching*. Mineola, NY: Dover, 1933.
Raymond, Anan. "Prairie Fire: A Footnote to Contemporary History." *American Bar Association Journal*, Vol 38 November 1952, 911–14, 972–75.
Read, Nicholas Cabell, and Dallas Read. *Deep Family: Four Centuries of American Originals and Southern Eccentrics*. Montgomery, AL: NewSouth Books, 2005.

Reed, Linda. *Simple Decency and Common Sense: The Southern Conference Movement, 1938–1963.* Bloomington: University of Indiana Press, 1991.

Reynolds, Quentin. *Courtroom: The Story of Samuel S. Leibowitz.* New York: Farrar, Straus & Giroux, 1950.

Rittenberg, Sidney. "We're C.I.O.s from Alabama." *Jacobin* 28 (winter 2018). Jacobinmag.com.

Robinson, Amelia Boynton. *Bridge across Jordan.* Rev. ed. Washington, DC: Schiller Institute, 1991.

Rogers, William Warren, Sr. *The One-Gallused Rebellion: Agrarianism in Alabama, 1865–1896.* Tuscaloosa: University of Alabama Press, 2001.

Roll, Jarod. "Reading Religious Belief as Working-Class Intellectual History." *Journal of Southern Religion* 13 (2011): 28–40.

———. *Spirit of Rebellion: Labor and Religion in the New Cotton South.* Urbana: University of Illinois Press, 2010.

Rosen, Dale, and Theodore Rosengarten. "Shootout at Reeltown." *Radical America* 6 (November/December 1972): 71.

Rosengarten, Theodore. *All God's Dangers: The Life of Nate Shaw.* Chicago: University of Chicago Press, 1974.

Ross, Malcolm. *Machine Age in the Hills.* 1933. Reprint, n.p.: Forgotten Books, 2006.

Ross, Nat. "The NRA in the South." *Communist*, December 1933, 1185–87.

Rossi, Faust. "The First Scottsboro Trials: A Legal Lynching." *Cornell Law Forum* 29, no. 2 (winter 2002): 1–6.

Ryan, James G. *Earl Browder: The Failure of American Communism.* Tuscaloosa: University of Alabama Press, 1997.

Salmond, John A. *Miss Lucy of the CIO: The Life and Times of Lucy Randolph Mason, 1882–1959.* Athens: University of Georgia Press, 1988.

Scales, Junius Irving, and Richard Nickson. *Cause at Heart: A Former Communist Remembers.* Athens: University of Georgia Press, 2005.

Schechter, Dave. "How Solomon Schechter's Daughter Became a Card Carrying Communist." *Forward*, September 29, 2015.

Schwartz, Ted. *Marilyn Revealed: The Ambitious Life of an American Icon.* Lanham, Md.: Taylor, 2009.

"Scottsboro—What Now?" *Militant* 5, no. 47 (November 1932): 1–2.

Segrave, Kerry. *Lynchings of Women in the United States: The Recorded Cases, 1852–1946.* Jefferson, NC: McFarland, 2010.

Sellers, James. *The South and Christian Ethics.* New York: Association Press, 1962.

Shapiro, Herbert. *White Violence and Black Response: From Reconstruction to Montgomery.* Amherst: University of Massachusetts Press, 1988.

Sharpe, Kimberly. "Tuscaloosa, Alabama, 1933: A Summer of Violence." Civil Rights and Restorative Justice Clinic, Northeast University School of Law, summer 2015.

Shaw, George Bernard. *Everybody's Political. What's What.* London: Constable Press, 1944.

Shay, Frank. *Judge Lynch: His First Hundred Years.* New York: Ives & Washburn, 1938.

Shover, John. "The Communist Party and the Midwestern Farm Crisis of 1933." *Journal of American History* 51 (September 1964): 248–66.

Smith, Lillian. *Killers of the Dream.* New York: W. W. Norton, 1949.

Smith, Sharon. "The 1930's: Turning Point for U.S. Labor." *International Socialist Review* 25 (September–October 2002), online edition.

———. "The Sit-Down Strikes." SocialistWorker.org, June 10, 2011, accessed May 3, 2018.

Solomon, Mark. *The Cry Was Unity: Communists and African Americans, 1917–1936.* Jackson: University Press of Mississippi, 1998.

Soodalter, Rod. "The Price of Coal, Part II." *Kentucky Monthly*, October 31, 2016, accessed November 2016.

Sosna, Morton. *In Search of the Silent South: Southern Liberals and the Race Issue.* New York: Columbia University Press, 1977.

Southern Exposure. Review of *The Ethnic Southerners*, by George Tindall. *Southern Exposure* 5, no. 1 (January 1980): 98–99.

Stanton, Mary. *Hand of Esau: Montgomery's Jewish Community and the Bus Boycott.* Montgomery, AL: River City, 2006.

———. *Journey toward Justice: Juliette Hampton Morgan and the Montgomery Bus Boycott.* Athens: University of Georgia Press, 2006.

Stone, Olive. "Agrarian Conflict in Alabama: Sections, Regions and Classes." PhD diss., University of North Carolina at Chapel Hill, 1939.

Storch, Randi. "Moscow's Archives and the New History of the Communist Party of the United States." *Perspectives on History: The News Magazine of the American Historical Association* (online), October 2000.

Straus, Robert K. "Enter the Cotton Picker: The Story of the Rust Brothers' Invention." *Harper's* 173 (September 1936): 386–95.

Sullivan, Patricia. *Days of Hope: Race and Democracy in the New Deal Era.* Chapel Hill: University of North Carolina Press, 1996.

———. *Lift Every Voice: The NAACP and the Making of the Civil Rights Movement.* New York: New Press, 2009.

Tanenhaus, Sam. *Whittaker Chambers: A Biography.* New York: Modern Library, 1998.

Taub, Allan. "Prelude to a Lynching." *New Masses* 8, no. 2 (August 1933): 6–7.

Taylor, Gregory. *The History of the North Carolina Communist Party.* Columbia: University of South Carolina Press, 2009.

Terry, Paul W., and Verner M. Sims. *They Live on The Land: Life in an Open-Country Southern Community.* Tuscaloosa: University of Alabama Press, 1993.

Theoharis, Jeanne. *The Rebellious Life of Mrs. Rosa Parks*. Boston: Beacon, 2013.

Uhlmann, Jennifer Ruthanne. "The Communist Civil Rights Movement: Legal Activism in the United States 1919–1946." PhD diss., University of California at Los Angeles, 2007.

Watkins, T. H. *The Hungry Years: A Narrative History of the Great Depression in America*. New York: Henry Holt, 1999.

Wechsler, James. *Age of Suspicion*. New York: Random House, 1953.

Weller, Jack E. *Yesterday's People: Life in Contemporary Appalachia*. Lexington: University of Kentucky Press, 1966.

West, Don. "Romantic Appalachia." In *Appalachia in the Sixties: Decade of Reawakening*, edited by David S. Walls and John B. Stephenson, 210–16. Lexington: University Press of Kentucky, 1972.

"What Happened in Tallapoosa County?" *Labor Defender*, February 1933, 4.

Wheeler, Tim. "We Charge Genocide: The Cry Rings True 52 Years Later." *People's World*, February 21, 2003. www.PeoplesWorld.org.

Willie, Charles V. "Walter R. Chivers, an Advocate of Situational Sociology." *Phylon* 43, no. 3 (1982): 242–48.

Wilson, Edmund. "The Freight Car Case." *New Republic*, August 26, 1931, 38–43.

Wood, Robert. *To Live and Die in Dixie*. Pamphlet. New York: Southern Workers' Defense Committee, 1935.

Wright, W. C. "A Klansman's Criterion of Character." *Imperial Knight Hawk*, February 6, 1924, 2.

INDEX

AAA. *See* Agricultural Adjustment Act
Abernathy, H. S., 19, 79
Abraham Lincoln Brigade, 164
ACLU (American Civil Liberties Union), 103, 136, 139–40
Adams, Oscar W., Sr., 15–16, 71–72
Adirondack Life (magazine), 170
Adkins, Addie, 21
AFL. *See* Alabama Federation of Labor
Agricultural Adjustment Act (AAA), 88–89, 140, 170
Agricultural Adjustment Administration, 88–89, 116
agricultural labor, 17–18, 47–50, 133, 145–47. *See also* sharecroppers
Alabama Christian Movement for Human Rights, 158
Alabama Commission on Interracial Cooperation, 74
Alabama Federation of Labor (AFL), 23, 130
Alabama Foundry Company, 169
Alabama Policy Committee, 148
Alabama Share Croppers' Union (ASCU), 44, 49, 80, 123, 129–30, 133–34, 146
Alabama State National Guard, 144
Alabama Supreme Court, 36–38, 71–72, 90, 98, 122
Alberta, Alabama, 53
Allen, Isabelle, 22, 24, 34–35, 162, 165–66
Allen, James, 22–25, 28, 34, 54, 66–67, 162, 165–66
Allen, Marion, 56
alliances, 103, 153
Allied victory, 156, 162
All-Southern Anti-Lynching Conference in Chattanooga, 30–31

All Southern Conference for Civil and Trade Union Rights, 129–30
All Southern Conference on Scottsboro, 20, 79
All-Southern Scottsboro Defense Conference, 48
Altman, John, 71–76
American Civil Liberties Union. *See* ACLU
American exceptionalism, 145
Amis, B. D., 48
Andrew Memorial Veteran's Hospital, 86
antebellum era, 17
anticommunist ordinance, 157
anti-insurrection statute, 101, 104–5
antilabor laws, 130
antilabor violence, 133, 139–40, 147–48
antilynching campaigns, 154
antilynching legislation, 25, 30–31, 149–50, 168
appeals: Herndon trial, 101–4; Martinsville Seven, 168; Peterson trial, 71–74; Scottsboro trial, 35–38, 90, 93, 98, 135, 159–60
Arrant, Ed, 132
ASCU. *See* Alabama Share Croppers' Union
atheism, 45, 59, 134
Atlanta, Georgia, 100–103
Atlanta Six, 123–24
Auerbach, Solomon. *See* Allen, James
"The Awakening Church" (West), 155

Bailey, H. G., 35
Baker, Frank, 58–59
Baldwin, Julius, 55–56
Baldwin, Martin, 83
Baldwin, Roger, 38, 40

Ball, Bessie, 48
Baltimore Afro American (newspaper), 37, 108
Bankhead, John, 151
Bankhead Cotton Control Act, 134
Bankhead-Jones Farm Tenancy Act, 135
Barbourville, Kentucky, 61
Barsky, Edwin, 167
Bates, Ruby, 33–34, 38–41, 93–94, 96, 99
Battle of Evarts, 54–56
Beans, John, 80
Beddow, Roderick, 70, 73
Bell, Sherman, 32
Bell County, Kentucky, 54–59, 61
Benson, Sid: All Southern Conference for Civil and Trade Union Rights, 129; biography, 166; district 17 restructuring, 78–79, 133, 146–47; Gelders, 142; leaving Communist Party, 162; Norman Thomas Study Club, 82–83
Bentley, Milo, 86–87
Bernstein, Solomon. *See* Benson, Sid
Bessemer, Alabama, 143
Bethell, Thomas, 58
Big Sandy Creek, 107–8, 112–13
Birmingham, Alabama: about, 13–14; Allen (James), 22–25; anticommunist ordinance, 157; antilabor violence, 139–44; attitudes toward communists, 20–21; district 17, 13–16; Fish Committee, 17; Gelders, 140–44; miners, 18–19; movement culture, 158; police brutality, 32, 77, 87; radicalism, 153; Robinson indictment, 28; Ross, 78–79; Scottsboro, 49, 94–95; Shades Mountain, 62–76; Southern Conference for Human Welfare, 148–51; Southern Negro Youth Congress, 154; Tennessee Coal, Iron and Railroad Company, 144; unemployment, 14–16, 77
Birmingham Age Herald (newspaper), 37, 51
Birmingham City Council, 157
Birmingham Industrial Union Council, 169

Birmingham News (newspaper), 39–40, 51, 63, 95
Birmingham Post (newspaper), 87, 88
Birmingham's Interracial Commission, 74
Black Bolshevik (Haywood), 165
black churches and fraternities, 154
Black equality, 160–61
black insurrection, 50
black labor–civil rights coalition, 153
black leaders, 30
black middle class, 15–16, 146, 153
Black Odd Fellows Hall, 30, 48
Black Pythian Temple, 87
Black Star Mountain Coal Company, 54
black women, 21
Blair, John Henry, 55–56
Blakemore, H. C., 98
B'Nai Brith Hillel Foundation, 166
Boyd, Clarence, 25–27, 29
Boyd, Grover, 26–29
Boykin, John A., 104
Bracy, Ed, 132
Braden, Anne, 40–41
Bridges, R. R., 96
Brodsky, Joseph, 36–38, 90, 92, 94, 97–99, 135–36, 162, 170–71
Brooks, Dan, 54–56
Browder, Earl, 91, 105, 129, 138–39, 145–46, 152, 156, 162
Bryant, Jap, 143
Burke, Alice, 79, 103, 162
Burke, Donald, 79, 87, 103, 162
Burns, Frank, 14–15, 19, 22
Burton, Ted, 138
Bush, Clarence, 27
Butler, J. R., 134

Cade, E. S., 76
Calhoun, John Henry, 52
Callahan, William Washington, 97
campaign for president, 1936, 145
Camp Hill, 17, 47–52, 80, 84
capitalism, 78, 139, 145–46, 162–63

Capitol Park, 21
Carlock, Eula May, 124–25
Carlock, Levon, 124–26
Carr, Joe, 19
Cason, Clarence Elmore, 111
Catchings, John, 141–42
Central Committee, CPUSA, 79, 123
Chamberlain, Bart, 28
Chambers, Whittaker, 90
Chambers County, Alabama, 116, 130
Chamlee, George W., 24, 36–38, 51–52, 87, 92
change of venue, Scottsboro, 35, 92, 94–95, 99
Charlton, Louise O., 148
Chattanooga, Tennessee, 15, 22–25, 30–32, 34, 48, 129–30, 154
Chellis, Joyce, 105
Chicago, Illinois, 59–60
Chicago Defender (newspaper), 36, 52
Chicago's Workers' School, 59
Chinese Communist Party, 165
Chivers, Walter, 29–30, 108
Christianity, 42–45, 59–61
Christian Patriotic League, 61
Christian segregation, 44–45
Christian socialists, 44
CIC. *See* Commission on Interracial Cooperation
CIO. *See* Congress of Industrial Organizations
Citizens' Committee, 74
Citizen Scottsboro Aid Committee, 81–82
Citizens' Protective League, 112–14, 120–21
civil liberties, 144
Civil Rights Congress (CRC), 156–57, 167–68
Clark, Elmore "Honey," 109–16
clemency, 72–76
Coad, Mack, 47–50, 77, 79–80, 124, 153, 164–65
coalition building, 139, 145, 153, 158
coal operators, 44, 54–61, 155–56
Cobb, Cully, 89
Cobb, Ned, 86

Coe, John, 157
collaboration, 129, 133, 146, 153–54
collective action, 25, 43
Colley, Roy, 17
Colored Ministers' Alliance, 34
Comintern (Communist International), 90, 138, 156, 166
Commercial Appeal (newspaper), 126
commissary system, 17–18, 134
Commission on Interracial Cooperation (CIC), 29, 51, 116
Committee for the Rehabilitation of Sharecroppers, 169
Committee on Un-American Activities (HUAC), 106, 150–51, 154, 167, 168
communism: All Southern Conference for Civil and Trade Union Rights, 130; anticommunist ordinance, 157; Camp Hill, 47–50; capitalism, 78, 139, 145–46, 162–63; Carlock campaign, 126; Christian Patriotic League, 61; Citizens' Protective League, 112–13; Committee on Un-American Activities, 106, 150–51, 154, 167, 168; Congress of Industrial Organization, 146; Fish Committee, 16–17; Gelders, 140–43; NAACP, 50–52, 81; National Miners' Union, 54–56, 58–60; organized religion, 42–46; organizing, 16, 19–21, 23–24, 153–55; Peterson trial, 67–68; Popular Front, 138–40, 152; radicals, 83–84; Scottsboro defense, 32, 37–38, 70, 137; Shades Mountain, 62–65; Southern Conference for Human Welfare, 150–51; Tuscaloosa lynchings, 121–22; value of, 159–63. *See also* district 17
Communist (magazine), 105
Communist Control Law, 157
Communist International (Comintern), 90, 138, 156, 166
Communist National Training School, 167
Communist Party of the United States (CPUSA): Fish Committee, 17; Gelders, 140–41; Herndon trial, 101;

Communist Party of the United States (CPUSA) (*continued*) membership, 162–63; Ninth Congress, 139; organized religion, 46, 60; outlawed in Birmingham, 157; Popular Front, 138–39, 152–53; presidential platform, 145; racial justice campaign, 105, 146, 159; Southern Conference for Human Welfare, 150, 151; value of, 159–63. *See also* district 17
Communist Workers School, 166
Community Chest, 21
community organizing. *See* organizing
Congress of Industrial Organizations (CIO), 138–39, 146, 148, 154–55
Congress of Racial Equality (CORE), 158
Connor, Theophilus "Bull," 149, 154, 156–57
Conservationist (journal), 170
constitutional guarantees, 81
constitutionality, 30, 104, 160
convict cage replica, 103
Corcoran, Deputy Sheriff, 98
CORE. *See* Congress of Racial Equality
Cothran, Ben, 51
cotton, 47–48, 88–89, 116, 130–31, 133–34
Cotton, Robert, 126
Cowley, Malcolm, 58
CPUSA. *See* Communist Party of the United States
Crawford, Bruce, 119
CRC. *See* Civil Rights Congress
credit, advanced to sharecroppers, 18, 88–89
credit suspension strategy, 47
crop liens, 17–18
Croppers and Farm Workers Union, 48, 49, 79–80
crop reduction program, 88–89
Cross, Dennis, 117–21
Crump, Edward, 123–24, 126
cultural Christians, 45
cultural Jews, 46
Cummings, Homer, 122

Dadeville, Alabama, 49, 51–52
Dadeville Record (newspaper), 51
Daily Worker (newspaper), 21, 34, 37, 39–40, 90, 94, 165, 169–70
Dallas County, Alabama, 130–32
Dalton, Mary, 24
Damon, Anna, 133–34
Daniels, Jonathan, 94
Darrow, Clarence, 36–38, 91
Davidson, Eugene, 50
Davis, Ben, Jr., 100–104, 123, 135, 162
Davis, Horace, 123–24
Davis, John P., 89
Davis, J. W., 131
Davis, Marian, 123–24
Davis, Red, 58–59
debt, sharecroppers, 18–19
Decatur, Alabama, 92–94
demonstrations, 14–16, 20–21, 23, 35, 37, 70, 74–75
denial of counsel, 110, 159–60
Denny, George, 141
Department of Public Safety, 157
Dial, Jesse, 27
Dial, Viola, 27–29
Dibble, Eugene, 85–87
Dies, Martin, 150–51
Dies Committee, 150–51
Dimitrov, Georgi, 138
district 17: coalition building, 153–54, 158; headquarters, 13–16; Herndon, 53–54; Memphis, 123–24; organizing, 17, 47; restructuring, 77–78, 133–34; territory, 146; Tuscaloosa murders, 121; unemployed worker councils, 15–16
Dombrowski, James, 129–30
Donaldson, Finley, 55, 59–60
Dorsey, Hugh M., 104
Dos Passos, John, 57
Double V campaign, 105, 156, 169
Douty, Kenneth, 151
Downs literature ordinance, 141–43
Draper, Theodore, 160

Dreiser, Theodore, 57
Du Bois, W. E. B., 36, 130
due process clause (Fourteenth Amendment), 92, 157
Dugger, Horace, 71
Durr, Clifford, 157
Durr, Virginia, 155–56

Eastland, James O., 151
East Thomas Blast Furnace, 141
economic conditions, 78, 147–51
economic freedom, 130
Eddins, Ben, 119
Elder, Witt, 85–87
Ellison, Ralph, 105–6, 162
Emelle, Alabama, 25–28
emergency relief bill, 134
Emergency Relief Office, 117, 118
émigrés, 162
Engdahl, J. Louis, 51, 90–91
equality, 20–21, 23, 78–80, 124, 130, 149–50
equal justice, 143
equal protection clause (Fourteenth Amendment), 159–60
evangelicals, 43–45
Evans, Hiram, 20
Evans, H. W., 45
Evarts, Kentucky, 54–57
evictions, 15, 87, 89, 134, 145, 149, 163
exclusion of blacks from juries, 36, 92–93, 96–97, 101, 135

false confessions, 108–9
farm bureau, 88
Farm Bureau and Extension Service, 89
farm-labor coalition, 145
Farm Labor Party, 166
Farm Relief Councils, 17, 47
Farm Security Administration, 135
farm tenancy system, 17, 47, 88–89, 134–35
fascism, 82, 138–39, 152, 156–57, 169
federal death penalty for lynchers, 130
federal election taxes, 156

federal employment insurance bill, 14–15
federal relief, 88–89, 113, 116, 122, 134, 135, 147, 149
Federated Press, 56–57, 132
female purity, 50
Field, Rose C., 105
First Amendment, 160
Fish, Hamilton, III, 16–17, 25
Fish Committee, 16–17
Flat Woods, 27
Fleenor, Lee, 56
Fleming, Martin, 24
folkways, 150
Ford, Beddow, and Ray (law firm), 70
Ford, James, 36, 91, 105, 145
Forsha, Harold, 124–26, 164–65
Foster, Henry, 109–11, 113–14, 120
Foundations of Leninism (Stalin), 140
Fourteenth Amendment, 92, 96, 104–5, 157, 159–60
Fowler, Leland, 107–8
Frank, Waldo, 57–58
Franks, Sadie, 83, 141
Free Angelo Herndon fund-raising tours, 104
free labor, 17
Freeman, J. P., 125
free speech. *See* First Amendment
Fries, Richard, 65
"From Mills, Mines & Farms" (Allen), 24
Fuller, H. W., 68–69
Fulton County Emergency Relief Center, 100
furnish merchants, 47–48

Gadsden, Alabama, 33–34, 118
Garland, Jim, 54
Gelders, Esther, 142
Gelders, Joe, 140–44, 147–48, 155–56, 162, 170
Georgia, 14, 80, 100–105, 133–34, 160
Giglio, James, 14
Goldstein, Benjamin, 81–84, 86–87, 94–95, 162, 166

Gordon, Hy, 24
Grace, Jim, 54, 57
gradualism, 30
graduated land taxes, 135
Graham, Frank Porter, 148–49
grand jury proceedings, 28, 58, 65, 109, 114–16, 119–20
Graves, Bibb, 27–28, 143, 151
Graves, John Temple, II, 119
Gray, Alfred, 47
Gray, Eula, 77, 79–80
Gray, Ralph, 47–50, 51, 80
Gray, Tommy, 47–48
Great Depression, 54, 140, 162–63
Green, William, 23
Greer, John H., 100–102
Group Theater Collective, 166

Hall, Grover, 50, 84, 150–51
Hall, Haywood. *See* Patterson, Haywood
Hall, Otto, 91
Hall, Rob: biography, 169–70; Communist Party membership, 162; district 17 restructuring, 133–34; enlistment in armed forces, 156; and Gelders, 142–43; in Kentucky, 59; Popular Front, 138, 146; Southern Conference for Human Welfare, 148–50; voter registration, 153
Hall, Sam, 155–57
Hall, Sylvia, 157
Hamilton, Rev., 53
Hanna, Walter J. "Crack," 143–44
Hanson, W. S., 86
Hardin, A. T., 107, 108–10, 111–16, 119
Harlan County, Kentucky, 54–59
Harlan County Coal Operators, 55–56
Harlem Renaissance, 91
Harper, Louis, 112
Harper's (magazine), 159
Haselden, Kyle, 44–45
Hawkins, Alfred E., 33–34
Hawkins, James, 20, 34–35, 65, 72, 74–76

Haywood, Harry, 31, 36, 91, 123–26, 146, 156, 162, 164–65
Heflin, "Cotton Tom," 71, 87
Heflin, Harrington P., 69–71
Henderson, Fannie, 125–26
Henderson, Jessica, 120
Herndon, Angelo: All-Southern Anti-Lynching Conference, 30; early participation in organizing, 15, 19–20; expelled from Communist Party, 162; police brutality, 63–64; sharecroppers, 53–54; Southern Negro Youth Congress, 153; trial of, 100–106; on Wood-Williams murder, 67; worker solidarity, 21
Herndon v. Lowry, 104–5, 160
Hersch, Harry. *See* Simms, Harry
Highlander Folk School, 129–30
Hill, Lister, 151
Hinton, A. J., 117, 120–21
Hinton Hardware, 120
Hirsch, Alfred, 120–21
Hitler, Adolph, 82, 138, 152
Holeman, Harley, 113–15
Holiness sect, 59–60
Holmes, Luther, 73
Horton, James, 93, 96–97
Horton, Myles, 129–30
Houston, Charles Hamilton, 72–76, 122, 139, 161
HUAC. *See* Committee on Un-American Activities
Hudson, Hosea, 21, 78, 138, 148, 153–54, 162, 169
Hudson, John H., 100–102
Huff, W. I., 113, 114–15
Huntsville, Alabama, 39–41
Huntsville Times (newspaper), 34, 39–41

ILD. *See* International Labor Defense
Imperial Night Hawk (newspaper), 45
inciting insurrection charge, 20, 24, 100–105, 123, 160
industrial labor campaigns, 146

industrial organizing, 14, 146, 153–54
Industrial Workers of the World (IWW), 13, 22
inquest, murders of Pippen and Harden, 114–16
institutional racism, 21
integration, 16, 83, 100–103, 129–30, 134–35
Internal Security Subcommittee, 151
International Brigade's 15th Brigada Mixta unit, 164
International Day of Protest Against Government Inaction Regarding Unemployment, 23-24
International Labor Defense (ILD): Citizens' Protective League, 112–14; Civil Rights Congress, 156; constitutional protections, 159–60; Engdahl, 90–91; Harden, Pippen, and Clark, 111, 114; Herndon trial, 104; mass defense tactics, 36–38; miners, 55–59; national leadership, 133–34; Patterson, 35–36, 91–92; Peterson, 67, 70, 72, 74–75; police brutality, 123, 125; Scottsboro defense, 84, 96–99, 135–36; Scottsboro Supreme Court petition, 81; southern district office, 32; as working model, 158
International Publishers, 166
International Unemployment Day, 14
International Workers' Order (IWO), 22, 59, 123–25
interracial cooperation, 25
interracial meetings, Mine, Mill and Smelter Workers, 134
interracial membership, Louisiana Farmers' Union, 134
interracial organizing and organizations, 30, 67, 78, 153–54
interracial protests, 100–103
interracial sex, 119
interracial southern social justice coalition, 158
Irwin, Frank, 110–12, 114–15
Israel, Boris. *See* Owen, Blaine

IWO. *See* International Workers' Order
IWW. *See* Industrial Workers of the World

Jackson, Albert. *See* Murphy, Al
Jackson, Emory, 153
Jackson, Harry, 13–17, 19–20, 22–23, 32, 64, 77–78
Jackson, James, 153, 156
Jackson County, Alabama, 37
James, Cliff, 85–87
Jamison, Willie, 120
Jefferson County, Alabama, 144, 153
Jemison, Will, 109
Jewish Daily Bulletin (newspaper), 95
Jewish membership, Communist Party, 45–46, 81–82, 123
Jewish Telegraphic Wire Service, 95
Jim Crow statute enforcements, 112
Johnson, Alice, 117–21
Johnson, Clyde, 103, 129, 131–35
Johnson, Gerald W., 159
Johnson, Joe Spinner, 132
Johnson, J. R., 67–69, 70–73
Johnson, Tom, 13–17, 19–20, 22, 24, 30, 32, 47–48, 77, 123–24
Joint Anti-Fascist Refugee Committee, 166–67
Jones, Claudia, 106
Jones, D. C., 56
Jones, Jimmie, 20–21, 63
Jordan Funeral Home, 87
Judge Horton and the Scottsboro Case (docudrama), 41

Kaufman, Bea, 81–83
Kaufman, Louis, 81–83, 86, 95
Kazin, Michael, 161
Kelley, Robin, 153, 170
Kentucky Advocate (newspaper), 61
Kentucky Coal Wars, 54–59, 61
Kentucky State Police, 59
Kester, Howard, 44, 52, 95, 119
Khrushchev, Nikita, 161, 163

King, Martin Luther, Jr., 30, 158
Kleiman, Ida. *See* Allen, Isabelle
Kleinman, Ida, 22
Knight, Hartford, 153
Knight, Thomas E., Jr., 37, 96–97, 114–15, 120, 135
Knight, Thomas E., Sr., 37
Knox County, Kentucky, 54, 58, 61
Kone, Sol, 98–99
Kourier (newsletter), 20
Ku Klux Klan, 16, 19–21, 45, 51, 84, 101, 120, 139

Labor Defender (newspaper), 22, 39, 97
labor discrimination, 50
labor organizing, 13–16, 125–26, 154
LaFollette, Robert M., 56, 144
LaFollette Committee, 144
La France, Charles, 109–10
land furlough, 113, 116, 133–34
Landon, Alf, 145
land purchasing program, 134–35
law enforcement: Citizens' Protective League, 112–13; dispersing demonstrators, 15–16, 24, 78–79; Gelders beating, 143–44; Gray murder, 49–51; Hardin, Pippen, and Clark murders, 113–15, 121–22; Johnson beating, 77; Kentucky Coal Wars, 57–59; and the KKK, 19–21; legal lynchings, 31–32, 120; in Memphis, 123–26; Vaudine Maddox murder investigation, 107–9
Lawson, Elsa, 24
Lawson, Green, 57–58
leadership, 21, 30, 59, 74, 129, 133–34, 161
League for Industrial Democracy (LID), 136
League of Struggle for Negro Rights, 24, 30–31, 48, 95–96, 125, 139
League of Young Southerners (LYS), 154–58
Le Craw, L. Walter, 101–2
Lee County, Alabama, 130, 132
legal lynchings, 31–32, 120
Leibowitz, Samuel, 91–94, 96–99, 135–36, 171
Lenin, Vladimir, 155, 161

Let Me Live (Herndon), 101, 105
Lewis, John L., 60, 139, 146, 154, 157
Lewis, Walter, 14
Leyton, James. *See* Johnson, Tom
Licht, Amy, 23–24, 30–31
LID. *See* League for Industrial Democracy
Lincoln Brigade, 167
Linder, Douglas, 137
livestock liens, 85–87
Lobman, Bernard, 83
Lobman, Dorothy, 83, 141
Logan, Bart and Belle, 143
Long, Helen, 21
Long, Jim, 65, 72
longshoremen strike, 20, 126
Louisiana Farmers' Union, 134
Lovestone, Jay, 145
Lowell, Ben. *See* Goldstein, Benjamin
Lowndes County, Alabama, 130–32
Lowry, James, 104
Lumpkin, Grace, 119
Lynch, Marvin, 96
lynchings: All-Southern Anti-Lynching Conference, 30–31; antilynching legislation, 25, 30–31, 149–50, 168; Civil Rights Congress, 169; of Cross, 117–22; federal death penalty, 130; of Gray, 51; legal lynchings, 31–32, 120; of Pippen and Hardin, 113–16; prosecutions of, 102; of Robinson, 25–32; Southern Commission on the Study of Lynching, 29–31
"Lynch Law at Work" (Allen), 24–25
Lynne, Seybourn, 157
LYS. *See* League of Young Southerners

Maars, Charlie, 29
Macedonian Church of God, 171
Macon County, Alabama, 85–86
Maddox, Vaudine, 107–12, 115–16, 121–22
Maddox, W. T., 107
Magic City. *See* Birmingham, Alabama
Marcantonio, Vito, 171
Marchetta, Mississippi, 27

march on Washington, 134, 156
Marcy, Helen. *See* Allen, Isabelle
Marrs, Charlie, 26
Martinsville Seven, 166–67
Marx, Karl, 42
Mary Church, 49–50
Mason, Lucy Randolph, 147–48
mass protest tactics, 146, 160
Maxey, Fred, 155
May Day parade, 78–79
Mayer, Ernest, 94–95
Mayfield, Henry, 153
McAdoo, Walter, 28
McCarthy, Joseph, 159
McClung, James, 143–44
McCoy, J. P., 19
McDuff, Fred, 16, 19–20, 22–23, 25, 64–65, 72, 75–76, 157
McElroy, J. Russell, 68–69
McGee, Willie, 166–67
McGuire, Jack, 109–10
McKay, Claude, 91
McKenzie, Doug, 32, 34
McMullen, Jim, 85
McPherson, Charles, 67–68, 71–75
McQueen, John D., 110–11
McQuire, Ralph, 131
mechanical cotton harvester, 133
membership in CPUSA, 59, 101, 123, 140–41, 162–63
Memphis, Tennessee, 32, 123–26
Memphis Appeal (newspaper), 124
merchants, 17–18, 47–48
Merriweather, Annie Mae, 131–32, 134–35
Merriweather, Jim Press, 131
Methodist Federation for Social Services, 136
Midlo, Gwen, 165
militant movements. *See* Southern Negro Youth Congress (SNYC)
Miller, Arlie, 58–59, 61
Miller, Benjamin Meek, 33–37, 74–76, 87, 94, 97, 114, 122, 132

Milner, Estelle, 47, 49, 52
Mine, Mill and Smelter Workers union, 141
miners, 15, 18–21, 44, 53–61, 67, 142, 156
mistrial, Peterson case, 68–69, 71, 73
Mitch, William, 130, 148
Mitchell, B. B., 113
Moe, Iver, 165
Monteagle, Tennessee, 147
Montgomery, Alabama, 80–84, 94–96, 130
Montgomery, Olen, 33–36, 79, 136
Montgomery, Viola, 36, 79
Montgomery Advertiser (newspaper), 37, 39–40, 50, 87, 95, 132, 151
Montgomery Examiner (newspaper), 94
Moody, Milo, 35–36
Moon, Henry Lee, 161
Mooney, Milo, 34
Moore, Joe, 55–56
Morris, Ruby, 125
Moscow, 162
Moton, Robert, 51, 74, 86–87
Mountain Brook community, 62–63, 66
Mullinicks, Lewis, 76
Murphy, J. C., 16–17
Murphy, Marcus "Al," 80–82, 85, 123, 129–30, 132, 138, 162, 168–69
Murray, Philip, 154–57

NAACP (National Association for the Advancement of Colored People): Camp Hill, 52; Carlock campaign, 125; constitutional guarantees, 81; counsel, 34; Patterson, 91; Peterson trial, 68–75; Popular Front, 146; Scottsboro defense, 36–38, 50, 135–36; Southern Negro Youth Congress, 154; Trenton Six, 168; voter registration, 153
Narkeeta, Mississippi, 27–28
National Board of the Civil Rights Congress, 171
National Committee for the Defense of Political Prisoners (NCDPP), 57, 119–21, 125, 142–43

National Committee of the Communist
   Party, 105, 169
National Committee to Abolish the Poll
   Tax, 156
National Emergency Council, 147
National Farmers' Union (NFU), 134, 146
National Federation of Constitutional
   Liberties, 156
National Industrial Recovery Act, 61,
   139–40
National Labor Relations (Wagner) Act, 142
National Labor Relations Board, 142, 144
National Lawyers' Guild, 170–71
National Miners' Union (NMU), 15, 54–61
National Negro Congress (NNC), 139, 153,
   156, 158
National Negro Congress' Youth Division,
   105
National Training and Worker Schools, 78,
   142, 169
National Urban League, 154
NCDPP. *See* National Committee for the
   Defense of Political Prisoners
Negro Businessmen's League, 64
Negro Commission, 91, 165
Negro Quarterly (magazine), 105
Nelson, Steve, 161–62
New Deal, 139–40, 145, 150–51
New Jersey Supreme Court, 168
New Masses (newspaper), 110, 124
New Orleans, Louisiana, 134
New Republic (magazine), 58
New York Graphic (newspaper), 40
New York Times (newspaper), 51, 161
NFU. *See* National Farmers' Union
Ninth Congress, 139
NMU. *See* National Miners' Union
NNC. *See* National Negro Congress
Nollner, Charles, 62, 75
"No More Labor Wanted Until Further
   Notice: Camp Blanding, Florida"
   (Seeger), 155
Norman Thomas Study Club, 81–83, 96, 141

Norris, Clarence, 33–35, 98, 108–9, 135–36
Norris, Ida, 36
Norris v. Alabama, 135, 160
North Carolina Workers International
   Relief, 55
no-strike pledges, 156

Obama, Barack, 171
Ochs, Adolph, 22
O'Connor, Helen, 56–57
"On What Hateful Bread does Communism
   Feed?" 63
Oppenheimer, Daniel, 46
organized religion, 42–45, 59–60
organizing: Citizens' Protective League,
   112–13; CPUSA, 162–63; district 17, 13–16,
   53–55; Downs literature ordinance, 141–
   43; Eula Gray, 77–79; Herndon, 19–20, 53,
   100–102; International Labor Defense,
   32; mass protest tactics, 160; Memphis,
   123–26; Montgomery, 81; National
   Farmers' Union, 133–34; National Miners'
   Union, 54–59, 67; Patterson, 35–36; Ross,
   78; sharecroppers, 17, 47–48, 51, 78, 84;
   sit-down strikes, 154–55; *Southern News
   Almanac*, 155–57; Trade Union Unity
   League, 23–25; unemployment, 14–15, 77;
   women, 21
Organizing in the Depression South (Allen),
   54
Our Southern Home (magazine), 27
Owen, Blaine, 56, 78–79, 124–26, 132, 164

Pannal, J. L., 118
Parker, Walter, 85
Parks, Raymond and Rosa, 81
Pate, Murray, 113–15, 119
Patrick, Luther, 151
Patterson, Haywood, 33–36, 92–94, 96–98,
   108–9, 135–37
Patterson, Janie, 36, 84
Patterson, William: appeals, 74–75;
   biography, 167–68; Civil Rights Congress,

156–57; ILD participation, 90–92, 133–34; mass protest tactics, 35–37, 146; Party membership, 162; Pippen trial telegram, 111–12; Popular Front, 152
Pearson, J. T. *See* Price, Charles
penny auctions, 170
People's Front against Fascism and War policy, 138
perjury, 41, 71, 136
Peterson, Henrietta, 67–68, 70, 72, 74–75
Peterson, Willie, 64–76, 109
Pine Mountain, Kentucky, 56
Pineville, Kentucky, 57–58
Pippen, Dan, Jr., 108–15, 119–20
Pippen, Dan, Sr., 109, 120
Pippen, Lucinda, 109–11
Pittsburgh (PA) Courier (newspaper), 37, 66–67, 121, 156
"The Plight of Tuscaloosa: Mob Murders, Community Hysteria, Official Incompetence—A Case Study of Conditions in Tuscaloosa County Alabama," 121
police brutality, 15–16, 19–21, 31–32, 49–51, 77–79, 95, 123–26, 142–44. *See also* law enforcement
Political Bureau, 78
Pollard, Charles, 83
poll tax, 134, 147–49, 154–56
Popular Front Against War and Fascism, 138–39, 145–46, 149–50, 152–53, 165
posthumous pardons, 137
postwar anticommunism, 157
poverty, 50, 134–35, 147–50
Powell (man from Maddox case), 108
Powell, Ozie, 33–34, 136–37
Powell, Paul, 116
Powell v. Alabama, 90, 159
prejudicial statements to jury, 71
President's Commission on Farm Tenancy, 134–35
Price, Charles, 98–99
Price, Victoria, 33–34, 38–41, 93, 96–99, 136

Prince Hall (Colored) Masonic Temple, 79, 154
prison practices, 103
production control, 88–89
propaganda, 63, 121
prostitution, 39
protests: after Camp Hill, 80; antilynching movement, 31; Downs literature ordinance, 141–43; Fish Committee, 16; Herndon, 100, 102; International Day of Protest Against Government Inaction Regarding Unemployment, 23–24; mass protest tactics, 146, 160; Murphy, 169; National Miners' Union, 57; Peterson trial, 74; police brutality, 125; of Scottsboro death sentences, 35–37; sharecroppers, 89; women, 21
Provisional Committee to Defend Angelo Herndon, 103
Pruitt, Jack, 114, 119
publicity campaigns, 55, 70–72
Puerto Rican Communist Party, 167
Pullman Plant demonstration, 16
"Pulpit in Print" (Maxey), 155

race: and communism, 50–52, 63, 130; CPUSA, 46, 105, 123, 146; organized labor, 147; organizing, 14, 67, 78; recruitment, 80, 146; Southern Conference for Human Welfare, 149, 153–54
racial discrimination, 101
racial equality, 20, 80
racial etiquette, 84
racial justice, 159
racial purity, 82
racism, 130, 156, 169
racism, institutional, 21
radicalism, 16, 105, 139, 153
radicalization, 44, 145
radical politics, 45, 134
Randolph, A. Philip, 139
Ransdell, Hollace, 38–40, 120

Raper, Arthur, 17, 29–31, 37, 109, 113, 118, 121–22
Rappaport, Morris, 165
Raymond, Anan, 145–46
Read, Jean, 83, 87
Read, Nash, 83
Red Cross, 21, 55
Red Squad, 157
Reeltown, Alabama, 85–87, 90–92
Reese, Louie, Jr., 72, 76
relief agencies, 21
religion. *See* organized religion
Report on the Economic Conditions of the South, 147–51
Republic Steel, 141
Rice, Fleetwood, 110
Right to Vote Club, 153
Roach, J. T., 67–73
Roberson, Willie, 33–34, 136
Robeson, Paul, 168
Robinson, Andrew, 28
Robinson, Bryant, Jr., 171
Robinson, Dock, 26–27
Robinson, Elbert, 28
Robinson, Esau, 25–29, 171
Robinson, Frank, 28
Robinson, Jacob, 28
Robinson, James, 28
Robinson, John, 26–29
Robinson, Jordan, 28
Robinson, J. P., 69
Robinson, J. W., 28
Robinson, King, 26–29
Robinson, Ollis, 26–29
Robinson, Tom, 26–27, 28–29, 31, 171
Roddy, Stephen, 34–36
Roosevelt, Eleanor, 105, 147–49
Roosevelt, Franklin D., 88–89, 134–35, 139, 145, 147–48, 161
Rosenberg, Nat. *See* Ross, Nat
Rosenthal, Albert, 32, 67
Ross, Nat, 77–80, 82, 103, 123–24, 129–30, 133, 140–42, 156–57, 162, 166

rural poverty, 135
Rust, John, 133
Ryles, Vaughn, 131

Sacco and Vanzetti, 36, 91
Sampson, Flem, 61
Sanders, O. D., 125
Sanders, Virgil, 73
Saturday Review (magazine), 105
Scales, Will, 26–28
Schechter, Amy, 23–24, 162
Schneider, Isadore, 97
Schriftman, Daniel, 98–99
SCHW. *See* Southern Conference for Human Welfare
Schwab, Irving, 52, 87, 110–12
Scottsboro: All Southern Conference, 79; announcement, 32; appointment of counsel, 33–34; arrest of teens, 33; bribery bombshell, 98–99; change of venue, 35, 92; consequences of, 50; Darlie Speed on, 95–96; demonstrations, 37; denial of counsel counterpoint, 110–11; equal protection clause, 159–60; four trials, 34–38; Goldstein's involvement, 94–95; ILD campaign, 35–38; last rounds of, 135–37; new trials, 90–94; petition, 49; sharecroppers, 47; Supreme Court decisions, 90; underground organizing, 81; Victoria and Ruby, 38–41
Scottsboro Bar Association, 33–34
Scottsboro Defense Committee, 49, 136, 168
Scottsboro Defense Funds, 99
Scottsboro Defense Rally, 95
Scottsboro Mother tours, 35–36
"Secret Speech" (Khrushchev), 161, 163
sedition, 24, 78, 126, 130
seditious literature ordinance, 141–43
Seeger, Pete, 155
segregation, 21, 43–45, 95, 123, 130, 149–50, 153, 162
self-determination, 19, 30, 50, 80, 101, 103, 145, 165

Selma, Alabama, 132
Selma Times Journal (newspaper), 53
Senate Education Subcommittee, 56
Seventh World Congress, 129, 138
Seymour, Whitney North, 104
Shades Mountain, 62–76
Shamblin, R. L., 109, 113–15, 119, 122
sharecroppers: Camp Hill, 48–52; Citizens' Protective League, 113; Communists, 50–51; credit suspension strategy, 47–48; Deputy Elder incident, 85–87; displacement of, 88–89, 116; mechanization, 133; Norman Thomas Study Club, 82–83; organized religion, 42–44; overview, 17–18; Popular Front, 146; Ross, 78; Tallapoosa, 82–84; union organizing, 53, 134
Shaw, B. G., 95
Sheppard, Tom, 69
Shut, Elmer, 41
Shut, Lucille. *See* Bates, Ruby
Shuttlesworth, Fred, 158
Simms, Harry, 47, 57–59, 61, 77, 79
Simpson, Judson, 86–87
sit-down strikes, 154–55
Sixth Amendment, 159–60
slavery, 17–18
slave statute, 1861, 100
Slinger, Dan. *See* Brooks, Dan
Sloss-Sheffield Steel and Iron, 18
Smith, Norman, 126
Smith, R. E., 63
Smith, Walter, 71
Smith Act, 106
SNCC. *See* Student Non-Violent Coordinating Committee
SNYC. *See* Southern Negro Youth Congress
social equality, 43, 111, 130, 150, 161
social Gospel tradition, 44–46
social insurance bill, 14–15, 23
socialism, 44, 145
social justice, 21, 80, 84, 126, 154–55, 158, 164
social responsibility, 60

soup kitchen, Evarts, 55–57
South (region), 147–51
Southern Christian Leadership Conference, 158
Southern Commission on the Study of Lynching, 29–31, 118, 121–22
Southern Conference Education Fund, 40
Southern Conference for Human Welfare (SCHW), 148–51, 154–56, 158
Southern Farm Leader (newspaper), 134
Southern Freedom movement, 154
Southern Negro Youth Congress (SNYC), 153–54, 158
Southern News Almanac (weekly tabloid), 155–56
Southern Railway yards, 23
Southern Scottsboro Defense Committee, 48
Southern Tenant Farmers' Union (STFU), 44, 131, 133, 134
southern wage differential, 134
Southern Worker (newspaper), 19, 22–25, 28, 30, 34, 37, 39, 63–64, 66, 143
Soviet model, 162–63
Special Committee to Investigate Communist Activities (Fish Committee), 16–17
Speed, James Buckner, 83
Speed, Jane, 83, 87, 95, 138, 145, 162, 167
Speed, Mary Craik (Darlie), 83, 87, 95–96, 162
Spivak, John, 94
spy program, 17
Stalin, Josef, 140, 152–53, 156, 161, 163
Starnes, Joe, 35
state courts, 160
state extension service networks, 88
stay of execution, 35–38, 74
Steel Workers' Organizing Committee, 138, 169
Stern, George B. *See* Goldstein, Benjamin
STFU. *See* Southern Tenant Farmers' Union
Stone, Olive, 82–83, 96
Street, Katharine. *See* Price, Victoria

Street, Walter, 41
Streit, Edward "Buck," 64–65, 68
strikebreaking, 154
strikes, 20, 44, 54–59, 126, 131–33, 141–42, 154–56, 170
Strong, Ed, 156
Student Non-Violent Coordinating Committee (SNCC), 158
Sumter County, Alabama, 25, 28
surplus crop reduction plan, 88, 116
Swingler, Lewis O., 125
syndicalism, 13, 55, 57
syphilis study, 86

Tallapoosa County, Alabama, 17, 47–49, 51, 77–80, 82–83, 86, 130, 170
Talmadge, Eugene, 103
Tasker, Capitola, 80–81
Tasker, Charles, 80–81, 132
Taub, Allan, 34–36, 57, 110–12
Taylor, Wirt, 79
TCI. *See* Tennessee Coal, Iron and Railroad Company
Temple Beth Or, 81–84, 94–95
tenant farmers, 17, 42–44, 51, 80, 101, 131, 133–34, 169
Tennessee Coal, Iron and Railroad Company (TCI), 14, 18, 20, 23, 143–44
Tennessee Socialist Workers' Party, 147
Tennessee Valley Authority, 82, 151
Third Communist International, 91
Trade Union Unity League (TUUL), 14, 20, 23–25, 30, 138, 155
Trenton Six, 168
Tuscaloosa, Alabama, 69, 107, 108–14, 117–22, 141–42
Tuscaloosa News (newspaper), 107, 111, 114–15, 150
Tuskegee Institute, 51
TUUL. *See* Trade Union Unity League

UMW. *See* United Mine Workers
unconstitutionality, 97, 101

underground network, 25
underground resistance movements, 80–81, 129
unemployed worker movement, 19–21, 23–24, 32
unemployment, 14–15, 112
unions: of agricultural workers, 17; Alabama Share Croppers' Union, 49, 129, 133–34; All Southern Conference for Civil and Trade Union Rights, 129–30; antilabor violence, 139; busting, 48–49; Croppers and Farm Workers Union, 48–49, 79–82, 146; district 17 restructuring, 134; industrial, 22–23; integrated, 16; leadership, 129; Mine, Mill and Smelter Workers union, 141; National Farmers' Union, 134, 146; National Labor Relations (Wagner) Act, 142; National Miners' Union, 15, 54; organized religion, 44, 59–60; organizing, 47–48, 54–55; Popular Front, 139; Reeltown, 85–86; segregated, 130; sharecroppers, 53, 116, 130–31; Southern Tenant Farmers' Union, 131, 133–34; Tennessee Coal, Iron and Railroad Company, 144
United Cannery, Agricultural, Packing and Allied Workers of America, 146
united-front policy, 152–53
United Mine Workers (UMW), 23, 54–55, 61
U.S. Constitution, 122, 135, 160
U.S. Justice Department, 122
U.S. Postal Service, 17
U.S. State Department, 159
U.S. Steel, 144
U.S. Supreme Court, 72–76, 90, 98, 103–5, 110, 135, 160

vagrancy, 16, 19–20, 22, 24, 33, 64, 157
Veterans' Commission, CPUSA, 166
vigilantes, 51, 63–64, 86, 114, 119
violence. *See* lynchings; police brutality
vocational education programs, 154
voter registration, 153–54

Wakefield, Jesse, 32, 54–55, 162, 165
Wakefield, Lowell, 32, 34–36, 64, 78–79, 162, 165
Walker, Stanley, 105
Wallace, George, 136
Wallace, Henry, 88
Wann, Matt, 33, 35
Ward, J. Monroe, 109–10
Washington, Robert, 132
Watkins, Thomas, 126
"We Charge Genocide" petition (Patterson), 168
Wechsler, James, 139
Weems, Charlie, 33–35, 136–37
Welfare Board, 21
Weller, Jack, 60
Wellman, Ted. See Benson, Sid
West, Don, 155
White, Walter, 21, 36–38, 68, 70, 75, 89, 139, 168
white croppers, 43, 53, 80, 86
white privilege, 45, 89, 133
white supremacy, 42, 97, 104, 150, 153
Whitfield, Owen, 169
"Why Communists are Valuable" (Johnson), 159
Wilcox, Mamie Williams, 36
Wilcox County, Alabama, 53
Wilder, Tennessee, 44
Williams, Augusta, 62–68, 73–75
Williams, Clark, 65, 68, 76
Williams, Dent, 65–67, 70, 72–74, 143–44
Williams, Eugene, 33–36, 136
Williams, Frank, 138
Williams, Helen, 65, 68, 70
Williams, Nell, 62–76
Williamson, John, 16
Wilson, Henry, 69–70

Wilson, Matt, 49–50
Witcher, Willie, 131
Wobblies. See Industrial Workers of the World (IWW)
Women's International League for Peace and Freedom, 83
Wood, Frank, 116
Wood, Jennie, 62–68, 72–75
Wood, Robert, 133, 142
Wood, Wade, Jr., 76
Wood, Wade, Sr., 62, 72
Woodruff, R. E., 131
Woodstock, Alabama, 113
Woodward, C. Vann, 120
Woodward Iron, 18
Workers International Relief organization, 23, 55
Workers' International Relief rally, 57–58
Workers' School, 167
World Congress of International Red Aid, 90
World War II, 105, 165, 170
Worthy, Seaten, 17
Wright, Ada, 34, 36, 90, 95
Wright, Andy, 33–36, 90, 136–37
Wright, Cleo, 169
Wright, Reuben H., 110
Wright, Roy, 33–36, 136
Wright, Wade, 94
Wright, W. C., 45
Wyatt, Lee B., 100–101, 104

YCL. See Young Communist League
Young, B. J., 132
Young, J. Kyle, 47–49, 51–52, 80, 85–87, 132
Young Communist League (YCL), 15, 24, 79, 105
YWCA national convention, 161